T0330400

ECONOMIC THEORY AND REALITY

ECONOMISTS OF THE TWENTIETH CENTURY

General Editors: Mark Perlman, *University Professor of Economics, Emeritus, University of Pittsburgh* and Mark Blaug, *Professor Emeritus, University of London, Professor Emeritus, University of Buckingham and Visiting Professor, University of Exeter*

This innovative series comprises specially invited collections of articles and papers by economists whose work has made an important contribution to economics in the late twentieth century.

The proliferation of new journals and the ever-increasing number of new articles make it difficult for even the most assiduous economist to keep track of all the important recent advances. By focusing on those economists whose work is generally recognized to be at the forefront of the discipline, the series will be an essential reference point for the different specialisms included.

A list of published and future titles in this series is printed at the end of this volume.

Economic Theory and Reality

Selected Essays on their Disparities and Reconciliation

Tibor Scitovsky

ECONOMISTS OF THE TWENTIETH CENTURY

Edward Elgar

Published by
Edward Elgar Publishing Limited
Gower House
Croft Road
Aldershot
Hants GU11 3HR
England

Edward Elgar Publishing Company
Old Post Road
Brookfield
Vermont 05036
USA

British Library Cataloguing in Publication Data
Scitovsky, Tibor
   Economic Theory and Reality: Selected
   Essays on Their Disparities and
   Reconciliation. – (Economists of the
   Twentieth Century Series)
   I. Title II. Series
   330.01

Library of Congress Cataloguing in Publication Data
Scitovsky, Tibor.
   Economic theory and reality: selected essays on their disparities
and reconciliation / Tibor Scitovsky.
      p. cm. — (Economists of the twentieth century)
Includes bibliographical references.
1. Economics.   I. Title. II. Series.
HB34,S34   1995
330—dc20
                                                      94–32262
                                                         CIP

ISBN 1 85898 139 5

Printed and bound in Great Britain by
Hartnolls Limited, Bodmin, Cornwall

Contents

Acknowledgements

The papers here assembled originally appeared in the following publications, to whose publishers and editors the author and present publisher are grateful for granting permission to reprint: 'The benefits of asymmetric markets', *Journal of Economic Perspectives* (1990); 'The debate on socialist economic planning in today's perspective', presented at the 1993 Budapest conference of the Osterreichisches Ost- und Südosteuropa-Institut in the original German; 'Lerner's contribution to economics', *Journal of Economic Literature* (1984); 'The demand-side economics of inflation' in D. Worswick and J. Trevithick (eds), *Keynes and the Modern World* (Cambridge University Press, 1986); 'Moral sentiments and welfare of nations' *De Economist*, Educatieve Partners Nederland (1991); 'How our economy stands up to scrutiny', acceptance paper for the 1990 Seidman Distinguished Award in Political Economy; 'Growth in the affluent society', the 1986 Fred Hirsch Memorial Lecture, printed in *Lloyds Bank Review* (1987); 'Towards a theory of second-hand markets', *Kyklos*, Helbing & Lichtenhahn Verlag, Basle (1994); 'The political economy of Josef Steindl', *Review of Political Economy* (1994); 'Economic Development in Taiwan and South Korea: 1965–81', *Food Research Institute Studies*, Stanford University (1985); 'Why the US saving rate is low – a conflict between the national accountant's and the individual saver's perceptions', in J. Cohen and G. Harcourt (eds), *International Monetary Problems and Supply-Side Economics* , Macmillan (1986); 'The meaning, nature and source of value in economics, in M. Hechter *et al.* (eds), *The Origin of Values* (New York: De Gruyter, 1993); 'Hindsight economics', *Quarterly Review*, Banca Nazionale del Lavoro (1991).

Introduction

The 14 papers assembled in this volume are the work of my old age: all have been written in the 1980s and 1990s, my 70s and 80s. They seem at first blush to deal with a bewildering variety of subjects, though actually all but two contain my contributions and reviews of my colleagues' contributions to two of my closely related lifelong preoccupations.

One of those preoccupations was to make economic theory more realistic and thereby more useful. I tried to do that by bringing the exercise of market power from the periphery of the economist's model to its centre stage. Marx was right when he stressed the importance of the transacting parties' unequal bargaining strength in most markets and the exploitation that resulted from it; but he was wrong in attributing it to inequalities only of wealth and naked force. For a more pervasive and therefore more important source of unequal market power under competitive capitalism is the division of labour, which renders people knowledgeable experts in their own specialities but rather ignorant about all other people's specialities; and the resulting unequal market knowledge of the transacting parties is a more subtle and important source of inequality as well, because it has the redeeming feature of benefiting the exploited along with the exploiters.

I first broached that subject in my 1951 book, where I introduced the characters of price maker and price taker into the economist's model, with the former using his superior market knowledge to take the initiative in making market offers and profiting by it. The realism of that model greatly facilitated analysing market behaviour in depth, which led to its ready acceptance by the profession; but only a third of a century later, on learning of Domar's unpublished lecture on the subject (Domar, 1989), have I recognized and published (in 1985) its even more important merit, which was to explain our competitive economy's most valuable achievement: the inducement it provides for sellers to improve their products, cheapen their manufacture, create new products and so stimulate growth. That my realistic model of the economy not only exposed its shortcomings but also accounted for one of its main accomplishments, which the less realistic perfectly competitive model was unable to explain, was a wonderful surprise – worth as much as a Nobel Prize. The first paper reprinted here, *The benefits of asymmetric markets*, restates and puts the finishing touches to my work on that subject.

The second paper, *The debate on socialist economic planning in today's perspective*, deals first with the importance the profession attaches to prices as the indispensable tool for maintaining efficient allocation, and then proceeds to illustrate the significance of the first paper's previously overlooked message that limited exploitation in competitive asymmetric markets is an efficient driving-force of economic progress, thereby reinforcing the argument and clarifying its place in economic theory.

The third paper, *Lerner's contribution to economics*, discusses in more detail the important contributions one of the protagonists in the debate on socialism has made to that subject as well as to just about every aspect of economic theory. His work was something of a bridge between the classics' simplistic and the moderns' more realistic models of the economy. Especially innovative was his analysis of inflation and its classification into demand-pull and cost-push inflation. To the latter of those, the next paper makes a further contribution.

For when differences in the contracting parties' market knowledge is among the main sources of their unequal bargaining strength, it often happens that one of the same two parties that confront each other in several different markets has the upper hand in one, while the other has the upper hand in the other market. Such conflicts can exert inflationary pressures, which I first discussed in a 1976 article. A much later, simplified and improved version of that is the fourth paper reprinted in this volume, *When excessive claims cause inflation*.

The fifth paper, *Moral sentiments and the welfare of nations*, is a review article of a book by Robert H. Frank, which deals with the influence on economic behaviour of such noble human passions as honesty, fairness, compassion and love. All of those counterbalance the influence of the passion for power and desire to exploit it, and thereby add more realism to one's model of the economy.

My second lifelong ambition was to understand and explain the nature and sources of our real-life economy's shortcomings when those cannot be incorporated in a more realistic model. I was especially anxious to account for our economy's failure to maintain macroequilibrium and full employment. It seemed obvious that inflexible prices and wages were one of the culprits, lack of competition was another. I concentrated on the former, but the ninth paper, *The political economy of Josef Steindl*, summarized Steindl's work on the latter and so completes and rounds out my own.

I looked for the cause of price and wage inflexibility in the first three articles of my career (1940, 1941a, 1941b); here the very much later sixth, seventh and eighth papers deal with it. The sixth, *How our economy stands up to scrutiny*, short as it is, puts the welfare implications of our real-life economy in a nutshell and accounts for unemployment with a simple, plausible, but little-known explanation of the downward stickiness of wages, which is unduly neglected owing, presumably, to the untimely death of its author,

Arthur Okun. His explanation (published in 1981), a variant of the prisoner's dilemma, stems from employees' distrust as to their employer's honesty and applies to firms with many employees.

The seventh paper, *Growth in the affluent society*, was a lecture commemorating the premature death of another distinguished economist, Fred Hirsch, whose important 1976 book on positional goods considered another shortcoming of our economy, which theorists have long overlooked. My paper deals with one of the peculiarities of positional goods, the depressing impact on the overall economy of the market for one of those goods, antique paintings.

The eighth paper, *Towards a theory of second-hand markets*, is a generalization of the previous one. It introduces the hitherto much-neglected second-hand markets into the economist's model of the economy and shows that their presence can keep prices in their related first-hand markets from equilibrating supply and demand, mostly by delaying their response to a disequilibrating change in circumstances, but occasionally also by exaggerating their response, depending on the nature of the two markets' relationship. My primary aim in writing that paper was to cast in simpler and more useful language Keynes's own and my 1940 paper's explanation of why Say's Law has ceased to hold good in today's economies; and that last aspect of the paper is, I think, its main merit, because it also shows why today's great changes in our financial system have rendered Keynesian monetary policies increasingly ineffective.

The ninth paper, *The political economy of Josef Steindl*, presented at the Vienna Conference honouring Steindl's 80th birthday, deals, as already mentioned, with the decline of competition. It is a short summary of his excellent and impressive but unduly neglected 1952 book, which contained the most rigorously argued and best documented version of a neo-Marxist analysis of the depressing effect of the decline in competition under monopoly capitalism. In some form, its main thesis was already familiar to Lange, as mentioned in the second chapter of this volume, on The Debate. It is included here, not only because Steindl's argument is no less pertinent today than when he wrote it, but also and mainly because its discussion of the depressing macroeconomic effect of the lack of competition complements the eighth paper's discussion of the depressing macroeconomic effect of price and wage inflexibility.

The tenth paper, *Economic development in Taiwan and South Korea: 1965–81*, probably my best work on development, fits into this volume because it shows the great influence monetary policy has on firm size and confirms the sixth paper's theoretical argument by showing that wages and prices are more flexible and unemployment rates significantly lower in an economy where the average size of firms is small.

The eleventh paper, *Why the US saving rate is low*, is a technical note, written at a time when the media and some economists attributed US economic ills to the low and declining rate of personal savings, which they blamed on the public's profligacy. As a confirmed Keynesian, I did not buy that diagnosis; but curiosity made me look into the way in which the national accountants estimate personal saving and I found that their estimates differed from what the saving public itself considers its saving just as much as the theorists' economic models differ from the real-life economy. My paper deals with that difference but catches only one explanation of it, although it inspired Steindl (1990) to look deeper into the intricacies of the national accounts' saving estimates, only to find them even more misleading than I believed them to be.

The twelfth paper, *The meaning, nature and source of value in economics*, explains the economist's use of the concept to laymen and could also be considered an ABC of welfare economics, since it explains the meaning of externalities, internalities, merit goods and collective goods, as well as the uses and abuses of national income and product estimates.

The thirteenth paper, *What ails the United States of America*, my latest and probably last paper, tries to deal comprehensively with most of our social and economic problems, showing many of them to be by-products of our economic, technological and social progress.

The last paper, *Hindsight economics*, is included because it serves as a postscript to this volume. It is a survey of my professional life and thinking as an economist and so provides further background for the above papers, linking them not only together but also to my third lifelong preoccupation, which is only barely touched upon in the fifth paper of this volume. I am referring to my unease with the profession's overly simplistic assumption of consumer rationality and attempts to look deeper into the rather complex psychology of consumers' motivation.

References

Domar, Evsey D. (1989), 'The blind men and the elephant', *Capitalism, Socialism and Serfdom*, (Cambridge: Cambridge University Press).

Frank, Robert H. (1988), *Passions within Reason: The Strategic Role of the Emotions*, (New York/London: W.W. Norton).

Hirsch, Fred (1976), *Social Limits to Growth*, (Cambridge, Mass./London: Harvard University Press).

Okun, Arthur M. (1981), *Prices & Quantities: A Macroeconomic Analysis*, (Oxford: Blackwell), pp. 57–9 and chap. 3.

Scitovsky, T. (1940), 'A study of interest and capital', *Economica*, N.S. **VII**, 293–317.

—— (1941a), 'Capital accumulation, employment and price rigidity', *Review of Economic Studies*, **VIII**, 69–88.

—— (1941b), 'Prices under monopoly & competition', *Journal of Political Economy*, **XLIX**, 663–85.

—— (1951), *Welfare and Competition*, (Homewood, Ill.: Irwin).

—— (1985), 'Price takers' plenty: a neglected benefit of capitalism', *Kyklos*, **XXXVIII**, 517–36.

Steindl, Josef (1952), *Maturity and Stagnation in American Capitalism*, (Oxford: Blackwell).

—— (1990), 'Capital gains, pension funds and the low saving ratio in the United States', *Banca Nazionale del Lavoro Quarterly Review*, **173**, 165–77.

1 The benefits of asymmetric markets*

Economists have long been fascinated by the paradox that, given favourable conditions, people's selfish greed for power and profits can annihilate the very power and profits they lust after, and in the process turn the chaos and anarchy of unbridled greed into order and harmony. Ever since the paradox was first noted, generations of economists have admired, taught and argued it, and the Arrow–Debreu theory of general competitive equilibrium is the culmination of the profession's long struggle to understand fully all its conditions and implications.

The resulting theory of general equilibrium, with its careful setting out of the many conditions on which the conclusions depend and its clarification of the way in which conclusions and underlying conditions are interconnected, has rightly been hailed as a remarkable intellectual achievement. Of course, the conditions set out have been chosen with a view to obtaining the conclusions, not for their realism; and some of them are admittedly and blatantly unrealistic. Accordingly, the important and remarkable results of the theory pertain to an imaginary economy. However, the theory's portrayal of the market forces that govern resource utilization and allocation resembles our actual economy closely enough to be of great practical importance. Hence the great attention that the theory has received and the consensus it represents are an important milestone in our understanding of the market economy.

One must be careful, however, not to read more into general equilibrium theory than what it says. Everybody knows that the US economy is far removed from the theory's imaginary model of perfect competition – the empirical evidence on unemployment and capacity underutilization makes that clear – but the intellectual pleasure one gets from following the theory's elegant logic and beautiful results easily makes one forget its limitations. Economists are often so mesmerized by the magic of perfect competition that they neglect or fail to notice other, equally important achievements of the real market economy around us, most of which seem to result from monopoly tempered by competition and competition tempered by monopoly.

For, as Schumpeter pointed out more than 60 years ago, monopoly power over others and monopoly profits earned at their expense, though considered ethically reprehensible by some, often yield important benefits, especially when suitably curbed by competition or legal constraints. The powerful often

* This article first appeared in the *Journal of Economic Perspectives*, Vol. 4, no. 1, Winter 1990, pp. 135–48.

help the powerless as they try to preserve and increase their power; and they are prompted to introduce new products, cheaper methods of production and to create new productive capacity by their desire to secure and enhance their continued access to monopoly profits.

The preoccupation of general equilibrium theory with the perfectly competitive model hides those valuable services from view, because it precludes the monopoly power that creates them. Moreover, since perfect market information by all economic agents is a necessary condition of perfect competition, general equilibrium theory assumes away by implication the very basis of modern economic life – specialization and division of labour – for they are incompatible with the assumption of everybody's having perfect information, as will presently be shown. Yet it would be absurd to refer to specialization and division of labour as instances of 'market failure'. They are 'failures' only in the sense that they imply a departure from the model of the perfectly competitive market; but they surely are the roots of the actual success of market economies in the real world.

Let me now consider some of those benefits of real-world markets which the perfectly competitive model of general equilibrium theory leaves out and cannot deal with. The simplest way to introduce them and show how market forces lead to their creation is to drop the one assumption underlying general equilibrium theory that does perhaps the most violence to reality. I have in mind the assumption that all economic agents possess all the market information relevant to the transactions they enter or contemplate entering into. That is the crucial condition necessary to render markets perfect for buyers and sellers alike; and we must now look at the nature and operation of markets that come about when that condition is *not* fulfilled.

Asymmetric information and asymmetric competition

Theoretical models of the economy are always based on simplifying assumptions to abstract from the irrelevant and bewildering complexity of reality. The condition of perfect information postulated in the theory of perfect competition may seem to be such an innocent assumption to a casual observer of commodity exchanges, the closest approximations to the ideal of perfect competition. After all, grains, fibres, metals and other staples are so perfectly graded and standardized that they can be (and are) traded sight unseen. All the market-relevant information concerning such commodities is condensed into just three bits of easily ascertained information: the identity of the product, its grade and its price. What the casual observer may fail to notice is that such perfect standardization and grading become profitable only when the majority of the buyers are expert specialists.[1]

Perfect markets do not emerge spontaneously. Most markets are imperfect to begin with, in the sense that they deal in many different brands and models of a given product, each with its own strengths, weaknesses, special features, and its own different price. To render such a market perfect by grading and standardizing and equalizing the prices of identical products, most of its members on the buying and selling side would have to compete knowledgeably and, to do that, would have to assemble piecemeal all the bewildering volume and variety of information concerning the nature, quality, convenience, cost and availability of all the competing brands and models. That takes much time and effort and is not something every market participant can do or finds worth doing, which is why the assumption of perfect knowledge, crucial for rendering markets perfect, is unrealistic.

Moreover, the assumption not only simplifies reality but also distorts it, because market-relevant knowledge is not randomly distributed among market participants but, in most markets, biased in favour of one or the other side of the market. Such a bias has a great impact on market behaviour and market outcomes, because knowledge is power, and those on the better informed side of the market can exploit the people on its other side. Such power is the main source of monopoly power, its exploitation yields monopoly profit, and rivalry among market participants who wield such power is the main form of monopolistic competition.

That explains why buyers' and sellers' perfect (and hence *equal*) knowledge of relevant information is a necessary condition of perfect competition, whose very essence is the symmetrical status of transactors on the two sides of the market. At the same time, it also explains why perfect competition is so rare in real life.

The root cause of the unequal distribution of knowledge between buyers and sellers is the division of labour, which causes everybody to know more than others about their own speciality and less about other people's specialities than they know about them. The farther the division of labour proceeds, the wider becomes the gulf between the specialist's knowledge and the non-specialist's ignorance of each speciality. While specialization reserves most production activities for its own specialists, it cannot do the same for exchange activities, considering that the division of labour forces each one of us to obtain through market exchange everything we need but do not produce ourselves. Market exchange therefore is one of the few activities that specialists and non-specialists alike participate in. Moreover, exchange in markets for final products (and in a few other markets as well) takes place between unequal partners, with a specialist facing a non-specialist on the other side of his market.

Such disparity in the knowledge and preparedness of buyers and sellers to deal with each other and to stand up to each other is an important and unavoidable feature of today's market economy, which has received surprisingly little attention. That is why it will be the pivot around which most of the argument of this paper will revolve.

First, however, it is well worth asking how something so obvious and ubiquitous could have been so much neglected by the profession. The main reason, I think, is that differences between buyers' and sellers' marketing knowledge have not been too great and widespread until fairly recently; but another reason could also be the profession's desire to exorcise power from its idealized picture of the economy. Since knowledge is power, one way of doing that was to assume away one of its sources by assuming equality of the different economic agents' market-relevant knowledge – an assumption that was not as absurd in the 18th century as it has become today. Power was admitted into economic theory only as an exception, in the form of natural, state and conspiratorial monopolies. All other monopoly power was expected to be eliminated by competition.

The main thrust of this chapter is that today, superior knowledge and earlier knowledge are the main sources of monopoly power; that only by eliminating differences in knowledge could one eliminate such power; and that competition, while mitigating monopoly power and diminishing monopoly profits, works its main beneficial effects by harnessing the monopoly power created by superior knowledge to promote the social welfare.

Buyers' markets

The most important examples of the asymmetry of information between buyers and sellers are the markets for consumer goods: both those where producers sell them and those where consumers buy them. Producers in the advanced economy are obviously more knowledgeable about the goods they sell than those they sell them to, but retailers also know more than their customers about the goods they sell. Since consumers must know something about all the various markets they frequent, they must spread their time and expertise thin, whereas sellers naturally concentrate their attention on a single market and cannot help but learn much more about the cost, nature, quality, variety, availability and marketing of the products they sell than the buyers facing them. That is why the typical seller is a specialist, the typical buyer a generalist in virtually all markets for consumer goods.

That difference between the market-relevant knowledge of the two sides gives the sellers an advantage to exploit. Competition among the suppliers diminishes this advantage but cannot eliminate it completely, as long as the buyers remain inexpert and unable clearly to distinguish qualitative differences between competing offers. The asymmetry between the information of the two sides distinguishes monopolistic competition from perfect competition and bilateral monopoly. While monopolistic competition may reduce net profits to zero (by equating price to average cost), it retains its monopolistic character and works its beneficial effects as long as price makers can set prices above marginal cost.

The simplification of reality by the perfectly competitive model would be relatively innocuous if monopolistic competition merely added monopoly profits to adjustment profits, and diminished the efficiency with which perfect competition would utilize and allocate resources and products. As already mentioned, however, there is also a positive side to monopolistic competition. It creates a number of important services and amenities, not only for consumers, but for producers and society at large as well. That is why providing a complete survey of the functions and benefits of the real-world market economy calls for setting the model of the perfect market aside and analysing monopolistic competition in depth.

In primitive economies, where the division of labour is limited, sellers exploit their superior knowledge by striking bargains favourable to themselves. In advanced economies, however, the much greater specialization and division of labour leads to so great a disparity in both numbers and knowledge between the specialists on the one side and the generalists on the other side of the market that the former find it profitable to save the cost of the time and skill that bargaining requires by setting prices on a take-it-or-leave-it basis. The resulting price maker – price taker relationship is the well-known institutional form that asymmetrical market situations usually take in advanced economies; and since it gives all the market initiative to price makers, it provides the further advantage of enabling them better to exploit their superior knowledge.[2]

Not only do sellers set their prices unilaterally, they usually also take the initiative in deciding what kinds and qualities of products to sell and what services to offer. This tempts some of them to cheat by cutting corners, offering inadequate service, shoddy merchandise, and so on. In turn, this causes price takers to try to compensate for their lack of expertise by taking price makers' reputations, rankings and distinctions into account when they make market decisions and by insisting that professionals and servicemen be licensed and obtain diplomas before marketing their expertise. The importance buyers attach to such tokens of reliability renders their demand less elastic and competition more monopolistic in character. Sellers facing less than perfectly elastic demand find it profitable to add a mark-up or profit margin to marginal cost in setting their prices. Such mark-ups are an incentive for them to promote sales by non-price competition, because they can always benefit by selling more at a price above marginal cost, provided that the cost of promoting sales in this way remains below the additional profit it generates.

Non-price competition can take many forms and consists in offering customers any one and any number of a great variety of amenities and services. These include the free information that advertisements and window displays provide about the availability, advantages, nature, appearance and price of products; the convenient location of stores, the pleasant surroundings and polite service; charge accounts, credit and delivery facilities most stores provide; explicit or implied guaranties of the quality of what is sold; refunds for returned merchandise offered with a smile; and the seller's ample inventory, allowing instant delivery of whatever buyers want, in whatever model, size, colour and quantity they want it, and catering to random surges, unexpected shifts and the secular rise in demand.

All these and similar conveniences together constitute what is called a buyers' market. That term, sometimes used merely to denote the buyers' advantage in not being rationed but free to buy as much as they want at a set price, gains in meaning when it also denotes, as it usually does, the many convenient services and amenities sellers provide to attract and please customers thereby to effect more sales, either because they have an excess supply to get rid of or, as in the present case, because additional sales at prices above marginal cost add to their profits.

To the unwary, for whom monopoly and profit are dirty words, the use of the term 'buyers' market' may seem paradoxical in this last case, considering that it is the sellers, not the buyers, who earn monopoly profits, even if part of the profits are spent on pleasing the customer. But that is the wrong way of looking at the subject. Buyers clearly prefer having the information, the guaranties, the comfort and the many other conveniences created by non-price competition, and most people willingly and freely pay for the surcharge that the seller's monopoly profits represent.

These conveniences may be looked upon as ancillary services which the sellers provide as joint products with the goods they sell. Although the cost to the seller of providing such services must be less than the profits the seller hopes to generate with their aid (since otherwise the seller would not offer them), their value to most customers exceeds what they pay for them. Nowadays, discount houses sell many of the same goods for less but without the ancillary services, thereby providing buyers with an opportunity to buy the merchandise without the services attached. The fact that discount houses have captured only a small fraction of the market shows that most consumers prefer to buy *and are willing to pay for* both the goods and the conveniences that come with them.

If sellers did not provide those services, buyers would be inconvenienced, having to go without some of them and either performing the rest for themselves or buying them separately at increased cost. In general, economies of scale render credit cheaper to merchants than to consumers, transportation in bulk by sellers more economical than transportation piecemeal by buyers; the larger inventories of a few sellers probably add up to less than the combined small inventories of many customers which would otherwise be necessary. But the scope for economies of scale is the greatest in the provision of information. Advertisements provide buyers with some of the information they lack; and it is much cheaper for a few sellers to advertise and make generally known information they already have than it would be for each buyer to ferret it out individually. Each seller, of course, wants to provide only the part of information favourable to himself; but that bias is largely offset by competitive advertising and legislation enforcing truth-in-lending, truth-in-selling and the disclosure of ingredients in the food and side-effects in the pharmaceutical industries. Guaranties and warranties combine the advantages of added information and lower insurance costs. In short, non-price competition not only compensates buyers for the monopoly profits they pay, it also improves the Pareto efficiency of markets.

Very similar to the amenities created by non-price competition among retailers are those that result from non-price competition among producers of consumer goods. They too are prompted to hold inventories and also to invest in standby capacity; produce their goods in many sizes, models and variants; offer warranties and repair services to the final buyer; and to cater to the public's desire for variety by constantly improving products, changing designs and new fashion. Further, they are prompted to engage in the research, development and investment required for the introduction of new products and cheaper methods of production. All this benefits the economy as a whole. Finally, and perhaps most importantly, they too engage in advertising, not so much to inform their already established customers as to reach a wider public that previously hardly even knew the existence, let alone the affordability, of their products, thereby to secure a mass market. Advertising is almost as essential for creating a mass market as is a mass market for realizing the economics of scale in manufacturing. In short, non-price competition among producers is a most important driving-force of both product and process innovation even if it is not by itself a sufficient condition of technical progress.

The great benefits of innovation and technical progress as the engine of growth need no stressing, but it is worth noting one of their important side-effects: the rise in equity. Market-oriented innovation consists largely of the progressive exploitation of mass-production methods for cheapening and making generally available an ever-increasing number of goods and services that previously were the privilege of the rich. Accordingly, although the market economy tolerates substantial inequalities in income distribution, it nevertheless increases equity, because market-oriented growth is mostly oriented towards equity as well.

Let me note that all the above benefits, all the ingredients of the buyers' market, stem not from the sellers' monopoly positions but from competition among them as they try to encroach upon each other's markets or defend their own. The distinction is important, because a positive mark-up will not always give rise to non-price competition. For one thing, the seller's market may expand so rapidly that he has no need to seek deliberately to increase his sales. In the heyday of British imperialism, for example, the world market for British products opened up so fast that British manufacturers could barely keep up with the demand and wasted neither money nor effort on innovation and improving their products. That explains why many years later, when their continental and US competitors entered the export market, their design and technology had fallen so far behind that they were unable to hold their markets against the new competition (Tylecote, 1981, p. 26).

For another thing, non-price competition is only one of many ways to secure and preserve monopoly positions. Some of the other ways include monopolistic agreement among competitors, tacit collusion, the buying out of competitors, seeking political influence to impose protective tariffs, and restricting domestic competition or the entry of newcomers through licensing or regulation. Since non-price competition alone secures the many social benefits just discussed, it is desirable that price makers adopt it in preference to all the other restraints on competition. That is a strong argument for antitrust and anti-monopoly legislation, additional to and probably more important than the traditional one.

While the social benefits of non-price competition are of paramount importance, monopoly power itself also provides benefits as a source of both funds and superior market information for investment. That nonprice competition stimulates innovation and technical progress has been mentioned earlier, but firms will respond to that stimulus only if they can expect to reap a steady and enduring flow of monopoly profits sufficient to repay research, development and investment costs and make it worth their while to take the gamble that innovation involves. The ephemeral profits created by change (and adjustment to change) in a highly competitive market are not enough. This fact is generally recognized today, which is why most countries enact patent laws to assure monopoly profits to inventors in case secrecy or the difficulty of replicating their innovative technology fails to do so.[3]

Another important benefit a producer gets from market power is more information on which to base investment decisions than would be available under perfect competition. A perfectly competitive economy would transmit only price signals or rather, in view of the rarity of futures and contingent futures markets, only current price signals. Asymmetric monopolistic markets are superior in that respect because, in addition to price information, they also provide some additional information relevant to investment decisions. At a minimum, each price maker has available quantity signals, which (unlike price signals) show not only that investment would be profitable but also *how much* investment is likely to be profitable. The increase in a producer's sales and unfilled orders or the reduction in inventories represents that producer's share in the overall rise in market demand. Since that share is the part it can most easily capture and hold onto without encroaching upon its competitors' actual and prospective markets, this amount indicates a minimal and fairly safe scope for capacity expansion and investment. In addition, most price makers have an idea of the elasticity of the market facing them and so also know something about the ease or difficulty and danger of expanding their market at competitors' expense.[4]

Sellers' markets

The asymmetric relationship between buyers and sellers can, of course, also go the other way around, putting the buyers in the favoured position of price makers when they happen to have superior market knowledge and a large enough number of people or firms on the other side of the market – two advantages that usually go together.[5] Before unions were established and in sectors where they were not established, employers assumed the role of wage makers thanks to their knowing more about labour market conditions than workers. Similarly, before the advent of mass production, large wholesalers and trading companies became knowledgeable price makers in their market relations with the small craftsmen and manufacturers who were their suppliers.

The implications of such a relationship are the mirror image of those discussed in the previous section. The sellers' lesser knowledge of the market gives the supply curve facing the price-maker buyers an upward slope, which enables them to maximize profits by setting their buying price *below* the marginal value product of the goods they buy or the labour they hire, by a profit margin that is the larger, the less elastic the supply facing them.

Capacity limitations permitting, the price- or wage-making buyer finds it profitable to absorb (and to stand ready to absorb) more input when more is offered at his set price, as long as that is below the marginal value product of the labour he hires or supplies he buys. That is the counterpart of the price-making seller's readiness to cater to surges in demand out of inventory or standby capacity. More input results, of course, in more output, which must be sold to render the added inputs profitable, and whose selling requires additional sales effort. That may slow the rate at which buyers can absorb unsolicited offers of supply, but does not prevent it if their calculations of the marginal value product of their inputs allows (as it should) for the selling costs of the extra output.

Firms that enjoy the advantage of being price makers in both the markets where they buy and the markets where they sell are especially able to absorb unsolicited offers of supply and cater to autonomous surges in demand. Witness the very fast growth of trading companies in Japan and 19th-century England, which absorbed the output of the fast-increasing number of small manufacturers, and the fast-increasing output of Britain's manufacturing industry during the industrial revolution, which enabled it to absorb fast-increasing supplies of labour.

Non-price competition by price-making *buyers* consists of the inducements they offer to increase the supply of their inputs beyond its natural increase. The scope for providing such inducements is greater the slower the natural rise in the supply of inputs and the larger the profit margin (or monopsonistic mark-down) between the buyer's marginal valuation of his inputs and the price at which he offers to buy or hire them. Examples of such inducements are good working conditions and fringe benefits employers offer their workers, and amenities like credit, transport, quality control, and help in acquiring raw materials. Also included is advice about design, quality improvement and the introduction of new products, which large trading companies offer to the small manufacturers whose products they market. The provision of such services justifies calling such a situation a sellers' market, since, here, the extra services the buyers (or employers) provide in the hope of reaping additional monopsony profits are in the sellers' favour.

The close parallelism between the non-price competition among sellers and buyers and between the buyers' and sellers' markets they respectively create makes one wonder why most of Britain's price-maker employers failed, during the industrial revolution, to engage in such non-price competition and provide their workers with amenities and conveniences corresponding to those shopkeepers provided for their customers. The probable explanation is the tremendous unemployment and poverty created by the enclosure movement, which increased the reserve army of industrial labour faster than the ability of industry to employ them. That is why the adversarial relations in the labour market of that time failed to soften. The workers, who felt exploited and resentful, used collective action to turn most of the labour market into a bilateral monopoly. By contrast, in the labour market composed of Japan's largest firms, non-price competition is as strong as in consumer markets, leading to much better relations between employers and employees.

Another difference between labour and consumer markets is that non-price competition for labour not only attracts workers and keeps them loyal, it also raises their morale and in many kinds of jobs increases the quality and quantity of their work.

Reconciling the advantages of price and non-price competition

My account of buyers' and sellers' markets may have seemed paradoxical, since it presented monopolistic competition, not as a market imperfection that abridges welfare, but as a creator of benefits that add to welfare. Non-price competition played a key role in the argument; and that raises three interrelated questions: (1) How do price makers choose between price and non-price competition? (2) Can the respective benefits of the two kinds of competition be reconciled? (3) Are the benefits of non-price competition peculiar to asymmetric markets or are they available in symmetric markets as well? In addressing these questions, I shall simplify the exposition by dealing only with the behaviour of price-maker sellers, omitting the parallel argument for the price-maker buyers.

How do price makers choose between price and non-price competition?
Asymmetric markets provide the price-making seller with many more policy variables than are (or would be) available to members of the symmetric perfectly competitive market. Such a seller will naturally choose the most profitable competitive weapon or combination of weapons, which depends on the nature of the market; and in an uncertain world, the seller's choice is bound to be difficult and uncertain. How the price elasticity of demand determines the seller's profit-maximizing price and profit margin is too well-known to be repeated here. Once a seller has set a price and mark-up at what he considers their best level, the scope for further price competition is exhausted. However, non-price competition may still add to the seller's profits, and its scope and effectiveness are greater, the larger the profit margin set. Since inexpert buyers lead to the price elasticity of demand being lower and the profit-maximizing price being higher, non-price competition prevails in inexpert markets. On the other hand, price is the dominant competitive weapon in markets where buyers are well informed and choosy – the limiting case being the perfect market, where every member has perfect information and sellers are restricted to price as their only competitive weapon.

Recall in this connection my initial statement above that monopolistic competition not only diminishes monopoly power and profits but creates positive benefits as well. It should now be apparent that price competition does the first and non-price competition accomplishes the second but may at the same time also affect the level of monopoly power in either direction. When the amenities of non-price competition increase marginal cost, they tend to diminish monopoly power as measured by the size of the profit-maximizing mark-up. On the other hand, non-price competition often also has the subsidiary effect of fragmenting the market by differentiating products and offers, and of creating goodwill, reputations and buyers' loyalty, all of which tend to secure and prolong monopoly power and raise the profit-maximizing price. Since these are important advantages for the price-making seller in the long term, they may bias the choice of competitive weapons in favour of non-price competition. In other words, when the price maker believes his set price to be above its profit-maximizing level, he may, rather than lowering the set price, keep it unchanged and use non-price competition to raise the level of the profit-maximizing price.

Oligopolistic markets are known to tilt the price maker's choice in favour of non-price competition even further, because they restrain price competition for fear of provoking retaliation and precipitating an all-round reduction of prices and profits. Of course, non-price competition can also be countered, but that is a much slower and more difficult process. One reason is that price reductions are more conspicuous, sooner noticed, easier to match or outdo and much harder to retract than most forms of non-price competition; another reason is that non-price competition requires skill and inventiveness, whose limited supply limits the length to which rivalry in offering its various amenities can go.

What is the trade-off between price and non-price competition?

Having dealt with the price maker's preferences between price and non-price competition, we can next look at their respective benefits from society's point of view. We know that price competition promotes price flexibility and narrows the mark-up between prices and marginal costs, thereby helping market forces to harmonize individual agent's economic behaviour and so to approximate the ideal of market clearing and efficient resource allocation more closely. On the other hand, those narrower mark-ups lessen the scope and inducement for merchants to create a buyers' market and for producers to innovate, provide variety and otherwise anticipate and cater to the public's tastes. Non-price competition creates these social benefits and, while it can raise or lower mark-ups, it is more likely to widen than to narrow them. Thus, the respective advantages of price and non-price competition are likely to be mutually incompatible.

In short, there is a trade-off between the social benefits of the two kinds of competition and I know of no way to compare or rank them. Common sense suggests that non-price competition should have priority, because it seems more important to have progress and continually to adapt and devise goods and services according to the public's needs and desires, rather than to cheapen existing goods and services to induce people to make fuller use of them. At the same time, it is also clear that society needs both. To get both, we have to compromise and accept less than perfect resource utilization and allocation for the sake of gaining some of the benefits of non-price competition. Since market forces cannot provide unaided a full (or even an adequate) measure of both kinds of benefits, they need to be supplemented by deliberate policies, like patent and copyright laws to buttress monopoly, antitrust action to encourage non-price competition, legislation for truth in lending and selling to block misleading advertising, and employment policies to increase resource utilization.

Note in this connection that the simple-minded argument for non-interference with market forces loses much of its force once one recognizes that efficient resource utilization and allocation are not the only benefits of the market economy, that its other benefits are no less important and that there is a degree of incompatibility between the two sets of benefits.

Can the benefits of non-price competition exist in symmetric markets?
The number, variety and importance of the social benefits that non-price competition creates in asymmetric markets makes one wonder whether they are absent in symmetric markets, which provide little or no scope for non-price competition, or, if they are present, who creates them and in response to what inducements.

A general equilibrium theorist might answer that, in perfect markets, demand for amenities whose benefits exceed their cost would be bound to elicit supplies. But this answer overlooks two facts. First, markets cannot signal consumers' hopes and desires for things not yet in existence and only transmit information about the urgency of demand for already available products, services and amenities. Secondly, such an answer also overlooks the risk of catering to a demand not yet formulated, which requires monopoly profits to pay for an investment that may easily misfire.

The problem here is not the static problem of whether demand for an amenity already known and found valuable would call forth a supply, but whether a product not yet even thought of would be dreamed up and developed by someone. The creation of buyers' and sellers' markets is a matter not of responding to consumers' wishes, but of anticipating them. In that it resembles, on its smaller and cheaper scale, the innovative process in the realm of production.

Only someone with imagination, initiative, willingness to gamble and the capital to gamble with can provide the amenities of a buyers' market. In asymmetric markets, price makers who have already seized the initiative and enjoy some monopoly profits are certainly the best-placed, if not the only ones to create these amenities. Credit cards, however, are an important example of a consumers' convenience often provided by third parties – banks.

In symmetric markets in which both sides lack marketing expertise, marketing experts can and usually do insert themselves as middlemen, providing information and other services and conveniences to both sides and reimbursing themselves for services rendered, sometimes by charging commissions but more often by assuming the price maker's role in both their buying and selling, thus reaping both monopsony and monopoly profits. The large wholesale houses of merchant capitalism and the trading companies (*shoshas*) of Japan already mentioned are the important historical examples; other examples are auction houses, real-estate brokers, used-car and antique dealers, and junk shops.

Symmetric markets in which buyers and sellers alike are expert professionals are bilateral monopolies and commodity exchanges. A good example of a bilateral monopoly is the market for armaments. There, one important amenity of the buyers' market is ruled out by its great expense: the seller's willingness to hold inventory to satisfy additional demand quickly. However, another very expensive amenity – product improvement and the development of new products – is important enough for the buyer to initiate it and pay for it directly, on a cost-plus basis.

Another important example of bilateral monopoly is the unionized labour market. There, the most important missing amenity is a counterpart to the readiness (under favourable circumstances!) of price-making employers to absorb additional labour. At the same time, many of the services and amenities that non-price competition among employers for scarce labour would provide, such as good working conditions, health insurance and pensions, are usually obtained by bargaining between union and management. Note the close parallelism between this and the previous example.

Concluding thoughts

I have purposely left commodity exchanges to the end. In these exchanges, expert professionals compete among themselves on both sides of the market, which brings us back to the subject of general equilibrium theory.

In designing their mathematical models, general equilibrium theorists made a deliberate decision to make prices and the quantities demanded and supplied the only dependent variables. They chose to regard all else, including the quality and variety of products and services, as exogenously given constraints. Their decision to have no other variables in their models must have been dictated by a mental picture of the main practical examples of perfect competition: the commodity exchanges that trade in cotton, wheat and other agricultural staples, and in raw materials, as well as in futures of those staples and raw materials.

In those exchanges, there is little need for the ancillary services and amenities discussed in this chapter. Technical progress in the production of staples and extraction of raw materials is mainly initiated and financed by agricultural research institutes, along with the monopolistic manufacturers of farm equipment and extractive machinery. As to the services and amenities that constitute buyers' markets, some of them, like advertising and window displays are redundant where buyers' and sellers alike are knowledgeable professionals and the merchandise is so highly standardized and graded that it can be bought sight unseen. Other amenities, like credit or transport, are provided or bought by each side for itself, since both sides can purchase these amenities with equal ease and at equal cost.

That still leaves unaccounted for the cost of the premises in which dealers transact their business, the communication and other equipment they need, and the services of the brokers and other personnel who run the exchange.

The cost of their pay and maintenance is negligible and usually paid for out of the very small commission (typically one-tenth of 1 per cent) that the exchange charges to both buyers and sellers.

In short, general equilibrium theory, which deals with an imaginary economy modelled on commodity exchanges, had good reason to ignore the social benefits of non-price competition. But for those who seek to understand the real economy in all its depth and complexity, the benefits of monopolistic, asymmetric, non-price competition cannot be ignored.

Notes

1. For the argument that the standardization of products is always the result of the buyers' expertise, see Scitovsky (1951 or 1971, p. 17).
2. For the first discussion of the subject matter of this section, see part III of Scitovsky (1951) or part IV of the revised 1971 edition.
3. For the argument of this and the previous paragraph, see Schumpeter (1942). For arguments that investment, innovation and technical progress require the inducements that monopolistic competition and the funds and information that monopoly provide, see Schumpeter (1926).
4. For a detailed discussion of the subject of this paragraph, see Richardson (1960).
5. For a detailed discussion of sellers' (as well as buyers') markets, see Scitovsky (1985).

References

Richardson, G.B. (1960), *Information and Investment*, (Oxford: Oxford University Press).
Schumpeter, Joseph (1926), *Theorie der Wirtschaftlichen Entwicklung*, (Munich: Duncker & Humblot).
—— (1942), *Capitalism, Socialism and Democracy*, (New York: Harpers).
Scitovsky, Tibor, (1951), *Welfare and Competition*, (Chicago: Irwin), revised 1971.
—— 'Pricetakers' plenty: a neglected benefit of capitalism' (1985) *Kyklos*, **38**, 517–36.
Tylecote, A., (1981), *The Causes of the Present Inflation*, (London, Macmillan).

2 The debate on socialist economic planning in today's perspective*

The debate took the form of articles, notes, rejoinders and two books published in England during the great depression of the 1930s. It had precursors, of course, because economists have long been intrigued by the problem whether and how a rational economic system could be organized in a centrally planned collectivist state. The first economist to raise the issue seems to have been Vilfredo Pareto (Pareto, 1897). As one of the founders of modern quantitative economics, he was well aware of the crucial role that the values attached to products and productive factors play in economic decision making, but he felt that the role which such 'real entities' as prices play in the market economy could equally well be performed by 'accounting entities' in a centrally planned economy without markets. It was Pareto's pupil and successor, Enrico Barone, however, who worked out his suggestion in a mathematical system of equations whose solution was to provide those accounting entities (Barone, 1908).

In 1920, when his country had a socialist government, the Austrian Ludwig von Mises published an important paper on the subject, apparently unaware of Pareto's and Barone's writings (Mises, 1920). He argued the impossibility of rational resource allocation without private ownership of the means of production, basing that conclusion on two arguments. First, he wrote that, if the socialist state owned all intermediate and capital goods, they would not pass through markets and so fail to acquire market prices reflecting their costs to producers and worth to users, without which their efficient allocation to alternative uses as well as the efficient allocation of resources to their production would be impossible. His second argument was that managers of plants are the people in the best position to recognize the possibility and advantages of innovative investments; but since, as managers of state property they would not be free to make their own decisions, they could neither take the initiative for innovative investments nor be made financially responsible for their outcome; yet without their ability to make such decisions and accept their risks, innovative investment and economic progress would be impossible.

In 1928, Fred M. Taylor made a contribution to the subject in his presidential address to the American Economic Association by arguing that the eco-

* This paper was presented, in the original German, at the 1993 Budapest conference of the Osterreichisches Ost- und Südosteuropa-Institut.

nomic authorities in a socialist state could establish prices for productive factors and capital goods on a trial and error basis, accepting their historical values for a start and then correcting them as necessary whenever their use led to shortages or surpluses (Taylor, 1929).

These were some of the more interesting precursors of the 1930s debate, which took place not only between the conservative Lionel Robbins and Friedrich von Hayek and the leftist Maurice Dobb, Henry D. Dickinson, Oscar Lange and Abba P. Lerner but also and even mainly among the members of this last group. The debate was greatly facilitated by von Hayek's having had the pertinent articles of Barone, Halm, Mises and Pierson translated into English and published in a collected volume along with a long historical introduction and an equally long postscript by himself (Hayek, 1935).

The debate began with a paper by Maurice Dobb, my kindest Cambridge teacher, a Marxist well known for his concern over the conflict between efficiency and equality. He argued for an equal income distribution and the central planning of the structure of consumer good production, the latter partly in order to protect unschooled and easily influenced consumers from their own mistakes, and partly to resolve (or evade?) the conflict just mentioned (Dobb, 1933). The other leftist participants were much more liberal and favoured free choice of occupation and consumers' sovereignty, in the sense of consumers' influence on what is produced and in what proportions.

In reply to Dobb, Lange (1936–7) argued that, in a socialist system where capitalist wealth is abolished and the state provides free education (to which today one would add free health care), the principles of equal income distribution and free choice of occupation need not be incompatible. For leisure time, a lazy existence and a simple, frugal life can be looked upon as consumers' goods that some people are willing to buy and pay for by accepting lower wages for work that is easier, less strenuous and requires less schooling. Moreover, should that and differences in innate talent or intelligence still create too great differences in incomes, these could be mitigated by the distribution of the social dividend. For the socialist state, as the sole owner of capital and land, would receive a sizable part of the national income, available not only for covering public expenditures and the cost of capital accumulation but also for distribution among the population.

More difficult and much more discussed was the problem of how to reconcile free occupational choice with consumers' sovereignty. Everybody agreed that its proper resolution required prices; the question was how best to ascertain the proper prices of goods for which no markets would exist, such as raw materials, parts, machine tools and other capital goods, because the collectivist state would be not only their owner but their user as well.

Robbins in a book (Robbins, 1934) and von Hayek in the postscript to his 1935 volume, accepted Barone's demonstration that theoretically those prices can be obtained as the solution of a system of equations; but they argued the practical impossibility of calculating millions of prices with the aid of the same number of equations on the basis of many more millions of statistical data. (Computers were unknown at the time; but I doubt if they would have changed that judgement.) Accordingly, several of the young leftist economists sought the solution in an imitation of the process with which markets generate prices; that is, by a sequence of trials and errors until the equilibrium prices that equate supplies and demands are attained. As already mentioned, Fred Taylor in 1928 was the first to propose that solution and later Dickinson independently had the same idea (Dickinson, 1933). Hayek's bibliography cites both their papers but either he had not read them or he lacked faith in that method.

The method's detail was worked out in the first part of Lange's article, already cited, which is altogether by far the most complete and thoughtful discussion of the whole subject. He presupposed that consumer goods' prices and workers' wages would be market-determined, just as in a market economy, proposed that all other prices (and interest rates) be determined by a central planning office and that those prices, along with the market prices for consumer goods and labour, be used by the managers of enterprises as the basis for all their cost calculations as well as their buying and selling decisions. Where demand exceeded supply, the planning office would raise the price, where it fell short of supply, it would lower the price, until equilibrium prices were reached. In short, Lange recognized Walras's insight that commodity exchanges with their auctions represent the only practical approximation to the theoretical ideal of perfect competition, and had the clever idea to imitate them in his plan for a socialist economy, with the central planning office acting as the Walrasian auctioneer and state enterprises acting as buyers and sellers. Lange then proceeded to prescribe the behaviour of enterprise managers: they would have to regard all prices as given parameters and, on that basis, aim at so combining the factors of production and determining the output produced as to minimize average costs of production.

Lerner, who then was editor of the review in which Lange's article appeared, published a note in the same issue (Lerner, 1936), criticizing a few of Lange's points, including his rule for managers to produce the output that minimizes its average cost. He proposed to replace that rule with two rules: one for plant managers to produce the output that equates the product's marginal cost to its price, the other for the manager of the whole industry to bring the number and size of the industry's plants to the level that minimizes the industry's average production costs, achieving that either by not replacing worn-out plants or by encouraging the building of new or the enlarging of old plants as the case may be. Lange accepted those corrections and incorporated them in the revised version of his paper (Lange and Taylor 1938).

The second part of Lange's paper dealt, in addition to his answer to Dobb already mentioned, with three topics: (1) externalities, (2) the motivation of public officials as plant managers and (3) investment. He rightly argued that a socialist collectivist state would be in a far better position to take external economies and diseconomies into account than private enterprise, although, since his writing, we have also learned, at least the principles, of how to make private firms deal with that problem.

On the second topic, Lange argued 'that the real danger of socialism is that of a bureaucratisation of economic life ... and we do not see how the same, or even greater, danger can be averted under monopolistic capitalism' (Lange, 1936–7, 127–8). He believed that the motivation of public officials would not be very different from that of corporate officials under monopoly capitalism, which may well be true; but he surely exaggerated when he implied that bureaucratic, hierarchically administered giant corporations have completely replaced private small-scale enterprises and failed to suggest the obvious remedy, which Lerner thought of later when he suggested providing socialist plant managers with financial inducement to follow the rules given to them.

On the subject of innovating investment, Lange had an excellent and admirably concise presentation of the difference between competitive capitalism and monopoly capitalism. He juxtaposed the gains of a successful innovating investor and the losses his competitors suffer when he lures away their customers and depresses their prices. He pointed out that, during the early, competitive phase of capitalism, prices performed their parametric function and enabled innovation to proceed unhampered by competitors' losses; and since those losses were offset by their customers' gains, the economy grew and total welfare increased. Under the later phase of monopoly capitalism, however, the gainers and losers from most innovations were either oligopolists or the one-and-only monopolist, who weighed the gains and losses against one another, which slowed or impeded investment and so depressed the economy. (Essentially the same argument, already stated by Robbins (1934, p. 141), is one of the central themes of Josef Steindl's 1952 book.)

From that valid and important contrast between competitive and monopoly capitalism, Lange erroneously concluded that socialism would be more favourable to innovation, growth and prosperity than was private enterprise at that time because, by imitating perfect competition, it would resemble the early phase of competitive capitalism. His error lay in his only seeing the difference between the two phases of capitalism and overlooking their similarity, which was that both of them were capitalist. For the essence of capitalism is the exploitation of the weak by the strong in their market relations. The latter's superiority over the former can be based on any disparity between them, be it of physical strength, wealth, cleverness or, as is mostly the case in competitive economies, of knowledge. For in every market of our economy where producers sell what they produce and consumers buy what they consume, specialized experts sell to laymen and laywomen, using their superior knowledge to exploit them. Competition among them does not eradicate their superiority and therefore cannot eliminate exploitation completely; but it limits the degree of exploitation, partly by lowering prices and profit margins and partly or even mainly through non-price competition; that is, through currying favour with customers to lure them away from competitors by offering them better quality, more choice, technical or aesthetic improvements, innovations and whatever else renders their offers more valuable and attractive. Price reduction is the simplest competitive weapon but quickly leads to retaliation and so to the all-round reduction of profits. That is why most sellers prefer some of the various forms of non-price competition, which usually take longer, require more initiative, imagination, technical know-how and may also be more costly but are usually more effective, harder to retaliate against, need not lower mark-ups and may even raise them if they engender brand loyalty (Scitovsky, 1990).

I am going into all this detail because, paradoxical as it may seem, non-price competition for the custom of consumers to exploit is an important driving-force of innovation and the engine of growth under capitalism as long as that is competitive (Domar, 1989, Scitovsky, 1985). Competitive capitalism therefore was exploitation mitigated *but not eliminated* by competition. It was the driving-force of the tremendous progress which Marx was the first to draw attention to, as Lange well knew, because he quotes him extensively. Let me lift just one sentence out of his page-long quotation, which comes from the Communist Manifesto: 'The bourgeoisie, during its rule of scarcely one hundred years, has created more massive and more colossal productive forces than have all preceding generations together' (Lange, 1936–7, 128). Lange hoped to harness that engine of growth to his model of socialism, not realizing that his clever imitation of perfect competition, with its rule of equating marginal cost to price, would, if successful, eliminate exploitation completely, render non-price competition unprofitable and put an end to economic progress. The difference therefore between monopoly capitalism, competitive capitalism and perfect competition is that the first is unmitigated exploitation without growth, the second mitigated exploitation with growth, the third lack of both exploitation and growth.

Let me hasten to add that Lange's mistake was not peculiar to him. At that time, most of us still looked upon imperfect (or 'free' competition, as it sometimes was called) as the practical approximation to the theoretical ideal of perfect competition, from which it only differed in not fully realizing all the latter's remarkable advantages. It never occurred to anyone that it could also have an important advantage over that ideal, which would be eliminated if the ideal were attained. Joseph Schumpeter seems to have been the first exception to that rule. In his (1926) *Theory of Economic Development*, unknown in England at the time, he discussed at length the motivations necessary for accepting the risks of undertaking innovative investments and listed the prospect of substantial profits as the first of them; and that would certainly be missing under perfect competition or a successful imitation of it. Equally missing under both would be non-price competition, which my 1951 book may have been the first to discuss and whose stimulating impact on innovation was recognized only much later (Domar, 1989; Weitzman, 1984; Scitovsky, 1985, 1990).

Lerner's most important contribution to the debate was his classic *The Economics of Control* (1944). It summarized and rounded out his earlier writings on the subject, contained very much additional material, and was written in the style of a handbook for the use of a socialist-planned economy's managers and employees, with rules for plant managers and central government to follow, designed to imitate perfect competition, along the lines of Lange's article but in much greater detail and covering every possible eventuality. Nevertheless, I doubt if it ever was used as a handbook in any socialist country. Instead, it acquired fame as an excellent, clear, purely verbal explanation of the theory of perfect competition and welfare economics and was much used as a textbook in the United States. I may add here that not only Lerner's book but also the whole debate on socialist economic planning was most useful in making Western economists understand much better the meaning and functioning of their own market economies.

As a model for a planned socialist economy and handbook for its architects and managers, Lerner's volume had great merits but also a great drawback. Its representation of perfect competition, its remarkably elegant argument for an equal income distribution and its short summaries of such macroeconomic topics and policies as taxation, investment, unemployment, foreign trade and the trade cycle may have made it a useful background for the planning of a socialist economy. Equally useful was Lerner's recommendation that public officials be given a financial inducement for carrying out the rules prescribed for their management of enterprises. Lerner's much more liberal and democratic notion of socialism than that of the other leftist participants in the debate was, or rather would have been, a further advantage, had it been followed. For Lerner favoured the retention, even the encouragement of private enterprise within a socialist economic system, partly for the sake of its competition with the state enterprise, which was to reduce production costs and decide which of the two is to survive as the more efficient producer, and partly also because he considered the existence of private enterprise the best guarantee of individual freedom.

As to its drawback, one misses in Lerner's book any discussion or even mention of the question as to who might shoulder the risk of innovative investments in a centrally planned economy, which Mises raised and Lange discussed but then wrongly believed himself to have answered. Lerner's silence on it is all the more surprising because he analyses at length the more formal and analytic aspects of investment and its multiplier effects, proposing to make the setting of the rate of interest a political decision of the central government of socialist economies and prescribing the rule for managers of state enterprises to push investment to the point where its marginal efficiency has been diminished to equality with the rate of interest set by the central planning authority.

The book contains a dozen or more of such rules whose precision and apparent simplicity can be very deceptive. To estimate even such simple concepts as marginal cost and marginal product can be very difficult in actual practice; but the difficulty is especially great in the case of the marginal efficiency of investment, whose margin of error is likely to be a multiple of the estimate. One occasionally reads of cost overruns on a new weapon, which can be ten times the original cost estimate, while the same weapon's performance turns out all too often to be disappointing, falling short of what it was touted to be. Identical in nature and similar in magnitude are the difficulty and uncertainty involved in predicting the cost of investing in the manufacture of a new consumer good and the latter's popularity with the consuming public, both of which are essential parts of estimating the marginal efficiency of that investment. In short, to undertake innovative investment that benefits consumers is often a large gamble; and establishing who should be made responsible for taking such gambles in a socialist society is a very difficult problem.

Lerner, who published Lange's article, must have been well aware of that problem. It is true that his socialist model included private enterprise to which he assigned important functions and could also have assigned that function; but if this was so, he should and probably would have made it explicit. My guess is that he accepted Lange's erroneous conclusion as valid because he, too, like the rest of us in those days, may have believed that perfect competition and perfect economy were one and the same thing.

The conservative Manchester liberals, who participated in or watched the debate, were in no danger of overlooking that problem, because they had no faith in a socialist imitation of perfect competition. Their concern, however, was not so much civil servants' lack of inducements to undertake innovative investments as their ability to respond to such inducement. It seemed to them that managers of state-owned enterprises would be in no position to base investment decisions on their own judgement and consequently could hardly be held financially responsible for them.

By today (1993) we have learnt a lot about the economic problems that the former Soviet Union and the socialist countries of Eastern Europe have failed to solve. The officials of those countries probably paid little or no attention to the 1930s debate, but it is worth noting that many of their failures were due to their inability to resolve the problems discussed in it.

Consider first the low labour productivity, high production costs and technical backwardness of many of their industries and the depressing drabness and uniformity of many consumer goods in the Soviet Union and apparently also in the other East European countries. It seems that the socialist countries failed to resolve in practice the same problem which the left-wing economists were unable or unwilling to grapple with in theory. For lack of imagination, drive or technical know-how could not have been the cause of their backwardness, because the Soviet Union accomplished a lot in science, space exploration, atomic research and in her defence industries; and all the communist countries were outstanding in sports and athletics. So one must look for the causes elsewhere.

One could have been the excessive concentration of all investment decisions in the central government, which would explain the concentration of progress on the defence and prestige industries. Initiative for progress in the consumer good sector would have to have been taken by plant managers in that sector, because they would have been the most knowledgeable about the possibility and attractiveness of improvements; but they seemed to lack authority, inducement or willingness (or all three) to take responsibility for expensive changes that might prove a flop. Wealthy capitalists seem more willing to risk part of their wealth for the chance of a huge accretion to it than are state employees to risk their job or worse for mere praise or faster promotion. Fear of any departure from the status quo may have been another explanation, because it resembles too much a departure from the ruling political ideology.

Let me recall in this connection Professor Janos Kornai's well-known work on the softness of the budget constraint (Kornai, 1986), which he considered the main problem of socialist economies, and whose source is the fear of state officials to admit the failure of their past investments. Yet the occasional failure of risky investment is unavoidable in any economy, and the cost of those failures is part of the price society pays for the benefits of the successful ones. In the private enterprise economy, every businessman accepts willy-nilly the risk of failure, hoping of course that not he but his competitors will pay the price, while he reaps the benefit and may even acquire his competitors' customers in addition. Apparently, socialist economies have not succeeded in accepting the unavoidable gamble that innovative investment involves.

I was made aware of another problem of socialist economies by a Hungarian official who audited economics courses at Harvard on a State Department fellowship while I too was a visitor there. He said he was struck by the failure of his and his family's living standards to get any better during the many years that Hungarian statistics showed 6 to 7 per cent annual additions to their national product. He was sufficiently intrigued to look into the matter and discovered that the statistics showed the growth in production, not in sales, whose discrepancy explained the huge accumulation of unsold and unsalable inventories, which were only relieved by spoilage. He was an intelligent person who drew the obvious conclusion; I learnt only months later that he had held the prestigious job of secretary to the Communist Party's central committee in Hungary until the 1956 revolution. His account reminded me of the many news reports from the USSR of unharvested farm produce rotting on the ground for lack of transport, since both were evidence of faulty resource allocation, which Lange's imitation of perfect competition was supposed to remedy.

Let me mention yet another piece of evidence I found in a book in which the well-known French novelist and enthusiastic believer in communism, André Gide, described his disappointment on visiting the Soviet Union (Gide, 1937). That was the time when the world press reported the astonishing feat of some Russian workers (named Stakhanovites after the first of them) who managed to accomplish in a single eight-hour day the same amount of work that ordinary Russian workers took several days to perform. On his sightseeing tour, Gide came to a large Russian coalmine, where he met a delegation of French miners who had been invited by the Soviet miners' labour union to visit the USSR. To show their gratitude for the invitation, the French miners offered to take the place of their hosts for a single day's shift in the mine. As they reappeared on the surface at the end of their shift, they were surprised to find themselves applauded and celebrated as true Stakhanovites and heroes of labour, although – as they recounted the surprising event to Gide – they were merely following their accustomed, fairly comfortable and not particularly exhausting French routine. Gide rightly concluded that the celebrated Stakhanovites must, by French standards, be ordinary workers. The extraordinary ones are the great masses of Russian workers, extraordinary in their slowness and easy-going ways.

When I read about East German workers getting jobs in West German factories and being fired after a few months for their slowness and lack of work discipline, I remembered that story in Gide's long-forgotten book. The explanation of both, I suppose, must be the great merit of socialist economies, where work is regarded as a right as well as a duty. When youngsters reach working age, they must presumably be given jobs in the fields for which they trained whether or not there are vacancies. With a well-functioning price system, that would have led to increased production and/or investment in additional productive capacity in those fields; but surplus labour coupled with a shortage of goods and perhaps also of productive capacity was yet another indication of faulty resource allocation owing to mismanagement or the lack of a meaningful price structure.

References

Barone, Enrico (1908), 'Il ministerio della produzione nello stato collettivista', *Giornale degli Economisti*, English translation in Hayek (1935).
Dickinson, H.D. (1933), 'Price formation in a socialist community', *Economic Journal*, **43**.
Dobb, Maurice (1933), 'The problems of a socialist economy', *Economic Journal*, **43**.
Domar, Evsey D. (1989), 'The blind men and the elephant', *Capitalism, Socialism and Slavery*, (New York: Cambridge University Press).
Gide, André (1937), *Retour de l'URSS*, (Paris: Gallimard).
Halm, Georg (1926), 'Ist der Sozialismus wirtschaftlich möglich?', Berlin, English translation in Hayek (1935).
Hayek, Friedrich von (1935), *Collectivist Economic Planning*, (London: Routledge).
Kornai, János (1986), 'The soft budget constraint', *Kyklos*, **39**, (1).
Lange, Oskar (1936–7), 'On the economic theory of socialism', *Review of Economic Studies*, **4**.
—— and Taylor, F.M. (1938), *On the Economic Theory of Socialism*, (Minneapolis: University of Minnesota Press).
Lerner, A.P. (1936), 'A note on socialist economics', *Review of Economic Studies*, **4**.
—— (1944), *The Economics of Control*, (New York: Macmillan).
Mises, Ludwig von (1920), 'Die Wirtschaftsrechnung im sozialistischen Gemeinwesen', *Archiv für Sozialwissenschaft*, Bd.47, English translation in Hayek (1935).
Pareto, Vilfredo (1897), *Cours d'Économie Politique*, Vol. 2, (Lausanne).
Robbins, Lionel (1934), *The Great Depression*, (London: Macmillan).
Schumpeter, Joseph (1926), *Theorie der Wirtschaftlichen Entwicklung*, (Munich: Duncker & Humblot).
Scitovsky, Tibor (1951), *Welfare and Competition*, (Homewood, Ill.: Irwin).
—— (1985), 'Pricetakers' plenty: a neglected benefit of capitalism', *Kyklos*, **38**.
—— (1990), 'The benefits of asymmetric markets', *Journal of Economic Perspectives*, **4**.
Steindl, Josef (1952), *Maturity and Stagnation in American Capitalism*, (Oxford: Blackwell).
Taylor, Fred M. (1929), 'The guidance of production in a socialist state', *American Economic Review*, **19**.
Weitzman, Martin L. (1984), *The Share Economy: Conquering Stagflation*, (Cambridge, Mass./London: Harvard University Press).

3   Lerner's contribution to economics*

Abba P. Lerner was one of the most original and imaginative economists of his generation. He initiated more of the concepts, theorems and rules that today constitute our profession's workaday tools than anyone else. Lerner introduced the idea that monopoly is a matter of degree, measured by the ratio in which the divergence between price and marginal cost stands to price; he was the first to establish the 'Lerner–Hotelling condition' that marginal-cost pricing is a universal welfare-maximizing rule, which extends even to decreasing-cost industries; he and Oskar Lange were the main architects of the theory of market pricing in socialist economies; and he was the one to base the ethical argument for greater income equality on a logical footing.

In the field of international economics, Lerner was the first to assert and prove the complete equalization of factor prices by free trade in products; he established definitively that export and import duties have identical consequences; he seems to have been the first to raise the question of what might be the optimum currency area and what factors determine it; he was among the earliest advocates of variable exchange rates, probably being the first to advocate them in conjunction with counterspeculation (market intervention) by monetary authorities to smooth excessive fluctuations.

In the area of macroeconomics, Lerner provided the logical framework (functional finance) for Keynes's policy recommendations; he noted and expressed concern over the intolerably high unemployment needed to assure price stability decades before the rest of us did and many years before Milton Friedman presented the idea of a natural rate of unemployment; he introduced the concept and stressed the importance of sellers' inflation; he was probably the first to argue that only unexpected inflation has harmful effects, and the first to advocate the indexation of bonds.

Many of Lerner's contributions were so fundamental that today all economists know and constantly use them without knowing or caring who introduced them. Also the sheer variety and range of subjects to which he contributed spread his fame not only wide but also thin, which partly explains why an economist of Lerner's stature and originality has received such scant recognition. It is as if his many new ideas on so many disparate subjects had left him no time to develop and elaborate any to the extent that would

* This chapter appeared in *Journal of Economic Literature*, vol. XXII, December 1984, pp. 1547–71.

indelibly stamp them with his authorship. Another partial explanation was, perhaps, his footlooseness. All his life, he was on the move from university to university, never staying in the same place long enough to acquire a following of younger colleagues and graduate students who would use, test, spread and extend his ideas.

Another reason for his lack of recognition may have been his exceptionally sharp logic and undue faith in its power. He rightly trusted the rightness of his logic, however far it took him off the beaten path; unjustified was his trust in the power of logic to influence action and of *his* logic to convince others. Few economists dare to venture out of the security of the conventional wisdom to follow the dictates of logic more than one cautious step at a time; and the few who do want the reassurance of mathematical reasoning to vouchsafe its correctness. Because Lerner's logic was honed on rabbinical, not mathematical studies, his arguments did not have the persuasive power of mathematical reasoning – a serious lack at a time when mathematics were fast becoming the language of economics. Yet he was a wonderful expositor, who excelled at geometrical proofs and scientific writing, and he was a master at reducing arguments and policy recommendations to bare essentials, thereby clarifying their logic and exposing their full implications. Not only was Lerner's writing a model of clear, succinct and rigorous scientific prose, he also preached what he practised: almost single-handed, he started a journal, the *Review of Economic Studies*, to provide an outlet for short, substantive papers with no excess verbiage.

Combined with his gift for exposition was Lerner's willingness to use it. He was always ready to help students and colleagues who, trapped in established habits of thought, had difficulty in grasping an unfamiliar argument; and he took great pains to devise means that would help them out of that trap.

But, however helpful he was in making difficult arguments simple, Lerner was utterly unwilling to modify the presentation of his ideas and policy recommendations for the sake of making them look less revolutionary and so cushioning the shock they so often administered to his listeners' and readers' preconceived notions. For Lerner believed in presenting new ideas in their starkest, most paradoxical form, to shock students into thinking for themselves, thereby forcing them to examine and reconsider traditional ideas they had unthinkingly accepted. That pedagogical device could be very effective with the young, but it frequently misfired with the not-so-young, in whom the profession's conventional wisdom was often too deeply ingrained to be examined afresh. They were merely alienated by Lerner's paradoxes and deceptively simple ideas and quite frequently looked upon him as a crank. That was all the easier because he dressed the part, with his open neck, bare toes and (later in life) his prophet's beard. In short, Lerner was a great teacher but a bad salesman.

That, in a sense, was a surprising shortcoming for so ardent a believer in democracy, who ought to have known that, if ideas are to be accepted and become effective, they must be not only correct but persuasive and attractively dressed up as well. He considered salesmanship and the translation of logical rules into practical policies the task of politicians, not economists, somehow forgetting that, for a politician to sell an idea and translate it into practical terms, he himself must be sold on it first – usually in ways and by arguments not much different from those he will need to persuade others. To make matters worse, Lerner's logic and the stark way in which he presented it often offended not only the ruling conventional wisdom but the conflicting conventional wisdoms of several contending ideologies all at the same time.

Lerner called himself a socialist but believed, not in the *socialist means* of the public ownership of the instruments of production, only in what he thought of as *socialist ends*: democracy, individual freedom, a fair income distribution, full employment and an optimal resource allocation. He must have shocked his fellow socialists when he extolled private enterprise on the ground that 'alternatives to government employment are a safeguard of the freedom of the individual'.[1] They were probably even more shocked when he argued against minimum wages, because they interfered with the price mechanism, which he considered 'one of the most valuable instruments of modern society'. Again, he was a devotee of free enterprise but would have astonished his co-devotees had they known that he defined it as 'the freedom of both public and private enterprise to enter any industry on fair terms which, in each particular case, permit that form to prevail which serves the public best'. Lerner was also the most ardent of Keynesians, to judge by all he did to clarify, extend and spread Keynes's ideas; yet he must have dismayed other Keynesians when he 'spotted the fatal flaw in the Keynesian schema' and warned against the inflationary consequences of full-employment policies two decades before the rest of us did. That insight, however, let me hasten to add, led him to try developing a means of reconciling price stability and full employment rather than advocating stability at the cost of unemployment.

Lerner's utter reliance on logic hindered acceptance of the man himself as well as of his ideas. It goes a long way, I think, to explain his loneliness and why he had few friends. Most people form emotional attachments not only to family and friends but also to ideas, ideologies and institutions; and they feel closest and friendliest to those who share those attachments. Lerner's unrelenting logic, however, overruled whatever loyalties he started with, and that made him seem like a cold fish to just about everybody: people on the left, on the right, to socialists, Manchester liberals and to Keynesians alike. His one abiding passion was the good society and whatever policies would bring it closer, which placed him in direct succession to the classic figures of political economy but earned him few friends among contemporary economists, to whom most of his policy recommendations looked like gimmicks. His interest was in normative, not positive economics: how the economy ought to and could be made to work, not how it actually works. Most of his thinking and writing was policy-oriented. He wanted to improve the economy, not economics – and that, I think, was yet another, perhaps even the most important reason for his failure to win the recognition he deserved. For, at the beginning of his career in the 1930s, when he was only flexing his mind, Lerner made many contributions to economic theory, which economic theorists were quick to appreciate, for which he got plenty of recognition. Only from the 1940s onwards, when he focused almost exclusively on policy recommendations, was he denied recognition, and that for two reasons. First, policy recommendations are addressed not to thinkers but to doers: politicians and economists involved in policy making who, for obvious reasons, are the slowest and most reluctant to abandon standard policies for the sake of new, untried ideas. They are the ones who distrust or even suspect pure logic, which was Lerner's strength, and need to be converted by salesmanship, which is what Lerner lacked.

The second reason why Lerner's policy recommendations cut so little ice was his lack of interest in and limited knowledge of how real economies actually operate and what individual motivations influence them. That often made him blind to political realities; and his overly simple picture of economic reality led him to prescribe overly simple cures for its woes. That, together with his inability or unwillingness to sell his ideas by means more persuasive than their inherent logic probably explains why so able and imaginative an economist saw so few of his policy recommendations put into practice.

It is quite obvious from Lerner's writings that he was fully aware of why his policy recommendations made so little headway. He must also have known that he could have advanced his career and fame far more effectively by sticking to the purely theoretical writings of his early years with which, he knew, he could win instant acclaim. But Lerner was a singularly selfless man, all of whose work seems to have been motivated not by personal ambition but by a desire to serve the public good. That explains, for example, why such an imaginative and original thinker spent so much time and effort writing purely expository articles (at least six) to explain another's ideas (Keynes's): at that time, the profession's and the general public's acceptance of those ideas seemed most important to him. At the same time, he was quite negligent about publishing his own original contributions to pure theory. Two of his theoretical papers (1952a, 1983a) were published with delays of two and five decades, respectively, and then only at other people's urging. The first is one of his most brilliant (see below, pp. 34–5). The same desire to promote the public good also explains Lerner's single-minded preoccupation with the problem of inflation during the last quarter-century of his life. None knew better than Lerner the doctrine of comparative advantage and his own comparative *dis*advantage in the art of formulating economic policies; but he was not the man to let go by default what he considered the economist's most urgent task.

Welfare economics and socialism

Lerner's first three articles, written while still an undergraduate, are little more than exercises in economic geometry, with one exception of which more will be said later. However, 'The Concept of Monopoly and the Measurement of Monopoly Power' (1934a), one of five papers he published while a first-year graduate student, is among his most brilliant. Also, it is the first of a series that culminated and were summarized in his best-known book, *The Economics of Control*. Today, a half-century after its publication, that article, however simple and simple-minded, still reads like an exceptionally clear and comprehensive exposition of what the social optimum means, why marginal-cost pricing is its necessary and sufficient condition, how competition assures and monopoly prevents its attainment, and what role the related concepts of rent, consumer's and producer's surpluses play. All that is elementary to present-day economists, but only because Lerner has made it so.

The first clear, rigorous and definitive statement of Pareto optimality also comes, not from Pareto's *Cours* or *Manuel*, where, according to Paul Samuelson (1964, 172), it is 'obscure and a bit confused', but from Lerner's article. When Lerner opts for marginal-cost pricing and marginal-product-value costing as the conditions of optimality instead of the then more orthodox and more generally accepted equality of average receipts and average costs, he is not setting up a straw man just to knock it down but is referring to the authoritative opinions of the day. To quote Samuelson (ibid. 173) once again: 'I can testify that no one at Chicago or Harvard could tell me in 1935 exactly why $P = MC$ was a good thing'; and the situation was no different in England, as will appear presently from the debate on socialism.

Lerner's paper was written (though not published) before Edward Chamberlin's and Joan Robinson's books on monopolistic and imperfect competition became available: at a time, therefore, when only the limiting cases of perfect competition and pure monopoly were known to the profession. Accordingly, Lerner's discussion of *degrees* of monopoly and his proposal to measure them by their distance from the $P = MC$ optimum introduced a continuous spectrum between the previously known limiting cases – a device Lerner often used, as we shall see below.

The economists of the early 1930s were helpless in the face of the Great Depression and regarded it as a major malfunction of capitalism, which probably explains the lively debate in the contemporary English periodicals on the feasibility of the alternative: a socialist economy. Participants in the debate came from the whole ideological spectrum. On the extreme right, Ludwig von Mises argued the logical impossibility of efficient resource allocation without market transactions between private participants. Friedrich von Hayek and Lord Robbins, impressed by Enrico Barone's brilliant 1908 mathematical paper, 'The Ministry of Production in the Collectivist State', conceded the conceptual possibility of efficient resource allocation under socialism but questioned the practicality of the ministry's bureaucrats solving – and solving in time! – the millions of equations that the market solves by trial and error in our economy. The socialist contributors to the debate[2] accepted the Hayek–Robbins position and focused their efforts on formulating a model that would use market prices for a trial-and-error approximation to the economic optimum in the socialist economy. The idea for such a solution had already been proposed in Fred M. Taylor's presidential address to the 1928 December meetings of the AEA, but it was worked out in detail only during the 1930s by a group of able young economists.

Most of them proposed rules of behaviour for socialist planners and plant managers, the observance of which would replicate one or another feature of the perfectly competitive economy. Lerner, in his five contributions to the debate (1934c, 1935, 1936c, 1937 and 1938) never worked out a full set of rules but confined himself to reviewing and criticizing the contributions of others, correcting their mistakes, amending their proposals and standing up for consumers' freedom of choice. In that disjointed fashion, however, he made one of the two major contributions to what is now known as the economic theory of socialism (the other is Lange's). He pointed out that perfect competition is not a goal but merely a means to an end: efficient resource allocation, whose only necessary condition is $P = MC$. As he put it, price or average revenue, marginal revenue, average total cost and marginal cost all tend to equal one another in perfectly competitive long-run equilibrium; but of the six equalities between those four variables only one, $P = MC$, is the necessary and sufficient condition of optimal resource allocation – the other five are merely the consequences of everybody's behaviour being optimal. Accordingly, Lerner could fault Taylor's full-cost pricing rule ($P = ATC$), Lange's prescribing the output that minimizes costs ($MC = ATC$) and Durbin's fall-back rule that plant managers maximize profits ($MR = MC$).

Lerner's contributions to the subject, along with some of his other work, were restated, integrated and greatly expanded much later, in his 1944 book, *The Economics of Control – Principles of Welfare economics*. Though written in the style of a handbook for use by socialist planners and plant managers, with its propositions presented as rules for planners and managers to follow, the book is more accurately described by the second than by the first half of its title. For most of those rules are nothing but the first-order conditions of welfare optimality, presented with great care, in meticulous detail, taking into account all cases and every conceivable exception but without a hint of the practical obstacles to observing them. A typical rule is: 'If the value of the marginal (physical) product of any factor is greater than the price of the factor, increase output. If it is less, decrease output. If it is equal to the price of the factor, continue producing at the same rate. (For then the right output has been reached.)' It reads like a recipe from *The Hopeless Cook's Cook-book* but its simplicity is deceptive because the practical problem of estimating a factor's marginal product is nowhere mentioned. True, Lerner's excellent and detailed discussion of indivisibilities, later in the book, makes clear to the careful and observant reader the virtual impossibility of estimating marginal product and marginal cost in any but the simplest cases. But the reader must be careful and observant, indeed, because Lerner never put the two things together; and, apart from introducing and discussing the concept of *net* marginal product, he gives no advice on how best to estimate the marginal product or marginal cost from real-life data. In short, the book was addressed to thinkers, not doers, however clear and simple its language. As Keynes put it, in a 1944 letter to Lerner: 'It is a great book worthy of one's hopes of you. A most powerful piece of well organized analysis with high aesthetic qualities, though written more perhaps than you see yourself for the cognoscenti in the temple and not for those at the gate.' Indeed, the book is a wonderfully clear, non technical and helpful guide to lead thoughtful readers through most problems of welfare economics, the simplest and deepest alike.

The exposition begins with the simple exchange economy, proceeds to production, first with one and then with several factors, for both fixed and variable proportions between factors and products, with special attention to allocation problems when factors, products and/or productive processes are indivisible. As the discussion of indivisibility is broadened to include factor indivisibility over time (that is, fixed factors), it leads into the separate problems of efficient allocation in the short and the long run, into the discussion of rent, economic surplus, taxation, analysis of production over time, investment and, ultimately, of the macroeconomic welfare problem: how to avoid both unemployment and inflation.

Lerner's *Principles of Welfare Economics* therefore goes far beyond the original meaning of that subtitle. As perhaps it should, it includes the welfare-economic principles not only of resource allocation narrowly defined, but of taxation, macroeconomic policy, international trade and international finance policy as well.

By comparing Lerner's book to Pigou's *Economics of Welfare*, one realizes how narrow and one-sided was Pigou's interpretation of that term, and what enormous progress has been made in one generation. Had Lerner written his *Economics of Control* fully footnoted with a complete set of references, one would also realize the magnitude of his own contribution to that progress.

The only thing that is strangely missing from this book is any mention of externalities.

At the same time, it contains some other interesting material, whose inclusion is explained by the fact that *Principles of Welfare Economics* is only its subtitle, whereas its main title defines it as a handbook for socialists on how to run their economy. Since a socialist economy, for Lerner, meant the use of private enterprise in some sectors, nationalized plants in others, depending on which was the more efficient in each, the book discusses not only all aspects, limitations, conditions and extensions of Pareto optimality but also why and when perfectly competitive behaviour leads to optimality and why and when real-life competition falls short of being perfect. Finally, the book was the first to go beyond mere Pareto optimality by also introducing into welfare economics a logically based judgement on distributional optimality, which needs some discussion because it is the most remarkable and most controversial contribution of the book.

Lerner's 1934 monopoly article was the first to recognize the serious limitation of Pareto's definition of optimality that consists in its compatibility with any and every distribution of income. That made him the natural person to tackle the problem of an optimal income distribution. As a first step in that direction, Lerner asked what income distribution would maximize the sum total of individual satisfactions if the size of the national income were independent of its distribution and if the distribution of the ability to experience satisfaction were unequal, uncorrelated with income distribution and unknown. Assuming the law of diminishing marginal utility to hold, and employing the Bayesian equal ignorance argument (that is, assuming that a move away from equality is as likely to increase as to diminish total satisfaction), he obtained the answer that an equal distribution of income would maximize society's probable total satisfaction.

Milton Friedman's 1947 review article criticized both Lerner's use of the equal ignorance argument and his acceptance of the utilitarian approach, which regarded the sum total of individual satisfactions as the proper measure of social welfare; and he offered an alternative proof of Lerner's result that made no use of the equal ignorance argument. That review started a controversy that took the edge off Friedman's critique, generalized Lerner's conclusion and may have been partly responsible for the emergence of inequality as an important new area of study. Samuelson (1964, 175) defended Lerner's use of the equal ignorance argument and reasoned that Friedman's alternative approach was no better. Valid and unassailable, however, was Friedman's critique that Benthamite utilitarianism, which considers the sum of individual utilities the measure of social welfare, was not only *not* the egalitarian criterion for which Lerner (along with Marshall, Pigou, Dennis Robertson, Jan Tinbergen and many others) mistook it but was, on the contrary, a very anti-egalitarian criterion.[3] Amartya Sen, however, has shown (1973, pp. 83–5) that Lerner's conclusion (viz., an equal income distribution is best when the distribution of the ability to enjoy income is unknown) holds true not only on the questionable utilitarian definition but also on any other definition of social welfare that makes it a symmetric concave function of concave individual welfare functions. That is an important generalization and vindication of Lerner's original argument which, of course, has great intuitive appeal.

International trade
A main topic of Lerner's early work was international trade, his papers on which were the most celebrated at the time and show best his skill with geometry. His first paper, 'The Diagrammatical Representation of Cost Conditions in International Trade', written as an undergraduate in 1932, brought together for the first time Pareto's indifference map, Marshall's offer curves and Gottfried v. Haberler's production possibility curves into an integrated geometrical apparatus for demonstrating the free-trade optimum in the two-country, two-commodity case and also showed the geometrical addition of production possibility curves.

In that paper, Lerner still used collective indifference curves; but already two years later, in 'The Diagrammatical Representation of Demand Conditions in International Trade' (1934), he showed the possibility of dispensing with community indifference curves in the welfare analysis of international trade. The argument and geometry of those two papers have become standard in modern textbooks on international trade only partly displaced, 20 years later, by James Meade's use of his trade-indifference curves.

Lerner's next contribution to the field was the celebrated Samuelson factor-price equalization theorem. The classical economists realized that factor mobility would equalize factor prices; Bertil Ohlin showed that product mobility is a substitute for factor mobility and so tends to diminish international differences in factor prices; and Samuelson published a geometrical (1948) and a mathematical proof (1949) to show that, on the assumption of no transportation costs, identical constant-returns-to-scale production functions and no factor-intensity reversals, free trade would equalize not only product prices but factor prices as well – in all cases except the limiting cases of complete specialization between the trading partners.

His 1948 paper was one of Samuelson's most celebrated contributions; but Lord Robbins, on reading it, remembered having heard the argument in his seminar 15 years earlier from Lerner, a copy of whose paper he still had. At Robbins's urging, Lerner published his 'Factor Prices and International Trade' (1952a) as originally written – and it is a very elegant, clear and succinct version. Why it was not published in 1934 may be explained by a story, current among Lerner's students when I was one of them in 1935. A student had offered to type one of Lerner's manuscripts for submission to a periodical but on her way home she left it on the bus and could never recover it. That was Lerner's only corrected copy and, because he was working on several other papers at the time,[4] he could not be bothered to reproduce the lost manuscript.

Lerner's next important paper on trade was his 'The Symmetry between Import and Export Taxes (1936a). The classical economists, down to Marshall and Pigou, stressed that foreign trade was essentially barter and took it for granted that taxes on imports and exports were symmetrical, in the sense of having identical effects: after all, what difference could it make whether a tax on foreign trade was levied on the imports bought or on the exports that paid for them? Francis Y. Edgeworth, however, in his important and otherwise wonderfully clear and rigorous 'The Theory of International Values' (1894), slipped up on that point. He showed, correctly, that the effect of duties on trade depended on whether they affected the demand for imports or the supply of exportables and illustrated the one case by a vertical shift (parallel to the import axis), the other by a horizontal shift (parallel to the export axis) of the duty-imposing country's offer curve. He then interpreted the two cases, wrongly, as representing the effects of an import duty and an export duty, respectively. Charles Bastable (1897, p. 116) soon pointed out the mistake, but Edgeworth did not quite recant. Not until a generation later, when Lerner came along, was the controversy resolved and the matter fully clarified.

Lerner's paper may still be the clearest and most comprehensive discussion of the subject. He vindicates the classical position that export and import duties are symmetrical and have identical effects; but he also accepts Edgeworth's reasoning as showing the differing effects, not of how the duty is levied but of how its proceeds are spent. The less spent on imports out of the duty's proceeds, the more favourable its impact on the terms of trade. Lerner uses the elegant geometry of inserting between the trading countries' offer curves a pencil, whose width, position and intersection with the two offer curves depict the size of the duty, the apportionment of its proceeds between imports and exportables, its impact on the terms of trade and the resulting volume of trade. Where Edgeworth's argument and diagram can be made to apply only to the limiting cases in which all the proceeds are spent either on exportables or on imports alone, Lerner's geometry illustrates the realistic intermediate cases as well. His paper was also important for reminding modern economists of the need to pay attention to the spending of tax proceeds when analysing the economic effects of taxation. Ricardo was fully conscious of that need, always having a macroeconomic general equilibrium model at the back of his mind; but later economists lost the habit and Lerner was probably the first modern economist to bring back the practice by stressing and demonstrating its importance.

Lerner's other contributions to international economics are to be found in his *Economics of Control* (1944), whose last chapters discuss the international trade and finance aspects of the economic optimum. They deal, among other things, with the possible conflict between the interest rate and income level that are necessary to maintain the fixity of exchange rates and those required for pursuing the goals of full employment and adequate growth. Since Lerner attaches a higher priority to those goals than to the convenience of fixed exchange rates, he wants to make foreign-exchange values subservient to the maintenance of full employment and favours 'currency autonomy', as he calls variable exchange rates.

That, in turn, leads him to discuss two related questions. First, if currency autonomy makes it easier to maintain employment and growth, why restrict it to countries; why not give currency autonomy to every region, district and village? Lerner's answer to his own question is that the free movement of people, investment and goods into other regions of the same country diminishes the social loss inflicted by regional unemployment and stagnation to such an extent as to reverse the priorities and give top priority to the convenience of a common currency.

The second question Lerner raises concerns the stability of the balance of trade. If price elasticities of demand for other countries' products are low, reducing the exchange value of a country's currency may do little to improve its balance of payments or may make it worse. Accordingly, Lerner would leave to an exchange stabilization board, not to market forces, the task of determining the country's exchange rate and, by the device of counterspeculation, of preventing manipulators and small fluctuations in demand and supply from disrupting the even course of foreign trade.

The whole discussion is probably the first modern argument in favour of variable exchange rates; the part concerning the size of the optimum currency area and its determinants is undoubtedly the first discussion of that problem, which was revived and carried forward by Robert Mundell (1961) and Ronald McKinnon (1963). Lerner's derivation of the condition of stability in the balance of trade and his discussion of the attendant problems probably explain why it is so often called the Marshall–Lerner condition, although earlier and more complete statements of it have been made by Bickerdike (1920) and Joan Robinson (1937). Official counterspeculation, however, at least for the purpose of offsetting the impact of monopolistic manipulators on market price, was definitely first suggested by Lerner.

Keynesian theory
Lerner was probably the first economist outside Keynes's inner circle to grasp the nature and importance of the *General Theory*. He immediately realized that the loss of welfare due to the involuntary unemployment of

labour and equipment was much greater potentially than that due to the misallocation of employed resources. From then onwards the greater part of his economic writings revolved around Keynesian macroeconomics. Within eight months of the publication of the *General Theory*, he wrote a summary for non-economists (1936b); in 1951, he published his *Economics of Employment*, which went considerably beyond Keynes and contained what was probably the first detailed exposition of the nature and danger of stagflation; and he wrote many articles to explain seeming paradoxes in the *General Theory*, to elucidate some of its obscurities, and to carry the argument further.

Let me start with Lerner's elucidation of the paradoxes. Perhaps the most revolutionary aspect of the *General Theory* was its use of macroeconomic theorems that flatly contradicted the profession's established habits of thought, which at the time were exclusively microeconomic. There was plenty of discussion of macroeconomic problems before Keynes, in such fields as money and banking, business cycles, public finance and international trade; but those discussions hardly ever made use of arguments that went counter to what seemed common sense on the basis of a person's or business firm's own experience.[5] Such macroeconomic arguments that the desire to save more is *not* likely to increase society's saving, or that a general wage reduction is *not* likely to diminish unemployment were totally new in the *General Theory*; and most people, including most economists, found it difficult to switch from their accustomed microeconomic thinking to Keynes's macroeconomic arguments, which seemed to fly in the face of common sense.

To help them make that switch and understand Keynes's reasoning, Lerner (1962) bridged the gulf between micro- and macroeconomics and reconciled their seemingly contradictory conclusions by presenting them as limiting cases of a continuous spectrum, leading up to them after first discussing intermediate cases within that spectrum.

Thus he showed how the decision of a group of people to save a fraction, q, of their income, Y_g, affects the group's actual saving, S_g, defined as the difference, $Y_g - E_g$, between their income and their expenditures. Expressing the size of the group by r, the ratio in which their income stands to national income, $Y_g = rY$, he showed that their expenditure declines by:

$$\Delta E_g = qrY,$$

their income declines by:

$$\Delta Y_g = r\Delta E_g = r(qrY),$$

so that the change in the group's actual saving becomes:

$$\Delta S_g = \Delta E_g - \Delta Y_g = (1 - r)qrY.$$

It is apparent from the last equation that, for a small group and a small value of r, the group's actual saving approximates the reduction in its members' expenditure; whereas at the other extreme, where the group comprises the whole economy and r equals 1, actual saving becomes zero. Lerner avoided the use of even such simple algebra but his verbal exposition and numerical examples are models of clarity and simplicity.

Lerner used a similar approach in the same paper, also, for showing the continuous spectrum between the very different ways in which employment and output respond to a change in wages on the microeconomic and the macroeconomic level. After explaining and distinguishing the substitution, income and cash-balance effects of the wage change, he first showed how all three were effective in the microeconomic case, with the substitution effect predominating. He then showed how the substitution effect became smaller as the number of firms affected by the wage change increased, and how it tended to zero as the wage change extended to all competitors. At that stage the income effect became the dominant force, until it too was eliminated as the wage change extended to the entire labour force and so led to an almost proportional change in incomes as well. At that stage, the macroeconomic case was reached, where the change in wages could affect employment and real output only through its cash-balance effect – and even that was eliminated if wage rigidities caused the wage changes to engender the expectation of further wage changes in the same direction, or if a rising demand for money (brought about by the rise in wages) created irresistible political pressures for an accommodating rise in the supply of money also.

Time and again Lerner used this technique: taking two contrasting cases and exploring the ground between them, thereby both facilitating and deepening one's understanding of them and bringing into focus a whole new range of intermediate cases. His first use of it came as early as the monopoly article, which was discussed above.

Let me now proceed to the second category of Lerner's papers dealing with the *General Theory*, those which elucidate some of the obscurities. I only want to mention his note 'User Cost and Prime User Cost' (1943b), which renders Keynes's user cost concept much simpler to understand and to use; and his 1936–7 'Capital, Investment and Interest' (essentially repeated in Lerner, 1953) which clarifies the meaning of Keynes's marginal efficiency of capital, its dependence on both the stock and rate of accumulation of capital and its relation to the classical concept: the marginal productivity of capital.

The most important, however, in that category is Lerner's 'The Essential Properties of Interest and Money' (1952b), which explains Keynes's notoriously obscure and difficult Chapter 17, of the same title, in the *General Theory*. Many readers, perhaps most, have despaired over and abandoned that chapter; all the more so because its object and the usefulness of the concept it introduced (own rates of interest) were far from clear, and because omitting that chapter did not seem to create any gap in one's understanding of Keynes. That, at any rate, was my attitude. Yet Lerner's clarification of Chapter 17 contains the key to an issue that even today, a half-century after the *General Theory* was published, is still alive and unresolved – at least in the minds of those who have not read Lerner's paper.

I am referring to whether underemployment equilibrium hinges on the downward rigidity of wages and whether greater wage and cost flexibility would resolve the unemployment problem. Lerner's paper is clear, succinct and full of insights; but since the argument is complex, with many ramifications, I would perform a disservice by trying to summarize it. Let me, however, list his conclusions and say a few words about one of them.

(1) Downward wage rigidity keeps unemployment from setting equilibrating forces into motion by preventing the fall in wage and price levels that would increase the real value of an unchanged money supply and so stimulate investment and consumer demand.

(2) Limited downward wage flexibility, by causing reductions in wages and prices to be gradual and spotty, would engender expectations of further wage and price reductions that are likely to offset, or more than offset, the stimulating effect on effective demand of the increase in real cash balances.

(3) For falling wages and prices *not* to engender the expectation of a further fall, they would have to fall instantaneously and to the extent needed fully to restore full employment; but such perfect flexibility of money prices and wages is incompatible with a monetary economy, since imperfectly flexible prices are an essential property of money. Chapter 17 of the *General Theory* tried, and Lerner's article managed, to substantiate that last statement.

The argument revolves around the medium-of-account function of money. Market operations involve an accounting cost: the mental effort of learning and retaining the prices of commodities that one wants to buy and sell as those prices change during the period of one's marketing horizon. The superiority of a money economy over a barter economy consists in its greatly reducing accounting costs, because n commodities in a market economy have only $n - 1$ prices at any moment in time, against their $n(n - 1)/2$ prices in a barter economy. For a money economy to get established, however, it is not enough for the public to recognize its advantages: people must also agree on which commodity to use for the unit of account. That choice is not arbitrary but is determined by their desire to minimize the number of prices to be learned and remembered. For efficient marketing requires one to know not only the $n - 1$ prices of the moment but, also, how those prices have changed in the past and are likely to change in the future. To minimize accounting costs, therefore, one must choose for use as money the commodity in terms of which the prices of other commodities are the least changeable over time. In other words, the stability or rigidity of prices saves accounting costs and so is a great advantage for every buyer and seller; and their desire to secure that advantage automatically assures as much of it as can be obtained by a suitable choice of the monetary medium.

Lerner's argument is clear and convincing; and since I never could get any of it from Keynes's Chapter 17, I am crediting it to Lerner. Note that in 1978, a quarter of a century later, Jürg Niehans seems independently to have developed the same argument, which he spells out in more detail but he, unlike Lerner, does not use it as a part-explanation of underemployment equilibrium.

Keynesian policy

The conflict between Keynes's policy recommendations, contained and implied in his *General Theory*, and the conventional wisdom reflected in the principles of sound finance was every bit as great as the conflict between his macroeconomic theorems and such microeconomically rooted conventional beliefs that a wage reduction would increase employment and an increased desire to save would increase saving. At the same time, however, that Keynes stressed and made much of the conflict between his and the classics' thinking on those two points, he advocated deficit spending in depression without so much as saying a word as to how that related to and conflicted with the tenets of sound finance. That task was undertaken and carried out by Lerner in 'Functional Finance and the Federal Debt' (1943a) and in restatements and elaborations of that paper's argument in both his *Economics of Control* and *Economics of Employment*.

It is true that Keynes was anxious to see his policies adopted and would not have found it politic to make too explicit, let alone stress, the conflict between his policies and what everybody else regarded as sound finance in those days. But Keynes seems to have been not so much hiding that conflict as to have been genuinely unaware of it, or at least of its full extent – to judge by his initially hostile and shocked reaction to Lerner's exposure of it.

The principles of sound finance are microeconomic in origin, derived from what seemed appropriate for the individual household and applied, by analogy, to the public household. Thus the argument for a balanced budget may be traced to a Shakespeare's 'neither a borrower nor a lender be', or the earlier 'to cut one's coat according to one's cloth'. The rule of keeping the public debt within some reasonable limit is just a retreat from that too austere position to a second line of defence.

Lerner argued that the subject had to be placed in a macroeconomic setting and then examined anew.

[His] central idea [was] that government's fiscal policy, its spending and taxing, its borrowing and repaying of loans, its issue of new money and its withdrawal of money, [should] all be undertaken with an eye only to the *results* of these actions on the economy and not to any established traditional doctrine about what is sound or unsound ... The principle of judging fiscal measures by the way they work or function in the economy [he called] functional finance. (Lerner, 1943a, p. 39).

Lerner formulated three laws of functional finance. First, use and adjust government spending and taxing in a way that will keep the economy's total spending at a level that is neither less nor more than what will buy the full-employment output at current prices, thereby avoiding both unemployment and inflationary pressures. Government must not and need not be concerned if, in the process, it spends more than its tax receipts or collects more in taxes than it is spending. Taxing therefore must never be undertaken solely because government needs money to make its payments.

Second, government should borrow money or repay debt only as a means of changing the proportions in which the public holds money and bonds when, by changing those proportions, it wants to raise or lower interest rates, thereby curbing or encouraging investment and instalment buying. Accordingly, government should never borrow merely to finance a deficit. That purpose is better served by printing money, unless it is desired to raise interest rates and so curtail investment and instalment buying at the same time.

The third law of functional finance is subsidiary to the first two. Government should print and put into circulation or withdraw from circulation and destroy the amount of money necessary to reconcile policies instituted in observance of the first two laws.

These laws of functional finance certainly seem to fly in the face of the traditional principles of sound finance, yet the conflict between them is more apparent than real. For, as Lerner pointed out, the evils that the principles of sound finance are supposed to ward off are either guarded against more effectively by the laws of functional finance or they are imaginary evils.

To start with the former, deficit financing and financing by the printing press are feared primarily for their inflationary implications. But, when they exert inflationary pressures, they exert them exclusively through their influence on effective demand, whose inflationary impact, however, is fully prevented when the first law of functional finance is observed. A second legitimate fear, engendered by a too large or too rapidly accumulating public debt, is that by raising interest rates investment will be curbed unduly, thereby slowing economic growth. That danger, however, is again guarded against when the *second* law of functional finance is observed. In other words, while functional finance seems, at first blush, to throw all restraint on reckless spending and borrowing to the winds, in reality, it substitutes specific and selective restraints for the general, vague and flexible warnings of caution, embodied in the principles of sound finance.

As to imaginary evils that sound finance guards against, Lerner had in mind the fear that a large public debt, whose service requires heavy taxation, diminishes the reward for risk taking and thereby diminishes the inducement to invest. He allayed that fear by pointing out that 'the same high income tax that reduces the return on the investment is deductible for the loss that is incurred if the investment turns out a failure. As a result of this, the *net* return on the risk of loss is unaffected by the income tax rate, no matter how high that may be.' Surprisingly enough, neither Lerner nor any of his critics (with one exception) thought of another and possibly real danger of the high income tax rates needed to service too large a public debt: the diminished incentive to work. Apparently no one in those days could imagine workers owning enough financial assets or drawing enough unearned income from other sources for high taxes to affect their willingness to work.

Functional finance was not, of course, a policy prescription, only a framework of guidelines for government's fiscal policy. But Lerner's repeated discussions of what he expected its consequences to be leave no doubt as to what he hoped it would achieve. While allaying fears about the supposed dangers of a growing public debt, he also stressed that functional finance was no licence for the indefinite accumulation of debt because he expected anti-inflationary restriction to reduce both spending and debt by orders of magnitude similar to those by which expansionary policies increased them. Lerner was no believer in secular stagnation and consequently no advocate of offsetting policies for achieving secular expansion. His picture of the economy, painted in his celebrated 1941 parable, 'The Economic Steering Wheel', was a driverless car, without a steering wheel, running on a straight, wide highway whose edges turn up'. 'As [the car] approaches the rising edge of the highway, its front wheels are turned so that it gets back onto the road and goes off at an angle, making for the other side, where the wheels are turned again.' In other words, he envisaged a business cycle with underemployment and inflationary overfull employment alternating, and Keynesian fiscal and monetary policy as a short-run anticyclical policy, a kind of balancing wheel to dampen the amplitude of business-cycle fluctuations. The purpose of functional finance was to remove the unnecessary trammels that so-called 'sound finance' might impose on such a policy; but its substitution of pre-announced rules of fiscal and monetary behaviour for discretionary policies also fits into the rational expectations framework. However, of the practical obstacles to making policy responses sufficiently prompt to be truly anticyclical, Lerner was blithely oblivious.

To return now to Lerner's laws of functional finance and his proposal to substitute them for the principles of sound finance, they so outraged conventional wisdom that at first they shocked just about everybody. Evsey Domar recalls:

> ...on having read the statement in [Lerner's] Functional Finance article that income taxation did not discourage risk-taking because losses could be offset against other income, I became so enraged that I dashed out of my office (at the Federal Reserve Board) towards Musgrave's who in turn was running to mine for the same reason. We decided to write a paper together disproving Lerner and ended up ... proving that not only was he right, but that he had not gone far enough.[6]

Keynes's reaction was like most others': initial shock, followed by complete acceptance – except that Keynes expressed his shock by publicly shaming Lerner, criticizing his ideas in language so intemperate that he later felt moved to retract his words publicly and to substitute for them the highest admiration. The episode is recounted in Colander's note in this issue of *JEL*, on pp. 1572–3.

Once Keynes became an enthusiastic convert, his followers followed suit and Lerner's functional finance soon became the generally accepted framework within which many, perhaps most, economists think and argue about fiscal and monetary policy – including, of course, those who take it for licence to engage in unlimited deficit financing. For that Lerner is partly to blame. To begin with, the simplicity of his first law of functional finance was even more deceptive than the simplicity of the rule to equate marginal product or marginal cost to price, because the dividing line between unemployment and inflation is not a line at all but a fairly wide band, as Lerner soon discovered and stressed. Second, he often argued that the economic and human costs of unemployment are much greater than the cost of inflation, apparently not realizing until later the unstable nature of inflation, which renders inadmissible static comparisons between the relative costs of a given level of unemployment and a given rate of inflation. He soon became aware of those problems, however, and they and their implications became his next preoccupation, setting the direction in which he tried to extend and carry forward Keynes's ideas.

Inflation

Lerner was not only the person who, in his theory of functional finance, provided a logical framework for Keynesian demand management, thereby bringing into the open its full implications; he was also probably the first to recognize its inflationary dangers. According to him, he went to see Keynes in 1935 or 1936 to raise the question whether full-employment policies might not start an inflationary process before assuring full employment, but Keynes did not get his point. By the mid-1940s, Lerner's question became a conviction, voiced in many of his writings. His article, 'Money', in the *Encyclopaedia Britannica* (1946) says that 'The experience of high employment during World War II has shown that reductions in the volume of unemployment result in inflationary tendencies *long before* unemployment has been reduced to a satisfactory level' (my italics). In 1949, he wrote: 'The maintenance of full employment without inflation depends on the acquiescence and cooperation of labor organizations in permitting collective bargaining to be superseded by other techniques for determining wage rates' (p. 199).

When the editor (Seymour Harris) of a series of economic handbooks invited him to contribute 'a lucid, elementary account of Keynesian economics', his *Economics of Employment* devoted four chapters, almost 60 pages, to inflation and its problems. After that, he wrote many more articles as well as a book on inflation, but most of his ideas on the subject were already contained in his *Economics of Employment* (1951).

That is where Lerner first speaks of 'a region between depression and inflation where we have both depression and inflation', calls the two limits of that region 'low full employment' and 'high full employment', estimates their positions in the United States to be around 10 per cent and 3 per cent unemployment rates, respectively,[7] and warns that *only temporarily* can a level of employment above the low full-employment level – that is, with less than 10 per cent unemployment – be maintained. All that may sound familiar and commonplace today, but Lerner wrote it seven years before Phillips launched his Phillips curve and 17 years before Friedman introduced the concept of a natural rate of unemployment in his presidential address to the AEA.

To Lerner, who was so very conscious of the high social cost of unemployment, a long-run equilibrium unemployment rate of that order of magnitude seemed totally unacceptable; yet he saw no way out at the time. Given the kind of person he was, passionately interested in improving the economy rather than just economics, that probably explains why, from then onwards, so much of his time and energy was devoted to the study of inflation and ways to contain it.

To explain inflation, Lerner focused attention on the people who change prices, on their motivation for changing them, and on the circumstances that keep undiminished both their ability and the force of their motivation to keep changing prices despite the price changes that have already occurred. He distinguished three different kinds of inflation, according to the motivating forces behind them; and since he believed that each required a different remedy, he put great stress on the nature of those differences.

To begin with, he made a sharp distinction between what he first called 'buyers'-' and 'sellers'-' inflation but renamed 'overspending' and 'administered inflation'' in his 1972 book, *Flation*. Buyers' or overspending inflation is, of course, the classic form of inflation, which comes about when buyers are trying to buy more than 100 per cent of what the available labour force can produce with the aid of the available equipment. That is the kind of inflation whose only cure is a reduction in total spending to equality with the value of the producible output at existing prices; therefore it is also the kind of inflation that can be prevented or stopped by enforcing the first law of Lerner's functional finance.

Very different, according to Lerner, is sellers' or administered inflation, also known as 'cost-push', 'mark-up' or 'wage inflation'. Its first mention in the economics literature seems to have been in Keynes's *Treatise on Money*, under the name 'income inflation', but Lerner was the first to note its crucial feature, excessive claims of income, instead of excessive demand for output, as its motive force. Lerner put it this way: 'the owners of the factors of production claim, as their respective shares of the product, payments that add up to more than 100 per cent of the value of the product'. Since the excess of claims to income over the income generated does not depend directly on whether and to what extent those claimants *spend* their income shares, sellers' inflation is compatible with a wide range of levels of unemployment and degrees of capacity underutilization.

Lerner's inventing and introducing the name 'sellers' inflation' and the later term, 'administered inflation', instead of using one already established, illustrates how carefully he always chose just the right words, which enabled him to express complex ideas in simple, often strikingly simple, language. By speaking of 'sellers' inflation', he stressed one crucial feature of that kind of inflation: the symmetrical role and equal responsibility of the sellers of factors (especially labour) and of the sellers of products in pushing up prices and keeping inflation going. The use of such terms as 'cost-push', 'wage' or 'mark-up' inflation would inevitably have suggested that one or the other party plays the dominant role.

Equally significant is his subsequent switch of terminology from 'sellers'-' to 'administered inflation', which had two purposes. First, he wanted to stress that, while overspending inflation is driven by impersonal market forces, which exert their inflationary pressure whatever the nature and degree of competition, administered inflation only comes about in the presence of market imperfection and monopoly power. Excess claims cannot even arise without price and wage administrators, as Lerner called them: people who can consciously set prices (and wages), either unilaterally or in agreement with other price administrators. To use Lerner's language: their monopoly power enables the price and wage administrators to overrule market forces and raise prices even when market forces call for no change, or to keep them unchanged when market forces would lower them. Since he believed that to arrest a rise or initiate a fall in administered prices required altogether different policies from those that influence the movement of market-determined prices, he laid great stress on continually keeping his reader aware of the kinds of prices and inflation he was considering.

Lerner's other reasons for his terminological switch seems to have been the following. While, originally, he believed that collective bargaining between employers and organized labour was a necessary condition for the unholy combination of inflation with unemployment, he gradually came to change his mind. Already in his *Economics of Employment* (1951b) one reads: 'The tendency for wages to rise may be due not merely to *collective* bargaining but to the determination of wages by bargaining, whether individual or collective.' Elsewhere in the same book: 'Even if there were no trade unions at all, the mere idea that a certain wage rate is reasonable or right or proper or fair ... can make a low level of full employment [that is, 10 per cent unemployment] a stable position.'

Much later, Sir John Hicks's *The Crisis in Keynesian Economics* (1974) takes up or independently reaches Lerner's insight that the employer's desire to be fair to, and to be considered fair by, his employees gives them implicit bargaining power. Later, still, Arthur Okun's work on implicit wage contracts documented and analysed the idea in some detail. So, here again, Lerner was ahead of his time. By using his new terminology, Lerner made clear that administered inflation still depends on there being wage administrators, able and motivated to raise wages, but they are not always on the selling side of the labour market.

When the precepts of functional finance are applied and give full rein to administered inflation, 'tripartite administered inflation' results. Wage administrators raise wages, because prices are rising; price administrators raise product prices, because costs are being raised by the increase in wages; and the total-spending administrators, as Lerner calls the fiscal and monetary authorities, take steps to increase total spending in order to prevent depression, which would otherwise overwhelm the economy. Each set of administrators can quite honestly believe that it is only the fault of the others that it has to participate in the inflationary process.

Administered inflation therefore renders functional finance, not wrong, but insufficient, because not applying its precepts or applying them in reverse leads to a situation even more objectionable. If fiscal and monetary authorities fail to maintain spending at the high full employment level – or, fearing inflation more than unemployment – actively restrain spending, they lower output and employment before slowing the rise in prices and create an inflationary depression. Sufficiently drastic and prolonged restrictive policies would stop inflation completely if government were willing to accept the severe unemployment and depression necessary to deprive price and wage administrators of their power to go against market forces.

Lerner considered all three alternatives unacceptable and set out to develop some other anti-inflation policy that would contain administered inflation by fulfilling the difficult condition of stabilizing the *average* price level while keeping *relative* prices and wages flexible. However, at the time that he wrote *Flation*, Lerner had not yet developed his anti-inflation plan, and it was characteristic of him never to give a thought to the practical problem of what to do in the interim, what second-best solution to advocate when the first-best is unattainable. It is true that he made a detailed static comparison between the welfare losses inflicted by each percentage point of unemployment and each percentage point of annual price increases and convincingly argued that the first was more than a hundred times greater than the second; but, by stressing the instability of the inflation rate, he clearly implied that such static comparisons cannot serve as the basis for policy recommendations.

For Lerner distinguished and stressed the existence, also, of a third kind of inflation: expectational inflation, engendered when one of the other two kinds persists long enough to lead to an expectation of future inflation. Expectational inflation, like administered inflation, also depends on the presence of price and wage administrators;[8] but its distinguishing feature is that it is self-perpetuating (because the expectation is self-fulfilling) and tends to accelerate the rate at which prices rise. The important role Lerner assigns to expectations as a source of inflation and of the escalation of inflation leaves no doubt that he was far from belittling its dangers and the need to contain it.

Another important difference that Lerner stressed between his second and third kinds of inflation was that administered inflation is aggressive, because the parties aim at the unattainable when they claim income shares whose sum exceeds the total income generated; whereas expectational inflation is defensive, because the parties would be content to keep on getting (in real terms) the shares they are actually getting, and raise prices and wages merely to forestall expected future losses. Lerner used that difference to explain why, in his opinion, an incomes policy is doomed to fail when inflation is the administered kind but can keep the inflation rate from escalating when inflationary expectations are its main motivating force; for he believed that the acceptance and success of an incomes policy depends not only on whether it is but also on whether it seems just, and on whether it promises and delivers what the parties want.

While the sharp, analytic distinctions he draws among the different kinds of inflation render Lerner's approach quite different from Friedman's, some of his argument resembles Friedman's. For he, too, believes that only a very low employment level (Friedman's natural rate, his low full employment) is compatible with a steady (including a zero) rate of price increase. Any attempt to increase employment leads to unexpected and therefore accelerating inflation. Accordingly, there is no trade-off between inflation and unemployment of the kind implied by the Phillips curve.

Unlike Friedman, however, Lerner refuses to accept that state of affairs even as a temporary institutional framework within which to make policy recommendations; and he deplores his own earlier (1951a) carelessness in naming an unacceptably low level of employment 'low *full* employment'. For Lerner, again unlike Friedman, does not regard the whole 10 per cent unemployment implied by the low full employment level as voluntary unemployment, because he does not identify the revealed preferences of wage administrators with the preferences of the workers themselves, many of whom are unemployed or newly employed, and most of whom do not belong to unions.

Because overspending, and therefore also overspending inflation, can be guarded against effectively by applying the laws of functional finance, Lerner's *Flation* is focused on the problems of containing administered and expectational inflation. That is why more than half the book deals with non-fiscal and non-monetary measures for controlling inflation. Lerner sets out the aims of policy (keeping the increase in average wages within the limit set by the increase in average productivity while keeping relative prices and wages flexible), lists the conditions of the parties;' and the public's acceptance of it (referred to eight paragraphs earlier); and then discusses what was or went wrong with the wage-price freeze, wage-price guideposts and related policies tried by the Nixon administration, and why incomes policies in some other countries (especially Brazil), with their different political structures, were more successful. His discussion is insightful and incisive, although this was probably Lerner's first attempt to face up to the clash between economist-designed ideal policies and practical, political reality.

Flation, however, despite the many interesting new concepts and discussions it contains, is an unsatisfactory book. For one thing, it is a somewhat incomplete treatment of its subject. Unlike Lerner's *Economics of Control* and *Economics of Employment*, which consolidated and rounded out his earlier writings on those subjects, *Flation* neither repeats nor supersedes several of his relevant and important earlier contributions; for example, his (1949) distinction between expected and unexpected inflation and his argument that only the latter inflicts a welfare loss. For another thing, inconsistencies in the book point to a confusion in the author's mind between accelerating and non-accelerating inflation. Lastly, the book leaves one unsatisfied because one senses that it left its writer unsatisfied. Lerner was used to providing solutions, often brilliant if not always practical, to economic problems. He must have felt frustrated not to come up with a solution to what he considered the most pressing economic problem of the time. His anti-inflation plan, which will be discussed below, was worked out many years later.

Reform

Lerner's economics had a strong welfare orientation, because he was a reformer at heart, always hatching schemes to improve the economy or the world. He clearly had a messianic streak in his character, which perhaps originated in his Talmudic training. No economist understood better or appreciated more than Lerner the workings of the market economy; but given his messianic streak and his awareness of the market's shortcomings as well as of its achievements, his appreciation was the hands-on, not the hands-off variety, forever bent on improving the market's performance or extending its scope.

His best-known reform proposal, the only one actually adopted (by central banks in foreign-exchange markets), was governmental counterspeculation, proposed in the *Economics of Control* (1944) to nullify the socially harmful effects of monopolists' aggressive speculation, while leaving unhindered 'productive speculation' and its beneficial effects.

The example I propose to discuss here, however, is Lerner's 1980 plan to diminish OPEC's monopoly power, thereby to resolve the oil crisis. The plan called for oil-importing countries to levy on the sale of oil a variable excise tax (he called it 'extortion tax') whose amount would equal OPEC's monopolistic mark-up over the 'fair' price and would be adjusted in a way to keep matching that mark-up whenever OPEC changed its price. The proposed extortion tax would have greatly increased the price of oil, of course, but its proceeds would have been used to compensate those on whom the price increase imposed too great a burden. The imposition of such a flexible tax would have roughly the same effect as a doubling of the price elasticity of demand facing oil producers, because, by making the price changes consumers face twice as large as those decreed by producers, it would also double the response of the volume of sales to the change in producers' prices. That would halve producers' monopoly power and, with it, their inducement to stay within the coalition (as well as the inducement of others to become 'free-riders' by charging OPEC's price without joining the coalition).

The idea seemed brilliant when I first saw it in the mimeographed typescript, handed out personally by Lerner to the audience at the 1979 AEA meetings as they entered to hear Solow's presidential address; and hindsight confirmed that judgement when we saw how vulnerable the OPEC coalition was to every fall in its sales.

As to Lerner's plans to extend the scope of market forces, the earliest, I believe, dates from the outbreak of World War II, when he wanted to replace the army's standard TOE (table of organization and equipment), with its rigid and uniform assignments of personnel and equipment, with a flexible system that would give every commander a budget of ration points with which to 'buy' all types of specialists, ranks of personnel and kinds of equipment, in order to assemble officers, NCOs, privates; and weapons, tanks and other equipment in whatever combination he regarded as the most effective for accomplishing his assigned task.

Lerner's friends, however (myself among them), seemed to have more faith in the army's collective wisdom than in the judgement of its individual commanding officers and dissuaded him from writing the book in which he wanted to publish and elaborate so fanciful an idea, fearing that it would worsen rather than improve his chances of professional advancement. Yet, if some such plan had been in force in the 1930s, it might have enabled the allied armies to prepare for fighting the next instead of the last war. In France, the young Colonel de Gaulle might have been able to demonstrate the need for a mechanized army instead of unsuccessfully pleading for it and, who knows, he might have changed the course of history.

The market anti-inflation plan

Lerner's best, most impressive plan, however, which he developed gradually, in the course of several publications, is his market anti-inflation plan (MAP). Written jointly with David Colander and published in its most complete and final form as a book (1980), it is a model of clear presentation and meticulous attention not only to detail and special cases but also to start-up difficulties and problems of administration, enforcement, auditing and acceptability. Since Lerner had always disdained mundane matters of that kind in his earlier work, I would give Colander the lion's share of credit for that part of the plan. My summary must be short, however, and will, also for that reason, concentrate on the aspects that carry Lerner's unmistakable imprint.

Individual price changes are essential for the working of our economy but all too often create an externality as well: they may affect the general level of consumer goods prices. They may raise it or lower it and, accordingly, we distinguish upward and downward externalities. I use the word *may*, not *will*, advisedly, because certain increases in factor prices leave the level of product prices unchanged, in view of the secular rise in productivity.

Since we want individual prices to be flexible but the general level of consumer goods prices to be stable, we want the upward and downward externalities to exist because they are manifestations of price changes, but we want them to exist in such proportions that they mutually offset one another's impact on the cost of living. Accordingly, the values of the two kinds of externalities must somehow be made equal. Since upward externalities always exceed downward externalities in our economy, their values have to be made equal by discouraging the former and encouraging the latter.

The best means of doing that is to internalize externalities by putting a price on them: exacting payment for price changes that raise, and paying a reward for those that lower, the cost of living. The way to establish the price whose levying and paying will fully balance the upward and the downward thrust of individual price changes on the cost of living is to give creators of downward externalities the right to create equivalent upward externalities and let them sell those rights at their market price, in a market organized for the purpose, to whoever wishes to exercise them.

That, in a few lines, is the idea behind Lerner's plan. To implement it requires direct constraints; but these may be imposed only on global quantities if the flexibility of individual prices is to be fully preserved. The price level, however, is a statistical construct, not a global quantity; but it can, at least, be expressed as the ratio of one global quantity to another: of total spending or total sales to the total physical volume of goods sold.

Functional finance (that is, monetary and fiscal policy) can constrain the total spending of consumers and businesses on final goods; but since they are quantity adjusters with no direct control over prices, constraints on their spending have more impact on quantities than on prices, which is why they are appropriate safeguards only against overspending inflation. To contain administered and expectational inflation, created by the actions of price administrators, who are price adjusters with no direct control over the quantities they sell, it is the value of total sales that has to be rationed – and rationed in proportion to the total quantity of goods sold.

That is what MAP proposes to do. It calls for legislation to turn the freedom to sell into rights to generate a limited amount of sales. Since each firm buys inputs from other firms, the limit would apply only to its value added, here called net sales. Each firm's allowance of transferable rights to make net sales would be set to equal its actual past net sales but corrected for changes in its input of labour and capital and for the estimated percentage increase in the economy's average productivity, in order to make adjustment for the probable change in its output. The firm's allowance of sales rights therefore is based on a rough estimate of what its current net sales will be worth at pre-existing prices. The estimate is rough, because the firm's productivity may rise by more or by less than the national average, because the change in its labour and capital inputs may have more to do with its investment or R&D operations than with current production, and also because the output it sells may not change by the same amount as the output it produces.

The sum of allowances, summed over all firms, is the estimated worth of the economy's total sales at pre-existing prices. If the total of actual sales is kept within the limit set by the sum of allowances, the average level of product prices cannot rise, except to the extent that the estimate is too high. The estimate of total sales, however, is bound to be much more accurate than the individual estimates of which it is the sum, because most of the above-mentioned possible errors in the individual estimates are randomly distributed and so cancel out when they are summed. Even so, the authors expect the enforcement of MAP to stabilize the price level only on average, over a number of years, rather than from one year to the next.

So much for the stability of the general level of product prices. How about the flexibility of individual prices? To begin with, the constraint is not on factor prices but on the net sales or value added; the share of wages and profits (which are the components of value added) would continue to be determined by bargaining between labour and management. For example, if the expected productivity increases were 2 per cent, wages and profits could both rise by 2 per cent or one could rise by more at the expense of the other's rising by less or not at all.

Secondly, each firm can add to its rights to increase net sales beyond its allowance by buying other firms' unused rights. That allows plenty of freedom for relative prices, wage rates and profits to move, provided that the market price of those rights remains reasonable. To satisfy that proviso, the authors stress the need for a well-organized, well-integrated market to bring buyers and sellers of sales rights together; and – what is even more important – they call for supplementing MAP with functional finance; that is, with restrictive fiscal and monetary policies to contain the overspending part of inflation.

The advantages of the former are self-evident. As to the latter, restrictive policy diminishes the excess of the demand for unused sales rights over their supply and so lowers the market price that will equate them. Lerner believed that restraint on spending is the only remedy for over-spending inflation; MAP was designed to deal only with expectational and administered inflation. In practice, of course, different kinds of inflation may be inextricably intertwined, the more so because expectational inflation may have both over-spending and administered components. (See note 8.) An attractive feature of MAP as an anti-inflationary device, however, is its close substitutability for that other anti-inflationary device, fiscal and monetary restriction. Each lightens the task and the social cost of the other; their combined costs may well be minimized by their simultaneous application.

One advantage of MAP, alluded to earlier, was that it cannot be accused of bias against labour because it limits increases in net sales, not in wages; but that advantage is obtained at the cost of including profits along with wages in the limitation. That raises the question whether MAP would not militate unduly against venture capital. The spectacularly successful new firms of the electronics industry are the engine of growth in our economy. Had MAP been in effect when they started in business, would they not have been discouraged by their need to buy a lot of sales rights, whose cost would have transferred part of their profits to their less successful brethren?

The answer to that question is reassuring. First, a new firm would begin to earn sales rights on the day it made its first investment and hired its first workers. Since it takes months, even years, before a saleable output is produced, the firm would begin its sales with an accumulated stock of sales rights, enabling it to recoup its initial expenses on labour and the interest on invested capital while providing an extra allowance for entrepreneurial profits as well. Second, the reduction of a successful innovator's initial high profits, by his need to buy additional sales rights, is counterbalanced by the reduction of the unsuccessful innovator's losses by his ability to sell his unused sales rights. Therefore the inducement to innovate is not much diminished because the size of the risk is reduced by almost as much as the reward for taking it. The argument resembles Lerner's 1943 argument (p. 42) that income taxes do not discourage risk taking when losses can be offset against other income, because, in that case, taxes diminish the net profits obtainable and the potential net losses in equal proportions.

Apologia

My account of Lerner's lifetime contribution to economics is unavoidably incomplete and unbalanced. It is incomplete because his 160 papers and eight books contain many more new ideas on many more subjects than I am able and competent to survey. For example, I have no judgement, and am therefore silent, on his contributions to such subjects as spatial competition, duopoly or the theory of price index numbers, even though I know from Samuelson's 1964 review that Lerner's paper on the last-mentioned topic carried forward the work of others. I have also refrained from discussing his many proposals for avoiding nuclear war: they are outside the purview of this article.

My account is unbalanced because I naturally need much more space to present his lesser-known works than those that, however new and revelatory when first presented, have since been thoroughly incorporated into the established doctrine of the new generation of economists so that they now seem commonplace or mere common sense. The latter appear to be the more important if we judge by their readier acceptance; nevertheless, my focus on Lerner's less well-known works also has advantages. First, they are his contributions that still retain some novelty and so are better able to convey the freshness, originality and elegant logic of their author's mind. Second, some of his unorthodox ideas are gaining and may continue to gain acceptance. Lerner's logic was the more compelling for his refusal to obscure it or water it down for the sake of expediency. His friends used to despair over his blindness to political realities, which they knew would diminish his influence on policy in the short run. The long run, however, is different. Initial resistances to the unusual wear off with time; also, when problems prove intractable by orthodox methods, unorthodox remedies become more acceptable. At that stage, the clear and impeccable logic of Lerner's arguments and recommendations makes them more convincing precisely because they were presented in an uncompromising fashion.

There are several instances of the gradual acceptance of Lerner's initially shocking or outlandish ideas. The one already discussed is functional finance. However shocking it was at first, by now it is the framework of many economists' thinking about macropolicy, without their even being aware of it. A second instance is governmental counterspeculation to counter aggressive speculation by monopolist manipulators, designed to keep the market functioning as it should. Even Meade (1945), the most favourable reviewer of Lerner's *Economics of Control* (1944), where counterspeculation is first presented, saw 'serious difficulties' connected with the idea; yet it is one of the few of Lerner's policy recommendations to pass into general practice.[9] Another idea, decried as absurdly unrealistic when Lerner first presented it, was the notion that socialist planners should opt for private or public enterprise, depending on which is more efficient in which industry. A few years ago, something closely resembling that had been adopted in socialist Hungary and seems to explain much of that country's economic success.

Notes

1. Throughout this chapter, I have tried to use Lerner's own terminology and language as much as possible. Passages in quotation marks are taken verbatim from his writings. I used no quotation marks when the requirements of style made me change his grammar or word order. It seemed unnecessary and unduly cumbersome to give references for the quotations.
2. They were, in addition, to Lerner, Henry D. Dickinson, Maurice H. Dobb, Evan F.M. Durbin, Oskar Lange and F.M. Taylor.
3. It implies that, if some people were known to have a greater capacity for enjoying life than all others, they would have to be given more income than all others in order to maximize the sum total of utilities – a conclusion that goes counter to one's sense of justice.
4. Lerner published 29 articles and notes between 1933 and 1939.
5. One of the very few macroeconomic theorems that predated the *General Theory* was the credit multiplier: viz., the idea that the banks are not passive recipients of their customers' deposits but create them.
6. The quotation is from a personal letter of Domar's. The paper mentioned is Domar and Musgrave (1944).
7. Actually, he speaks of six million and two million unemployed as the two limits; but, given the size of the labour force at that time, they correspond to the above percentage rates of unemployment.
8. I would distinguish between expectational overspending inflation and expectational administered inflation, according to whether the expectation of future inflation leads consumers to increase their spending in an effort to reduce their holdings of money and other financial assets (the Germans call that 'flight into real assets'), or whether it leads wage and price administrators to raise wages and prices. Before Lerner, the economics literature dealt only with the former type of expectational inflation; Lerner, in most of his writings, concentrates on the latter type.
9. The Bank of England's Exchange Equalization Account of the 1930s antedates Lerner's recommendation, but the market interventions of today's central banks serve a different purpose, which comes much closer to what Lerner had in mind.

References

Publications marked with an asterisk have been reprinted in *Selected Economic Writings of Abba P. Lerner* (ed. David C. Colander, 1983b).

Barone, Enrico (1935), 'The Ministry of Production in the Collectivist State', in Friedrich A. von Hayek (ed.), *Collectivist economic planning*, English translation of 1908 Italian original (London: Routledge & Kegan Paul), pp. 245–90.

Bastable, Charles F. (1897), *The Theory of International Trade with some of its Applications to Economic Policy*, 2nd edn (London/New York: Macmillan & Co).

Bickerdike, C.F. (1920), 'The Instability of Foreign Exchange', *Economic Journal*, Mar. 1920, **30**, 118–22.

Dickinson, Henry D. (1933), 'Price Formation in a Socialist Community', *Economic Journal*, June, **43**, 237–50.

—— (1934), 'Problems of a Socialist Economy', *Economic Journal*, March, **44**, 152.

Dobb, Maurice H. (1933), 'Economic Theory and the Problems of a Socialist Economy', *Economic Journal*, December, **43**, 588–98.

—— (1935), 'Economic Theory and Socialist Economy: A Reply', *Review of Economic Studies*, February, **2**, 144–51.

Domar, Evsey and Musgrave, R.A. (1944), 'Proportional Income Taxation and Risk-Taking', *Quarterly Journal of Economics*, May, **58**, 388–422.

Durbin, Evan F.M. (1936), 'Economic Calculus in a Planned Economy', *Economic Journal*, December, **46**, 676–90.

—— (1937), 'A Note on Mr. Lerner's "Dynamical" Propositions', *Economic Journal*, September, **47**, 577–81.

Edgeworth, Francis Y. (1925), 'The Pure Theory of International Values', *Papers Relating to Political Economy*, vol. 2, (London: Macmillan & Co.), pp. 63–125. This is a reprint of part of the much longer 'The Theory of International Values', *Economic Journal*, parts I–III, March, September and December 1894, **4**, 35–50, 424–43 and 606–38. The mistake is substantially repeated, although it was pointed out, and conceded by him, in 1897.

Friedman, Milton (1947), 'Lerner on The Economics of Control', *Journal of Political Economy*, October, **55**, 405–16.

—— (1968), 'The Role of Monetary Policy', *American Economic Review*, March, **58**, 1–17.

Hayek, Friedrich A. von (1935), 'The Present State of the Debate', in *Collectivist Economic Planning*, (London: Routledge & Kegan Paul), pp. 201–43.

Hicks, John (1974), *The Crisis in Keynesian Economics*, (Oxford: Basil Blackwell).

Keynes, John Maynard (1930), *A Treatise on Money*, (London: Macmillan).

—— (1936), *The General Theory of Employment, Interest and Money*, (London: Macmillan).

—— (1944), unpublished letter to Lerner, dated 27 September.

Lange, Oskar (1936–7), 'On the Economic Theory of Socialism', *Review of Economic Studies*, parts I–II, October 1936, February 1937, **4**, 53–71 and 123–42. The paper, corrected to take care of Lerner's criticism, has been reprinted, together with F.M. Taylor's presidential address in Oskar Lange and Fred M. Taylor, *On the Economic Theory of Socialism*, (Minneapolis, MI: University of Minnesota Press, 1938).

Lerner, Abba P. (1932), *'The Diagrammatical Representation of Cost Conditions in International Trade', *Economica*, N.S., August, **12**, 346–56.

—— (1934a), *'The Concept of Monopoly and the Measurement of Monopoly Power', *Review of Economic Studies*, June, **1**, 157–75.

—— (1934b), *'The Diagrammatical Representation of Demand Conditions in International Trade', *Economica*, N.S., August, **1**, 319–34.

—— (1934c), *'Economic Theory and Socialist Economy', *Review of Economic Studies*, October, **2**, 51–61.

—— (1935), 'Economic Theory and Socialist Economy: A Rejoinder', *Review of Economic Studies*, February, **2**, 152–54.

—— (1936a), *'The Symmetry between Import and Export Taxes', *Economica*, N.S., August, **3**, 306–13.

—— (1936b), *'Mr. Keynes' General Theory of Employment, Interest and Money', *International Labor Review*, October, 435–54.

—— (1936c), 'A Note on Socialist Economics', *Review of Economic Studies*, October, **4**, 72–6.

—— (1936–7), 'Capital, Investment and Interest', *Proceedings Manchester Statistical Society*.

—— (1937), 'Statics and Dynamics in Socialist Economics', *Economic Journal*, June, **47**, 253–70.

—— (1938), 'Theory and Practice of Socialist Economics', *Review of Economic Studies*, October, **6**, 71–5.

—— (1941), *'The Economic Steering Wheel', *The University Review*, (Kansas City), June, 2–8.

—— (1943a), *'Functional Finance and the Federal Debt', *Social Research*, February, **10**, 38–51.

—— (1943b), 'User Cost and Prime User Cost', *American Economic Review*, March, **33**, 131–2.

—— (1944), *The Economics of Control: Principles of Welfare Economics*, (New York: Macmillan & Co.).

—— (1946), 'Money', *Encyclopaedia Britannica*.

—— (1949), *'The Inflationary Process: Some Theoretical Aspects', *Review of Economic Statistics*, August, **31**, 193–200.

—— (1951a), 'Fighting Inflation', *Review of Economic Statistics*, August, **33**, 194–6.

—— (1951b), *Economics of Employment*, (New York: McGraw-Hill).

—— (1952a), *'Factor Prices and International Trade', *Economica*, N.S., February, **19**, 1–15.

—— (1952b), 'The Essential Properties of Interest and Money', *Quarterly Journal of Economics*, May, **66**, 172–93.

—— (1953), 'On the Marginal Product of Capital and the Marginal Efficiency of Investment', *Journal of Political Economy*, February, **61**, 1–14.

—— (1962), 'Macro-Economics and Micro-Economics', Ernest Nagel, Patrick Suppes and Alfred Tarski (eds), in *Logic, Methodology and Philosophy of Science: Proceedings of the 1960 International Congress*, (Stanford: Stanford University Press), 474–83.

—— (1972), *Flation: Not Inflation of Prices, not Deflation of Jobs*, (New York: Quadrangle Books).

—— and Colander, David C. (1980), *MAP: A Market Anti-inflation Plan*, (New York: Harcourt Brace Jovanovich).

—— (1983a), *'Paleo-Austrian Capital Theory', unpublished, printed in David C. Colander (ed.), *Selected Economic Writings of Abba P. Lerner*, (New York Press), pp. 563–79.

—— (1983b), *Selected Economic Writings of Abba P. Lerner*, ed. David C. Colander, (New York: New York University Press).

MacKinnon, Ronald I. (1963), *American Economic Review*, September, **53**, 717–25.

Meade, James E. (1945), 'Mr. Lerner on "The Economics of Control"', *Economic Journal*, April, **55**, 47–69.

Mises, Ludwig von (1935), 'Economic Calculation in the Socialist Commonwealth', in Friedrich A. von Hayek (ed.), *Collectivist Economic Planning*, (London: Routledge & Kegan Paul), pp. 87–130.

Mundell, Robert A. (1961), 'A theory of optimum currency areas', *American Economic Review*, September, **51**, 657–65.

Niehans, Jürg (1978), *The Theory of Money*, (Baltimore: Johns Hopkins University Press).

Okun, Arthur M. (1983), *Economics for policymaking: Selected essays of Arthur M. Okun*, ed. Joseph A. Pechman, (Cambridge, Mass., MIT Press).

Robinson, Joan (1937), 'The Foreign Exchanges', *Essays in the Theory of Employment*, (London: Macmillan & Co.), pp. 183–209.

Samuelson, Paul A. (1948), 'International Trade and the Equalisation of Factor Prices', *Economic Journal*, June, **58**, 163–84.

—— (1949), 'International Factor-Price Equalisation Once Again', *Economic Journal*, June, **59**, 181–97.

—— (1964), 'A.P. Lerner at Sixty', *Review of Economic Studies*, June, **31**, 169–78.

Sen, Amartya K. (1973), *On Economic Inequality*, (Oxford: Clarendon Press).

Taylor, Fred M. (1929), 'The Guidance of Production in a Socialist State', *American Economic Review*, March, **19**, 1–8.

4   When excessive claims cause inflation*

When I was asked to speak on inflation at this centenary celebration of Keynes, I admit that I was at first puzzled. Inflation was not a problem Keynes gave much thought to, since it was not a problem of his country in his time. What little he wrote about inflation showed good sense and shrewd insight; but we look up to Keynes for much more than just those qualities, however rare and precious they may be. As I started to think about it, however, I realized that the subject does belong to this conference. For one thing, inflation is a major macroeconomic problem; and macroeconomics, as we understand it today, is largely of Keynes's making. For another thing, it was Keynes who reformed our thinking about monetary problems by departing from his contemporaries' exclusive preoccupation with the supply of money and directing their and our attention to the motivation, and the determinants of the motivation, for holding money. A similar reform is badly needed also in our thinking about inflation. There is nowadays an excessively one-sided preoccupation with the supply of money as the restraining force on inflation, as if prices had an innate, automatic tendency always to rise to the level at which the demand for holding money equalled its supply. I shall try here to restore the balance by focusing attention on the factors that motivate price increases and so motivate the demand for additional holdings of money.

Macroeconomics deals with general economic tendencies that permeate many markets and industries, persist over time and seem very different from isolated economic changes. We have long taken for granted the existence of those economic tendencies, which seem to develop a momentum of their own, spreading from market to market and retaining their force over time – as if the law of the conservation of momentum governed not only the physical world but economics as well. Yet one must look to economic forces to explain economic phenomena; and if we want to control them, we must fathom the laws of their behaviour and find out how, why and when isolated economic changes become general, economy-wide tendencies.

General equilibrium theory provides a part, but only the lesser part, of the answer to that question. It shows that the relation of substitutability causes a given economic change to spread laterally to other markets and to be dissipated in the course of its becoming generalized by affecting more and more markets. The other and more important part of the answer we owe to Kahn

* This chapter appeared in D. Worswick and J. Trevithick (eds), *Keynes and the Modern World*, (Cambridge: Cambridge University Press, 1986).

and Keynes, whose multiplier theory showed when and how changes in income and output were transmitted vertically from market to market and, far from being dissipated in the process, got magnified – or multiplied, to use Keynes's expression.

Everything that we know about inflation suggests that there, too, a multiplier-type vertical transmission process must be at work, which generalizes isolated price increases into a general price increase and gathers enough momentum to keep the process going. In the following, I shall take up that suggestion, look into the mode of operation of the cumulative price increase and try to find the conditions that make it gather momentum and become self-sustaining.

Prices perform important functions in the market economy: they allocate resources and distribute income. Changes in prices, brought about by changing conditions, adapt resource allocation and income distribution to those changing conditions; and most economists believe that market prices perform better than any other system known today at least one of those functions, the allocative function.

Yet even the price system does not perform well all the time. Its allocative and distributive functions depend on relative, not absolute, prices; and there are circumstances in which a change in conditions that calls for reallocation and redistribution leads to a generalized and parallel increase in too many prices, which fails therefore to bring about the required reallocation and redistribution to the extent necessary. Moreover, because such a general rise in all or most prices fails to reallocate resources and redistribute income, it also fails to eliminate the initial cause of the price rise. That is why inflation, once it has started, tends to continue and is hard to stop. To find the causes of inflation, therefore, one must look for the special circumstances that turn specific price changes into general and parallel changes of most prices and thereby keep them from performing their reallocating and redistributive functions.

Let me begin the search for those special circumstances by analysing a familiar example: an increase in public sector expenditure. If we focus attention on a closed economy in which all resources were underemployed, so that the increased demand could be fully matched by an increase in supply without creating any upward pressure on prices, any obstacle to the rise in output would change it into a rise in prices. I shall concentrate on the obstacles and their consequences, and will begin by assuming perfect competition. That may seem like a strange assumption to make in a study of inflation but I will soon drop it and at that stage it will pinpoint the role that the lack of competition plays in generating inflation. I shall also go into more detail and differentiate the different obstacles to an increase in output. In equilibrium, of course, there would be not one but many and equally important obstacles, because all scarcities would be equalized on the margin. But we seldom are in equilibrium. Most of the time, one factor is more scarce than the others, and which is the most scarce makes a great deal of difference to the outcome.

For lack of time, I shall consider only three cases. Take first the one, especially common in developing countries, in which manufacturing equipment is the limiting factor. This is represented by the individual firms' rising marginal cost curves; and it causes production costs and product prices to rise along with output in response to the rise in demand. That lowers real wages, raises real profit rates and so redistributes income from labour to capital, all of which tends to reallocate resources in an equilibrating fashion. The shift in income distribution lowers the private sector's effective demand out of un-changed real income; the rise in product prices relative to wages renders profitable the increased utilization of existing equipment through overtime work and multiple-shift operation; and the higher rate of profit makes it profitable to invest in additional equipment and provides additional saving out of which to finance such investment.

In this case, therefore, there is a general rise in prices but no rise in wages, because there is no excess demand for labor.[1] Indeed, there may be continued unemployment, though not Keynesian but Marxian unemployment, due to the insufficiency of the tools of production with which to put labour to work. Product prices will continue rising if the public sector is unwilling to accept the reduction of its take (in real terms) owing to the rise in prices; but the cumulative process of rising prices will converge to a higher but stable level, because it causes output to rise, the private sector's share in output to fall, and also leads, in the long run, to a rise in productive capacity. This is the kind of slow rise in the general price level to which many distinguished economists, Lord Kaldor among them, have given their blessing – on the ground that it not only accompanies all fast economic growth but promotes it as well.

As the second case, consider a situation in which labour and productive equipment are both underemployed, but the economy is open and the limiting factor is foreign exchange. Assume further that exchange rates are flexible. Then an increase in public-sector demand will cause output and the price of foreign exchange to rise, along with the prices of imports and import-dependent domestic products, while wages and the prices of other products remain unchanged.[2] Since that means a change in relative prices, consumers and producers are put under pressure to reduce their consumption and use of imports and import-intensive domestic products. Here again, the prices of imports and import-dependent domestic products will continue to rise if the public sector refuses to accept the reduction in its real take caused by the price increases; but the rising import prices will converge to a stable level, which will be lower, the less dependent the economy on imports and the greater the foreigners' price elasticity of demand for its exports.

I now come to my third case, a closed economy with plenty of underemployed productive equipment but a shortage of labour; and you will see that in this case alone would excess demand lead to persistent inflation in a perfectly competitive economy. It is not easy, however, to find examples of this case, because businessmen are not so foolish as to build manufacturing capacity that cannot be manned. That is why this is an exceptional case, which usually occurs only in time of war. It may be useful to look at the most obvious example: the assignat period during the great French Revolution of the 1790s. That was the time of the first hyperinflation recorded by history and it is customarily associated in people's minds with that great French invention, paper assignats. A no less and perhaps even more important part of the explanation was compulsory military service.

With the threat of foreign invasion, compulsory military service enabled the French to increase the size of the army, in record time, from under 100 000 men to almost 800 000 men. In a country with barely 27 million inhabitants and a labour force which 60 years later was estimated at only 7.2 million (out of a then population of 36 million) that constituted a very large diversion of manpower, because the new recruits were conscripted not from the unemployable rabble of the Paris streets but mainly from among the most productive and active members of the labour force. The decree of the Committee of Public Safety did proclaim that 'young men will go to the front, married men will forge arms and carry food, women will make tents and clothing, and work in hospitals, children will turn old linen into bandages'; in effect, however, only the first part of that comprehensive plan for total war was actually carried out. Contemporary comments and scattered data showing a fall in output suggest that there must have been a sizeable reduction in the labour force – at least by 10 per cent and possibly by much more.

At the same time, of course, the need to equip, clothe, house, feed and transport so large an army greatly increased the public sector's demand for the diminished output of that diminished labour force. The way that demand was financed is explained by the disarray of the tax system and credit market of the time; but the only thing important to know about it is that it failed to diminish the private sector's effective demand. The result was a simultaneous excess demand for both products and labour, which led to a simultaneous rise of prices and wages, keeping income distribution more or less unchanged. Since that raised the money value of the unchanged output, private income and (in view of the unchanged income distribution) private demand in equal proportions, government, in order to keep maintaining, supplying and equipping its army, was forced to spend ever-increasing sums in order to keep outbidding the private sector, thereby raising prices, wages and presumably profits to ever-higher levels. Note that, with no significant change in relative prices and income distribution, the inflationary process generated no equilibrating forces to make the rising prices converge to a stable level.

That, in a nutshell, is the story of the French hyperinflation; and similar reductions of the labour force in the face of increased or undiminished demand for output occurred also in the Hungarian and Chinese hyperinflations of the mid-1940s and, at least for a while, in the German hyperinflation of 1923. In Hungary, following the siege of Budapest, in the winter of 1944, the city's entire adult population was commandeered (and generously paid) for clearing rubble away and building temporary shelters; in China, the civil war took many millions of people out of the labour force; in Germany, the entire labour force of the Ruhr, the country's industrial centre, went on strike, encouraged and financed by the German government to protest against the French occupation of the area, at the beginning of 1923.

In all these examples, the excess demand for products and the excess demand for labour arose simultaneously from the same cause, thereby short-circuiting the sequence of events people have in mind when they speak of a price–wage spiral and visualize rising prices to drive up wages and rising wages to drive up prices in turn. The simultaneous occurrence of excess demand in both product and labour markets may explain why the rate of inflation accelerated so easily and quickly in all those countries and reached such astronomic heights. Indeed, hyperinflation, defined as a ten fold or faster annual rise in the general price level, is probably limited to those exceptional circumstances in which a general shortage of labour is the main obstacle to supply's ability to respond to a rise in demand; and note that that was also the only one of our three cases that, on the assumptions so far made, was truly inflationary.

Let me now drop the assumption of perfect competition and consider what happens when some members of some markets have a conscious influence over some prices. Since people use their power over prices to claim a share in income, bringing them into the picture shifts the focus of attention from the allocative function of prices to their distributive function and, more particularly, from their occasional failure to perform the first function to their much more frequent failure to perform the second.

When owners of the factors of production ask a price for the services they perform or for the primary or intermediate goods they sell, they claim a part of the value of the output to whose production they contribute. For those prices to stick and the price level to remain stable, the sum of the parts to which they lay claim must not exceed the total of which they are the parts. When that condition is not fulfilled, inflation results, which I propose to call 'excess claims inflation', by analogy with excess demand inflation. A notable difference, however, between the two kinds of inflation is that while excess demand inflation can start only after supply has reached its physical upper limit, excess claims inflation can occur whatever the degree of utilization or underutilization of the capacity to produce. The reason is that claims to income are claims not to absolute quantities but to proportionate shares or parts of income. Accordingly, when the prices claimed for the inputs add up to more than the value of the output they generate, the excess can be eliminated by reconciling prices, by increasing productivity, but not by increasing activity.[3]

How does the market economy reconcile prices and distribute income? We have a theory of income distribution under perfect competition but know next to nothing about what happens when competition is imperfect. If one could separate the people with power to influence prices from those who, powerless, face prices on a take-it-or-leave-it basis, one would safely suppose the powerful to increase their share in income at the expense of the powerless; but what happens when no such separation is possible? What, for example, would happen in an economy in which all prices were set by the sellers and all buyers would be price takers? That may be an extreme and oversimplified model, but today's reality is a lot closer to it than it is to the model of perfect competition; and it is an inherently unstable and inflationary model – for reasons that become apparent as soon as one starts analysing it.

Since everyone of us is both a seller in some markets and a buyer in other markets, such an economy would give everybody a split personality, a kind of economic schizophrenia, by putting them into a position of power in some markets and a position of complete powerlessness in other markets. That is a natural and harmless position for middlemen to be in: most retailers regularly buy their wares at the wholesalers' set prices and resell them to consumers, with a mark-up added, at their own set price. But when all or most members of the economy are in that position, powerless against exploitation in markets where they do their buying but able to exploit their opposite numbers in the markets where they do their selling, then any change in economic conditions that calls for a reallocation of resources or redistribution of income will, instead, start a chain reaction of price changes, because everybody who finds his income diminished by a price change he cannot resist will try to recoup his loss by changing some other price in some other market in which *he* has the power to change prices and play the role of exploiter. To do so requires no increase in exploitation; indeed, it is reasonable to assume that everybody already exploits his market power to the full. But when prices are raised against anyone, he will find it profitable to raise his prices in turn by adding his unchanged profit-maximizing mark-up to his now higher costs. Once that process has started, it is self-sustaining and can only be ended by the providential presence of suckers, willing to take the reduction of their incomes on the chin, or by a rise in productivity, which allows some people to gain without causing others to lose. Moreover, since the economic model we are considering is one in which the sellers, not the buyers, are the price makers, the cumulative process whereby one price change leads to another will be biased in the inflationary direction.[4]

I dare say that many of the people who have already contracted the condition of economic schizophrenia in today's economy do not think of it as a disease at all, because they do not connect its ill effects to their cause. Yet the ill effects are inflation – or the miseries inflicted by attempts to combat inflation with restrictive monetary and fiscal policies – and I will try to show that those ill effects result not only in the oversimplified model I postulated but in practical and more realistic approximations to it as well.

Economists instinctively think of competition as the force that keeps prices stable; but that is false. The necessary condition of price stability is market symmetry; that is, competition among both buyers and sellers. Perfect competition provides that, because it means equally perfect competition on both the buyers' and the sellers' side of the market; but competition does not have to be perfect, it does not even have to exist for prices to be stabilized. All you need is the mutual offsetting of buyers' and sellers' market power as they exert their pressures on prices. The simplest form of this is when a buyer and a seller confront one another in an isolated market and haggle over price until they manage to hit upon a mutually agreeable one. That then becomes a stable price. In any single market transaction, the price agreed upon divides the gain from that transaction between the transacting parties; and that statement can be generalized from a single market to the whole group of factor markets in which a given producer buys his inputs, provided that the price of his product remains unchanged. The price he agrees to pay the suppliers of his inputs determines the shares of the contributors in the income his output generates; and the sum of all the shares necessarily equals the total income generated, because his own share, which he pays himself for his own input, is the residual that remains after he has paid for all the bought inputs.

That somewhat trivial result is true whether factor markets are competitive or monopolistic and whether the buyers or the sellers have the upper hand in those factor markets; but it ceases to be true, and the situation becomes very different, when product prices are free to change and the producer has the power to change them. For in that case, if, having signed all his factor market contracts, the producer finds that he has promised away too much and left himself too little, he can raise the price of his product, thereby unilaterally revising in his own favour the income distribution implicitly agreed upon in his factor market contracts. In short, costs can push up prices when, and only when, producers have power over the prices at which they sell their output.

I advisedly speak of power over prices rather than of monopoly or oligopoly power, because I want to include political power over prices, manifest in farm price support programmes and minimum wage legislation, and because

I want to extend the argument also to socialist economies. After all, excess claims inflation is endemic to socialist economies as well when plant managers have the power to set the prices of their products or to influence the level at which the central pricing agency sets them. That power is crucial, because one of the necessary conditions of excess claims inflation is the power over prices of the sellers of products, not the power over wages of the sellers of labour.

To raise prices, however, is a very different and much rarer thing than merely to have the power to raise them, because it is not always in the producer's best interest to exercise his power over product prices. Having agreed to or initiated an increase in the price of an input, he can reduce the resulting loss of his profit by raising product prices correspondingly; but that will not eliminate the loss completely if the higher prices of his products discourage their sales. Accordingly, the producer usually regards raising product prices in response to rising costs as a second-best policy, to be resorted to only if no better policy is available. His first-best policy is to resist cost increases and keep costs as well as prices unchanged – provided that that is possible and not more costly than the parallel increase in both costs and output prices.

Whether the producer can resist and avoid the rise in his input prices depends on whether he possesses superior bargaining strength in factor markets to match his superior bargaining strength in the markets where he sells his products. In my model of price-maker sellers and price-taker buyers, that, obviously, is *not* the case, since a price taker's market position is always weaker than the price maker's. Accordingly, under the conditions postulated in my model, the producer's second-best policy of raising product prices in response to rising input prices becomes his first-best policy. That explains one half of the cost–wage spiral that characterizes excess claims inflation: the half that consists in costs pushing up prices. But the same model also explains the other half of the cost–wage spiral, which consists in product prices pushing up costs. For, when the owners of the factors of production are price makers in selling their services, then they can and will raise the prices of their services in response to a rise in the cost of living which they are powerless to resist.

You will have noticed the important role asymmetrical market relations play in destabilizing the price system. My theoretical model postulates a particularly simple form of asymmetry; but that, while sufficient, is not a necessary condition for excess claims inflation to arise. Our next task therefore is to leave my model and look instead at the real world to see how, why, and since when its asymmetries approximate the asymmetry postulated in my model sufficiently to generate inflation. After all, quite a few economies have been remarkably stable until not so many years ago: what has happened in recent times to undermine their stability? It will be easiest to answer that question by tracing the gradual change in our economic relations from the atomistic competition in those early markets and periodic fairs, which posed for the economist's idealized picture of perfect competition, all the way to today's bitter conflicts between large oligopolies, organized labour, international cartels and others of their ilk. The beauty and stability of the early market relations lay in the perfect symmetry of buyers' and sellers' market positions, which resulted from bilaterally competitive bargaining, and which today is only preserved in the textbook model of perfect competition. In the real world, the symmetry and the stability slowly came to an end with the growing size of economic agents.

The first departure from bilaterally competitive bargaining came with the emergence of the wholesale trader as the dominant figure of merchant capitalism. The sheer size of his wealth and scale of operations enabled him to impose his terms on both the small retailers to whom he sold and the small manufacturers with whom he placed his orders. His superior bargaining position in both the market where he bought and in the market where he sold accounted for his large profits and fast growth to great size and wealth; but it did not diminish the stability of the general price level, because the asymmetries between buyers' and sellers' bargaining strengths in the two markets were themselves symmetrical and so mutually offsetting. The upward pressure the wholesaler exerted on the price paid by retailers and consumers was counterbalanced by the downward pressure he put on the price received by the small manufacturers and with it also on their workers' wages and suppliers' earnings. For, remarkably enough, the downward pressure of buyers' market power will counterbalance the effect on the general price level of the upward pressure of sellers' market power, not only when they are pitted against each other in a direct confrontation in the same market, but also when each of them presses against a different price in a different market, and even when the opposing pressures are exerted by the same actor or actors.

The last vestiges of merchant capitalism can still be found in Japan, whose large general trading companies retain to this day their dominance over the part of the country's export trade that originates in small manufacturing firms; and they also seem to have maintained their downward pressure on costs and wages in those small firms – to judge by the failure, during the 1950s and 1960s, of costs and wages in those firms to rise in step with the inflationary rise in the level of both consumer prices and wages in large firms and the service industries. That fact has been cited among the reasons why Japan's export prices and export performance were unaffected by her domestic inflation during that period.

In the West, wholesale merchants had already yielded their dominant position to manufacturers by the end of the 19th century. The development of precision machine tools for machining interchangeable parts and the invention of the assembly line on which to assemble them created great economies of scale which not only called for firms large enough to engage in mass production but also yielded the large profits that enabled manufacturing enterprises to grow to great size and market power. As a result, manufacturers gradually displaced wholesalers as the dominant members of the markets in which they sold their products and acquired the ability and habit of setting their prices on a take-it-or-leave-it basis.

At the same time, of course, their increasing size rendered manufacturers equally powerful in the markets in which they bought their inputs and so became wage or price makers also in those markets for many years to come. Accordingly, the period of wholesalers' domination was followed by an equally stable period of manufacturers' domination, because that too created a situation of symmetrical asymmetries, in which the impact on the general price level of producers' downward pressure on wages and input prices counterbalanced the impact of their upward pressure on product prices.

Needless to say, there were exceptions to that rule of the manufacturers' power over input prices; but those, at first, were too few and unimportant to endanger the stability of the system. As time went on, however, more and more exceptions were added, until the exceptions became the rule and turned the once symmetrical and stable situation into an asymmetrical, unstable and inflationary one.

An obvious exception to the rule could be found in the markets for intermediate goods, where producers faced producers and buyers and sellers could not both dominate the same market at the same time. But power relations in those markets and the way they operate are an internal matter of the manufacturing sector and do not diminish the stability of the system, because they do not affect its basic symmetry, which consists in manufacturers as a group dominating both the markets in which they sell to, and those in which they buy from, people outside their group.

A similar and equally harmless exception was provided by the markets in which large and powerful manufacturers sold to large and powerful wholesalers. Here again what happens in such markets is an internal matter of the business community and does not alter the balance of market power between businessmen and consumers on the one side and businessmen and the sellers of primary productive factors on the other. Exactly the same applies to yet another exception of more recent vintage, the formation of nationwide retail chains and their acquisition of countervailing power in their dealings with manufacturers. Their countervailing power redistributes profits within the business community but does not diminish retailers' power over prices in consumer markets.

More significant exceptions are the markets for primary products, like wool, cotton, corn and wheat, in which the standardization of the product assures bilaterally perfect competition and deprives even the largest buyers of any conscious influence on price. Note that the buyers in such markets are just as powerless to resist a price increase as they are when the price is unilaterally raised by price-maker sellers. This shows that price-maker sellers in input markets are a sufficient but not a necessary condition for creating the costs-pushing-up-prices half of the inflationary spiral.[5] Perfect competition in input markets does just as well. Perfectly competitive markets, however, were too few and transacted too small a part of the trade in inputs to endanger stability.

All the other exceptions to the rule of producers' domination in input markets came very much later, mostly as the result of defensive action taken by various groups of people who felt exploited by the large manufacturers' large profits. The most important of those groups was labour, whose organization into unions managed, in some countries, to substitute collective bargaining for the unilateral setting of wages by employers and to exert a fair amount of pressure in the course of such bargaining.

A second group or set of groups were producers of mineral resources, who formed international cartels in their attempts to reverse the balance of market power and assume the price maker's role in the markets where they sold. The most recent and spectacularly successful of those attempts was the concerted action of oil producers in 1973. The worldwide rise in price levels that immediately followed was a striking illustration of the way costs can push up prices; whereas the second oil crisis of 1978 showed how prices pushed up (oil) costs.

Farmers constitute a third group of sellers of inputs; they improved the terms of trade between their produce and manufactured goods, in some cases by cooperative marketing, in others by successfully pressing for the enactment of farm price support legislation. The latter is a form of price setting on the farmers' behalf, the more effective in promoting the inflationary spiral (both the cost–price and the price–cost halves of it), the more it stabilizes the farmers' share in income.

In all these instances, the concerted action of the suppliers of a given input either reversed the balance of market power in their own favour or at least substituted bargaining for prices set by the other side and so presumably brought the two sides' bargaining strength closer to equality. Since every reversal adds to the number of input markets dominated by sellers, each one brings the economy a step closer to my theoretical model of price-maker sellers and price-taker buyers, which we know to be inflationary.

But what are the consequences for price stability of a mere reduction in the disparity between the buyers' and the sellers' bargaining strength? In practical terms, that is the really important question one must answer, because complete reversals in the balance of market power, such as the one that created the 1973 oil crisis, are rare occurrences; and few of them have taken place in the markets for the most important input: labour. Collective bargaining as the main means of wage determination is confined to a handful of Western European countries; and labour does not, by any means, have the upper hand in all such bargaining situations. In the United States, collective bargaining determines the wages of only 29.8 per cent of all wage and salary earners,[6] the remaining 70 per cent are paid according to wage scales unilaterally set by employers. In Japan, about 35 per cent of the labour force belongs to unions; and they are probably the only ones whose earnings are determined by collective bargaining, given the importance in Japan of the closed shop. In most other countries, including the newly industrializing countries, all or almost all wages and salaries are still set by employers, except in small firms with few employees, where personal bargaining is probably the rule. In the newly industrializing countries that is not an unimportant exception. In Taiwan, for example, 10.1 per cent of the labour force in manufacturing works in enterprises employing less than ten people; and the percentage would be much higher if all sectors, including retail trade, were included. I also suspect that Japan in this respect is not very different from Taiwan.

What can one make of this variety of ways in which wages are determined? What, to begin with, is the impact of collective bargaining on price stability? It is generally believed to be destabilizing. I go along with that – not only when labour has the upper hand at the negotiating table but even when the opposing parties are evenly matched. After all, I have just argued (see p. 67 above) that perfect competition in input markets is inflationary, because it destroys the symmetry in market relations between input and output markets; and perfect competition is merely a limiting case of bilaterally competitive bargaining between buyers and sellers of approximately equal bargaining strength.

We now come to the puzzling behaviour of wage rates unilaterally set by employers. US experience shows that they tend to rise with the cost of living or faster than the cost of living whether or not there is unemployment in the firm's sector and even when there is general unemployment in the economy. Indeed, wages unilaterally set by employers do not seem to behave very differently from wages negotiated by unions, from which one must conclude that the market position of unionized workers is not much better than that of the workers who have no union to represent them.

The implication, however, is not that unions are unable to exert strong bargaining pressure but that individual workers themselves have also acquired a strong bargaining power of their own, which they exert even when they have no union to represent them. That, at any rate, seems to be the most plausible reason for the observed practice of employers to initiate wage increases on their own, thereby to keep their workers' earnings abreast of the cost of living and of other workers' earnings.[7]

What is the basis of the individual worker's growing bargaining strength? Often mentioned is the supposedly ever-present threat of forming and joining a union; but a more important basis, I believe, is technical progress, which is gradually but profoundly changing the character of work. What used to be considered the substance of factory work – the need to exert brute force and endure fatigue, monotony, danger, filth, noise and generally unpleasant working conditions – is slowly receding into the past as mechanical power is displacing muscular exertion, repetitive operations are increasingly performed by machinery, and hygiene and safety regulations are better enforced. At the same time, however, the new technology makes many new demands on the worker, requiring him to be vigilant, careful, always on the alert, ready at a moment's notice to avert or deal with unexpected mechanical breakdowns or mishaps, and able to exercise judgement and use his sense of responsibility. Needless to add, today's workers are fully able to meet the many new demands on their various skills and abilities, thanks to better training, better education and their greater sophistication and self-confidence.

The fact, however, that modern technology and modern work utilize such a great variety of the worker's faculties also means that the inevitable differences between different people's talents and abilities come to the fore and become apparent, because they greatly affect the quality and quantity of the work performed and output produced. Within limits, the employer must accept and accommodate these inevitable human differences and the resulting differences between different workers' performances; and in the process *he cannot help accepting and accommodating similar differences also in the same person's performance at different times*. The employer's forcible acceptance of such variability in the individual worker's work performance provides the latter with a secret but powerful bargaining weapon.

Work contracts specify wages, hours, working conditions, vacations, sick leave and so on but cannot, for the reasons just mentioned, specify the quality and quantity of the work to be performed. Accordingly, even when the employer is unencumbered by unions and free to draw up the work contract as he sees fit, he still leaves, and cannot help leaving, to his workers a large measure of influence over the profitability and success of his enterprise. They do not even have to make a conscious decision how well or how badly to fulfil their side of the work contract, because their morale, feelings towards the firm, and the ambition and enthusiasm they bring to their work depend very much on how well they are paid and treated and make a great deal of difference to their performance and productivity. The greater the influence of workers' morale on productivity, and the greater the producer's awareness of that influence, the more his ability unilaterally to set wages loses its advantage and becomes little more than an empty formality.[8]

My argument implies that modern technology and the resulting change in the character of work have had much the same impact on the balance of market power in labour relations as the collective action of workers through their unions. Moreover, as a moment's reflection shows, those two influences on the balance of market power are not additive but overlapping, which is why I argued earlier (see p. 68 above) that the similar behaviour of wages in unionized and non-unionized industries is no indication of the weakness of union power. All it shows is that the individual worker in the new industries has plenty of bargaining strength and is in very little need of a union to represent him and make his bargaining power more explicit. The fast, inflationary increase in money wages in such newly industrializing countries as South Korea, where industry is highly automated and collective bargaining unknown, would be hard to explain without the argument just outlined.

To sum up the argument, the producer's power over the prices at which he buys his inputs has been weakened in most markets over the years – by the sellers' collective action, by legislation and by the new technology. From the point of view of distributive justice, the change, on balance, was probably to the better; from the point of view of the stability of the pricing system, it was almost certainly to the worse, because it brought the pattern of market relationships in the economy's different markets very much closer to my theoretical model of an unstable system of markets.

The significance of an unstable system of markets is that it tends to amplify into an inflationary process any major price increase brought about by random shocks. Among such random shocks are not only wars, bad harvests and similar disasters, but also the kind of initially non-inflationary price increases discussed at the beginning of this chapter. For example, an increase in effective demand during a depression would raise the level of activity and employment in a stable system; and any worsening of the balance of payments and rise in import prices would be regarded as a small price to pay for an increase in real output and income. In an unstable market system, however, the rise in import prices may well turn into an inflationary wage–price spiral and stop the rise in real output in its tracks.

The above is a quick sketch of a very incomplete theory of inflation, with many important parts missing. After all, I have not even mentioned expectations, one of the main elements in the cumulative inflationary process, never discussed the growth of productivity and its anti-inflationary impact, said nothing about money, on the supply side of the subject, nor about finance, which has much to do with the initial impetus. The points I have covered are the neglected ones in present-day discussions; yet they constitute an important part of the background one has to understand and bear in mind in order to develop a satisfactory cure for inflation, less painful and less costly than the restrictive monetary policies that bedevil our economy today.

Notes

1. When the assumption of perfect competition is dropped, the conclusion that wages do not rise may have to be revised. See p. 70.
2. That conclusion may also have to be revised when the assumption of perfect competition is dropped. See p. 70.
3. Except to the limited extent that increased activity leads to a rise in productivity.
4. See my 'Asymmetries in Economics', *Scottish Journal of Political Economy*, vol. 25, 1978, 227–37 for the argument that prices set by sellers are more flexible in the upward than in the downward direction.
5. The other half of the spiral hinges on product prices entering the costs of inputs.
6. That percentage is considerably higher than the percentage of union members, because it includes workers who, though not union members, are covered by wage contracts negotiated by unions. It is based on surveys made between 1968 and 1972; today's percentage is probably somewhat lower. See Richard B. Freeman and James L. Medoff, 'New Estimates of Private Sector Unionism in the United States', *Industrial and Labor Relations Review*, vol. 32, 1979, 143–74.
7. See, however, my 'Market Power and Inflation', *Economica*, vol. 45, 1978, 221–33 for an alternative explanation, in terms of the fairness of employers.
8. The argument of the last two paragraphs owes much to the work of the late Arthur Okun on implicit contracts and what he called 'the invisible handshake'.

5 Moral sentiments and welfare of nations: a review of Robert H. Frank's *Passions within Reason**

Economic science owes to Adam Smith three of its fundamental insights: that specialization and the division of labour are the source of all progress; that two persons' trading with one another, each for his own selfish advantage, creates mutual benefits; and the latter's generalization, which is that competitive trading among *n* selfish people is in the public interest.

The profession built an imposing edifice on these (and a few other) basic insights; but it was too much enamoured of the elegance of a superstructure standing on so slender a base to heed Smith's warning that the division of labour also has a reverse side, because it unduly narrows each specialist's understanding of all things beyond his speciality; and we also overlooked or forgot his reminder that the rational pursuit of selfish interest is not enough; we also need morality, both as a motive force of individual behaviour and as a criterion for the economist by which to judge the economy. Our profession's failure to pay attention to these reminders has plagued it ever since.

In the 19th century, American and German institutionalists criticized 'the British School of Economists [for] recognizing, not the real man of society but the artificial man of their own system. Their Theory, occupied with the lowest instincts of humanity, treats its noblest interests as mere interpolations of the System ... The economist's science is that of material wealth alone, to the entire exclusion of the wealth of affection and the intellect.' Fritz Machlup (1972) who quotes the above sentences, wrote an eloquent survey of that vituperative attack and rightly blamed it on the early economists' careless, easily misunderstood language; but he failed, I believe, to notice another reason for the misunderstanding. The economic man, whose behaviour the British economists analysed, was not, as the critics thought, an unprincipled brute; on the contrary, they modelled him in their own and their friends' image on the perfect English gentleman of irreproachable honour, who would always pursue his self-interest within the limits of decency and decorum. Since that seemed to them self-evident and to go without saying, it never was said and made explicit – hence the misunderstanding.

Today, a century later, establishment economics is again being attacked for focusing its attention too narrowly on the implications of people's pursuit of

* This article appeared in *De Economist*, Educatieve Partners Nederland, 1991.

self-interest to the exclusion of all other motives of human behaviour; but this time the attack is the profession's own clear-sighted, sophisticated self-criticism, much of it launched by some of its leaders and sparked partly by the growing realization that such seemingly simple concepts as rational behaviour, self-interest and profit maximization, are much more complex than was once believed, and partly also by the recognition that the exclusion of ethical considerations from welfare economics has greatly reduced its scope.[1] An increasing number of economists also feel that the division of knowledge in the social sciences has gone too far and that we need more interdisciplinary work if we are to keep our field from becoming increasingly sterile.[2]

Those critics will welcome Robert Frank's *Passion within Reason*, which is the latest answer to the growing demand for broadening our discipline; for it provides plenty of raw material from neighbouring disciplines from which economists can draw important conclusions and gain new insights. Several of these are presented, though the author leaves one or two for the discerning and analytically minded reader to extract for himself. The ostensible purpose of the book is to stress the power and analyse the motivations of passions, emotions and principles, and to contrast and relate them to the motivation of the economist's stock-in-trade, the rational pursuit of selfish interest.

It is not, of course, the first book to do that: recall Albert Hirschman's similarly titled, elegant little volume on *The Passions and the Interests* (1977). The two books, however, are not only very different but exact opposites. Hirschman concentrates on such deadly passions as the lust for power and glory, which involve the subjugation of other people and whose competitive pursuit leads to war and carnage; and he contrasts them to the pursuit of profit and material interests, which is a lesser evil at worst and is made by competition to promote the public good. Frank, on the other hand, lists with approval such emotions as honesty, compassion, love, fairness, guilt, shame and sense of justice, and shows their promptings to be superior to those of self-interest. Also, while Hirschman argues that the early advocates of capitalism regarded the lust for lucre as a substitute, something of a countervailing passion to the lust after power and glory, which, they hoped, it would displace or at least diminish, Frank looks upon the righteous passions as a desirable complement to the pursuit of selfish interest.

Frank's book presents a kaleidoscope of striking real-life episodes, quoted from the media, memoirs and so on, along with a great variety of arguments and experimental findings partly from his own experiments, partly culled from an impressive array of sources in the social and behavioural sciences, genetics and evolution theory; with all of them showing the origin and persistence of passions, emotions and principles, their much greater force as motives of behaviour than most economists realize, as well as their ability to overrule selfish interests and increase social welfare as a result. The intrinsic interest of such variety of information and ingenious experiments, all of it presented in non-technical, plain, good English, makes for fascinating read- ing – the more so because much of it will be new to the many economists who keep their noses buried in their own technical discipline. Indeed, the sheer volume, variety and novelty of the bits of information packed tight into less than 300 pages is overwhelming and in danger of distracting the reader from some of the important insights the book leads up to but all too often fails to emphasize or to follow to their logical conclusion – perhaps because even the author himself could not always see the forest for the trees.

What are those important insights? To begin with, the book shows that honesty is a necessary condition of two of the main conclusions of econom- ics: (1) that economic transactions and associations between consenting adults are mutually beneficial and (2) that free competition causes people's rational pursuit of their selfish interests to ensure Pareto efficiency. One may well ask how such an important condition could have escaped the attention of genera- tions of economists. The answer is that it has not. At the very least two economists, Kenneth Arrow and George Akerlof (1983) have not only stated it but did so in connection with examples very similar to those given by Frank. Mostly, however, the condition has been stated in abstract, formalistic and much less meaningful terms. In the Arrow–Debreu theory of general competitive equilibrium, which so meticulously postulates a long list of necessary conditions of Pareto efficiency, honesty is an unstated practical condition of the stated theoretical condition that *every agent must possess all the relevant information* about every good. Similarly in the first main conclu- sion, honesty is the unmentioned condition of the stated condition that the parties must conclude their transaction *knowingly* and freely for it to yield mutual benefits.

Indeed, the need for equal information of all economic agents on the two sides of the markets in order to ensure economic efficiency has long been known and stressed. In actual markets, of course, the availability of informa- tion always fell short of that ideal, but earlier generations of economists seem to have accepted it as a reasonable approximation to the theoretical ideal and probably hoped that the spread of education would diminish the gap between theory and practice. They could not foresee our tremendous technical progress which rendered most goods much more complex, thereby increasing the sheer amount of knowledge informed economic agents needed to know; nor did they anticipate the great increase in the division of labour and consequent division of knowledge, which greatly enhanced the informational disparity between the two sides of most markets.

Today, we regard the asymmetric availability of market-relevant knowl- edge as a significant shortcoming of our economy and the inefficiencies that result from it have become the subject of the rapidly growing literature on 'adverse selection' and 'moral hazard'. The first theoretical paper on adverse selection was George Akerlof's (1970) analysis of the second-hand market for cars, one of the more conspicuous examples of asymmetry between buyers' and sellers' information; and most of the other papers in that literature also deal with important special cases rather than with the problem in general.

No less important than knowing the economic consequences of differential market information is to know the remedies. In a forthcoming paper, I have tried to deal with one of these, non-price competition; but a better remedy would be honesty. For honesty would diminish or eliminate those inefficiencies, either by providing the less knowledgeable parties with the additional information they need or by keeping the more knowledgeable parties from exploiting their advantage. The main merit of Frank's book is that it simplifies the argument by short-circuiting the information aspect and focusing directly on the connection between honesty and welfare, thereby bringing the discussion of some important, abstract issues down to the level of concrete, everyday, human experience. It even enables the reader to do that for himself in cases where that is close at hand but not spelled out in the book.

In contemporary discussions, the danger that selfish behaviour, when dishonest, can diminish social welfare, centres around the 'Prisoner's Dilemma' A.W. Tucker introduced in 1950. Unfortunately, however, Tucker chose to illustrate the important role honesty plays in economics with an anecdote taken from the upside-down underworld of criminals, where honesty means honesty-among-thieves and consists in not ratting on one's buddies, and where Pareto efficiency amounts to minimizing the sum total of the man-years criminals spend in prison. That paradoxical scenario probably explains why many economists still dismiss the prisoner's dilemma as a theoretical curiosity of little practical importance. It remained to Frank to correct that misperception by collecting and analysing a variety of non-paradoxical and realistic examples of the prisoner's dilemma, thereby to bring home the full significance of Tucker's insight that honesty and cooperation serve the social welfare better than dishonest selfishness.

Since that conclusion arises mainly in the static prisoner's dilemma game, when the players cannot guess and know nothing about each other's behaviour, Frank next considers the dynamic game, where the players learn something about each other's behaviour and responses to their opponent's behaviour by playing the same game repeatedly in succession. In that case, selfish behaviour gradually changes and becomes honest and cooperative with increasing frequency – a result Frank again tests against real-life examples (such as soldiers after months of trench warfare learning to slaughter each other 'considerately' by sparing mealtimes and hospital tents from shellfire) before arguing that a person's unswerving commitment to honesty becomes advantageous also to himself, provided that his commitment becomes known to or can be ascertained by others. Indeed, people known to be truthful and trustworthy will obviously be favoured in business and the labour market over others not so known, which clearly gives them an important economic advantage.

That conclusion leads Frank to his second important insight, which is that people's commitment to honesty is strengthened, and may even be explained, by their pursuit of selfish interests – but only to the extent that their honesty becomes *known* and their pursuit of self-interest is *rational*. Both these qualifications will be seen to be crucial. Frank fully recognizes the relevance of the first, which is why he devotes four chapters, almost a third of the book, to discussing the channels of communication through which people learn about one another's moral character. As to the second, he presents a model highly pertinent for analysing the rationality of choice but uses it in a lesser connection and fails to see or admit its relevance for the purpose at hand, leaving to the discerning reader (and this reviewer) the task of completing one of the more interesting conclusions of the book.

Much of the preceding argument concerning the economic effects of people acting out their righteous emotions, Frank generalizes to righteous behaviour prompted by such other emotions as fairness, altruism, compassion, love, anger, guilt, shame, rage, revenge and so on. He shows that righteous behaviour motivated by these emotions also contributes both to society's and to the emotionally committed individual's own welfare – though the latter again mostly on condition that his or her emotional commitment is known to others. Two examples should suffice to give the flavour of Frank's argument. A choleric person's outrage at being cheated, robbed or mugged may move her to take some precipitate action, different and more drastic than what the cold calculation of its costs and benefits would counsel; and if her hot-blooded appearance or reputation makes her adversary fear such vehement response to his villainy, the adversary may well restrain himself and so spare her the danger and possible costs of her foolhardiness. Note that such emotional behaviour is always in society's interest but may harm the emotional person herself and benefits her only if its threat makes her attacker desist. Similarly, a person indignantly refusing, or expected to refuse, advantageous but unfair and inequitable offers promotes social welfare but gains more equitable contracts for himself only if his initial refusal does not end the bargaining process.

The discussion of several of those emotions receives whole chapters in the book and is among its more innovative parts; but since the arguments concerning them are mostly quite similar to the book's basic argument about honesty, and since I have nothing to add to them, I will not deal with them further.

Let me return instead to Frank's main argument and deal with the question whether and to what extent material rewards can be relied upon to help maintain honesty. Earlier generations relied on religion, the law, the schools and the family to form people's character and make them into upright citizens. But now, when religion is losing its hold, law enforcement is lax and inefficient, the family is disintegrating and education is accused of failing to teach and inculcate values, it is high time to look at what, if anything, economic inducements have to do with people's character.

To derive people's ethical behaviour from their rational self-interest has been tried already by the utilitarians. In my college days, when I first encountered British agnostics and their high moral standards, I wanted to learn what made them that way and was advised to read Sir Leslie Stephen – an Anglican minister who, having lost faith in God but not in His teaching, relinquished the ministry and wrote *The Science of Ethics* (1882), a book on the utilitarian argument for ethical behaviour. It was a long book, its arguments difficult to follow and remember; but I persevered and recall coming away from it disappointed and unconvinced. The fact that the book now seems all but forgotten makes me feel that my judgement then was right.

Frank's attempt to show that material rewards encourage honesty is much more successful. He begins by discussing two imaginary limiting cases in which people's character is either stamped on their foreheads for all to see or completely impossible to judge and ascertain. In the first case, dishonest persons would be recognized by everybody and shunned by honest and dishonest people alike, depriving them of their livelihood and making it to everybody's advantage to become and remain honest. In the second limiting case, in which crooks and squares were utterly impossible to tell apart, it would become easy and advantageous for everybody to cheat, convincing even the most upright people that among crooks one must cheat to survive.

Between those extremes lies the real world, in which cheaters are hard but not impossible to recognize, and where crooked, upright and not-so-upright people coexist, in proportions determined by the cost (in terms of money and effort) of checking the honesty of prospective employees and business associates. For that cost is worth incurring only when it is smaller than the mathematical expectation of the loss suffered by those who fail to check their employees' and associates' character. Since that loss is the smaller, the fewer the cheaters in the population, so is the inducement to incur the cost and make the effort to weed them out. As a result, cheating is the easier and the more profitable, the fewer are the cheaters in a given society; and adding the assumption that the number of cheaters depends on the profitability of cheating, Frank shows that the ratio of cheaters to non-cheaters tends to stabilize at the level where the cost of ascertaining character equals the mathematical expectation of the loss incurred by assuming that everybody is honest.

That is the third and to my knowledge most original of Frank's important conclusions; but so far it is only the skeleton of a theory, which needs to be fleshed out with detail about how, and at what cost, information on people's honesty or dishonesty is transmitted, and about the way in which relative earnings affect the proportion of honest to dishonest people in the population. As already mentioned, the book deals at length with the first issue, but its treatment of the second is skimpy and vague, although the tool for dealing with it is at hand. I proceed to discuss them in that order, hoping to add something to the treatment of the second.

Note to begin with that small, stable communities, in which everybody knows everything worth knowing about almost everybody else, come fairly close to Frank's first limiting case, in which honesty prevails, because cheaters, being easily recognized, become outcasts. Only large urban agglomerations and the great mobility of the modern world have rendered information about people's character scarce and its transmission a valuable service.

The obvious reason why information about people's moral character is scarce is that the dishonest have even more to gain from an honest reputation than the honest themselves. That renders valueless people's advertising their own honesty. Credible information on the subject must come from the involuntary signals and unconscious telltale signs people give of their own character and from sources other than the person whose character is to be assessed.

Frank focuses his attention on the former and discusses at length facial expression, general demeanour, unconscious habits, shifty eyes, body language, blushing, sweating, changes in speech pattern and symptoms of nervous arousal, some of which are clues to general character while others are telltale signs of specific disreputable acts such as lying and cheating. Frank's discussion of all that is based on an impressive variety of sources, ranging from Charles Darwin to modern physiological psychology, and ending with an account of a series of experiments he and his psychologist colleagues designed and administered, which establish that ordinary people are well able to interpret such signs and assess a person's character surprisingly well, even on minimal acquaintance.

Character information from sources other than the subject himself he treats under the headings of affiliation and reputation. Affiliation as a clue to character is often easy to fake and so can mislead and aim to mislead but is used nevertheless. Frank cites the example of the New York rich who, trusting the Mormon's superior moral standards, recruit governesses by placing want ads in Salt Lake City's newspapers. Another example is France's exceptionally large number of family businesses, which is customarily explained by French people's distrust of anyone but members of their own family as business associates. In some European countries, former professional officers use their military rank as badges of impeccable honesty; and in the United

States, lawyers, brokers and small businessmen often join, or at any rate used to join, church groups to inspire confidence and make themselves known.

Reputation is probably the main basis nowadays on which people judge the honesty of prospective employees and business associates; and to ascertain it is costly in terms of time and money, because it involves collecting and weighing references, credit ratings, police records and so on. Frank at first casts doubt on the reliability of reputation as a predictor of future behaviour, pointing out that, instead of indicating character, it merely separates those caught cheating from others not caught, which latter category includes not only the righteous but also cheaters smart enough to get away with it and potential cheaters who have passed up as too risky previous opportunities to cheat. I would qualify that judgement partly on the ground that people too timid to cheat are only a notch or two less reliable than those who do not cheat on principle, and also because, ideally, references reflect the judgement of the candidate's character by the people best able to observe those telltale signs and involuntary signals Frank shows to be so reliable, though most people admittedly are reluctant to put down in writing impressions based on such intangible evidence, which means that their judgement must be read between the lines and inferred from the tone of wording.

Moreover, Frank himself reverses his initial judgement later, when his analysis of the way dishonest people choose between cheating and not cheating makes him conclude that most of them are not only amoral but irrational as well, seldom cautious enough to pass up risky opportunities and smart enough to get away with it. From that he infers that the proportion of cheaters not caught must be very small and so not likely to seriously impair the reliability of reputation as a predictor of future behaviour.

Franks' conclusion is interesting, but even more interesting is the analysis behind it, because I believe that the latter's relevance goes beyond the rather limited use to which he puts it. For I shall argue presently that an honest person's decision whether or not to stay honest is not significantly different from a dishonest person's choice between cheating and not cheating; and if that is so, then the same analysis will also be seen to help resolve the already mentioned question how economic reward affects the proportion of honest people in the population.

Frank analyses the individual's choice between the temporary gain from a criminal act and the long-run advantage of an honest reputation with the aid of Robert Strotz's 1956 dynamic model of consumer's choice. That model has been used extensively in economics, in the theories of money and public finance,[3] as well as in theories of consumer behaviour,[4] and also by psychologists for elucidating the addiction problem.[5]

It is well suited to Frank's purpose, since it deals with the problem of choosing between alternative future satisfactions of which one is smaller but closer in time, the other larger but more remote. Since both lie in the future, it is natural to expect their present values to be discounted; the question is why, on what basis, and by how much. In addition to discounting entitlements to money at the market rate of interest (which for simplicity's sake I shall ignore), many people discount all future events for the uncertainty of living long enough to experience them, and presumably set their subjective rate of discount the higher, the shorter their life expectancy. That is why the average person's enjoyment of smoking, drinking and rich diets is least inhibited by his fear of their long-term health effects in poor countries, where life expectancy is short, and among the aged.[6]

In addition, however, many people discount the present value of future satisfactions yet further, owing to what Strotz calls 'short-sighted imagination'. That additional rate of discount depends, not on one's life expectancy but on the remoteness of each satisfaction from the present and diminishes sharply as the passing of time brings it into the foreground of one's consciousness and thereby increases its attraction. Those two reasons for discounting the future affect one's ranking of alternative satisfactions differently at different moments of time, as illustrated in Figures 5.1 and 5.2.

All the curves are discount curves and show the discounted value of future satisfactions A and B at each point of time, with their slopes showing (in the semi-logarithmic diagrams) the rate of discount. Figure 5.1 shows only the uncertainty discount, whose fixed rate is represented by straight lines that are parallel and non-intersecting, considering that one discounts for the uncertainty of one's remaining lifespan at the same rate, whatever and whenever the future satisfactions are. In Figure 5.2, the two curves show the combined discount for uncertainty *and* short-sightedness; and since the latter depends on and diminishes with the proximity of each satisfaction, they can, and in the example do, intersect.

Accordingly, Figure 5.1 shows that, when a person discounts the future only for uncertainty, the satisfaction whose present value he considers higher to begin with will remain higher, and higher in the same degree, through time. Figure 5.2 shows that, when someone discounts future events for myopia as well as for uncertainty, and happens initially to prefer the later-but-larger satisfaction, then the passage of time will diminish the degree of his preference and may ultimately reverse it, because as it brings the smaller-but-earlier satisfaction within easy reach, it renders the allure of its instant gratification so dazzling that it temporarily blinds him to the greater merit of its larger but still remote alternative. Hence the paradox that, even when tastes and sources of satisfaction both remain unchanged, the mere passing of time can reverse one's choice between them, because their unchanged time distance from each other appears larger when seen from nearby than what it seemed while looked at from afar.

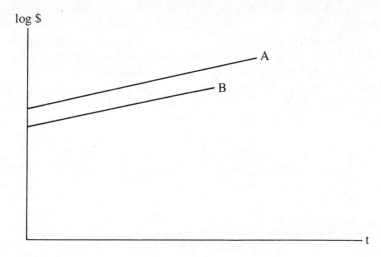

Figure 5.1

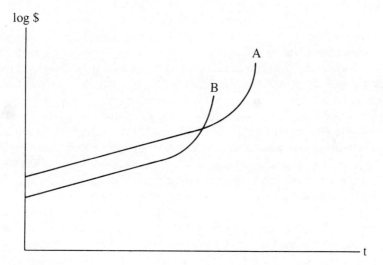

Figure 5.2

That argument has been used to explain why some people are improvident spendthrifts, why thrifty people sometimes splurge and go on a binge, why taxis in Mexico City are unavailable on the weekly payday when workers go on a spree, why even happily married couples occasionally cheat on their spouses, why people break self-imposed dieting rules, and why so many addicts to gambling, smoking, drinking and drugs are unable to break the habit, though fully aware that it is ruining their lives. Frank uses the argument to explain why people without a conscience to keep them honest and motivated only by material rewards so often throw prudence to the winds and take great chances to yield to the lure of cheating and stealing, thereby to risk losing the greater long-run benefits of an honest reputation.

Different authors give different names to the cause of such reversals of choice, calling it weakness of will (the Greeks), perverse desire (Hobbes), faulty telescopic faculty (Pigou), inability clearly to imagine distant goals (Böhm Bawerk), short-sighted imagination or myopia (Strotz), improvidence (John Stuart Mill), imprudence, impatience, and so on. Most people, including Frank, consider such behaviour irrational; but in the field of public finance, of course, the explanation is quite different; and also the individual consumer's reversal choice can have a variety of explanations, most of which are analysed in detail by Gordon Winston.

In the context in which Frank uses the model, the explanation clearly is irrationality, or more exactly a temporary suspension of rationality; and that throws new light on the meaning of rationality. Rational behaviour has long been known to be something much more complex than what the economist's casual use of the term suggests (see Sen's article in *The New Palgrave*); nevertheless, the use Frank and the psychologists make of Strotz's model seems to add something to our understanding of it. To begin with, rational behaviour appears to consist of two parts: rational thinking to establish goals and rational action to adopt and stick to those goals. The first is fairly straightforward, the second, as has just been argued, is not always easy, because it may require going against an inborn predilection. Psychologists have collected overwhelming evidence[7] showing that reluctance to give up present satisfaction in exchange for greater future satisfactions is an inborn, strongly ingrained instinct, common to animals and men, strikingly evident in young children, which to overcome requires self-discipline – an acquired skill difficult to learn and never fully mastered by a large part of mankind.

That, after all, is why people trying to behave rationally have developed so many aids to bolster their failing self-control. The earliest example was Ulysses having himself strapped to the mast to help him resist the lure of the sirens and so avoid wrecking his ship. Today, people join Christmas savings clubs and pension plans, smokers resolve not to light up before noon, prudent gamblers leave their credit cards at home when going to Las Vegas, drinkers put the bottle out of reach and sight, bet money on not drinking, join Alcoholics Anonymous or take Antabuse if all else fails.[8]

I mention all this in order to point up the close affinity between rationality and honesty. To begin with, they are surprisingly similar in their effects on behaviour. Both require self-control to resist temptation and many are the temptations that honest and rational people alike have to resist (such as cheating and thieving when they are risky). Yet not everything prescribed by honesty is in one's rational self-interest and much that is has nothing to do with honesty.

Secondly, commitment to honesty could, in some cases, also be regarded as one of the devices to strengthen the self-discipline one needs for rational behaviour. It is by no means obvious that self-control in the service of honesty is, by itself, easier to exercise than the self-control of rationality; but it is often bolstered by conscience, religion and the desire to avoid feelings of guilt and shame – a pair of strong emotions shown by Frank to be capable of generating or bolstering righteous behaviour. In short, temptations proscribed by both honesty and rationality are probably easier for a would-be rational person to resist if he is also honest at the same time. Frank does not spell it out in such detail but that is what I get out of the book.

Having dealt with the support honesty provides to keep people rational, we can take up the last topic yet to be dealt with by turning the question around: does the rational pursuit of economic reward support people's commitment to honesty? Frank argues that the main sources of a person's commitment to moral behaviour are emotional and that, while people's (and especially children's) character is formed mainly by their predisposition to imitate the behaviour of people in superior positions (adults), the brain is not a completely empty slate on which anything can be imprinted, because its receptivity is biased in favour of orderly standards and such innate emotions as empathy and responsibility. The argument, based largely on post-behaviourist psychology, is interesting; but it does not explain how changes in the material reward to honesty affect the degree to which honesty prevails.

Frank needs a constructive answer to that question in order to complete his theory of how the economy's mix of honesty and corruption is determined (see p. 77 above); but his position on the subject is far from clear. He seems to be looking for an evolutionary explanation *à la* Darwin but cannot find one. His argument that 'those with larger material payoffs have the resources to raise larger numbers of offspring' (p. 58) is not very convincing and seems, in any case, to be offered, not as an explanation, but as a model for someone else to follow and improve upon.

He is apparently unable to countenance the much simpler explanation that a change in the relative material pay-offs to honest and dishonest people might affect their own moral character. Strotz's analytical model is ideally suited for dealing with that possibility but Frank explicitly restricts his use of it to an *amoral* person's choice behaviour, presumably because he visualizes commitment to honesty as a way of life and as a refusal even to consider committing a dishonest act. The choice between honesty and dishonesty is admittedly more momentous than that between jam and marmalade to put on one's bread; but Frank seems to forget that the Strotz model is designed for dealing with the often equally momentous choice between rational and irrational behaviour, that honesty and rationality are alike also in that both require self-discipline, and that, while an honest person's self-control is arguably stronger than a rational person's, none of us is free from temptation. To me, it seems wrong to think of commitment to honesty as an either–or proposition as I believe Frank does; surely it resembles rationality also in that both come in many gradations. Once one accepts that, it also becomes easier to accept the idea that rational self-interest can nudge a person into becoming a little more or a little less honest. Both points have been made by Akerlof (1983) in an excellent but all-too-short paper, which Frank quotes but seems to overlook or disagree with.

Let me clinch the above argument with a piece of undocumented indirect evidence, similar in that respect to evidence occasionally also used in the book. Businessmen in this country traditionally look upon politicians as morally inferior to themselves and often corrupt. If that is justified, as it certainly seems to be today, the likely explanation would be that, in business life and the labour market of the private sector, honesty is highly valued, carefully checked, continuously audited, and valuable to the honest person himself; whereas all of that is much less true of elected officials (and political appointees) in the public sector. For the electorate, in most cases, cannot check and knows nothing about the candidates' moral character, which eliminates the latters' rational self-interest in being and remaining honest. It is conceivable that people who are dishonest to begin with go into politics and local government for that reason; but a more important explanation, I suspect, is that the average person's average honesty is nourished and made to grow under the private sector's continued pressure to be and remain honest, whereas similar people's similar honesty is allowed to wither in the public sector, where little attention is paid to honesty until the media uncover some scandal, by which time it is far too late.

I want to end this review with praise, because the book is full of information, ideas and food for thought. I learned a lot from it; but I must add a warning that learning from it is not nearly as easy as reading it, because it also requires work, fun work, from the reader.

Notes

1. Cf. Sen (1987) especially chapter 1.
2. Cf. Simpson (1988).
3. Cf. Fischer (1980); Persson *et al.* (1987) and the latter's bibliography.
4. Cf. Winston (1982); Deaton and Muellbauer (1985); Phillips (1974).
5. Cf. Ainslie (1975) and its bibliography; also his 1983 paper.
6. Indeed, the fully rational thing might be for all of us gradually to increase the rate of our uncertainty discount as advancing age and declining health shortens our life expectancy.
7. For an account of some of the evidence, see Ainslie (1975).

8. For a classification and detailed discussion of the various internal aids to self-discipline, see Ainslie (1975).

References

Ainslie, George (1975), 'Specious Reward: A Behavioral Theory of Impulsiveness and Impulse Control', *Psychological Review*, **82**, 463–96.

—— (1983), 'Beyond Microeconomics. Conflict among Interests in a Multiple Self as a Determinant of Value', in Jon Elster (ed.), *The Multiple Self*, (Cambridge: Cambridge University Press).

Akerlof, G.A. (1970), 'The Market for Lemons: Quality Uncertainty and the Market Mechanism', *Quarterly Journal of Economics*, **84**, 488–500.

—— (1983), 'Loyalty Filters', *American Economic Review*, **73**, 54–63.

Arrow, K.J. (1972), 'Gifts and Exchanges', *Philosophy and Public Affairs*, **1**, 343–62.

Deaton, A.S. and Muellbauer, J.N. (1985), *Economics and Consumer Behavior*, (Cambridge: Cambridge University Press).

Fischer, Stanley (1980), 'Dynamic Inconsistency, Co-operation and the Benevolent Dissembling Government', *Journal of Economic Dynamics and Control*, **2**, 93–107.

Frank, Robert H. (1988), *Passions within Reason. The Strategic Role of the Emotions*, (New York: W.W. Norton).

Hirschman, Albert O. (1977), *The Passions and the Interests. Political Arguments for Capitalism before its Triumph*, (Princeton, N.J.: Princeton University Press).

Machlup, Fritz (1972), 'The Universal Bogey', in Maurice Peston and Bernand Corry (eds), *Essays in Honour of Lord Robbins*, (London: Weidenfeld & Nicolson).

Persson, Mats, Persson, Torsten and Svensson, Lars E.O. (1987), 'Time Consistency of Fiscal and Monetary Policy', *Econometrica*, **55**, 1419–31.

Phillips, L. (1974), *Applied Consumption Analysis*, (Amsterdam: American Elsevier).

Sen, Amartya (1987), *On Ethics and Economics*, (Oxford: Basil Blackwell).

Simpson, David (1988), 'What Economists Need to Know', *The Royal Bank of Scotland Review*, no. 160, December, 3–11.

Stephen, Sir Leslie (1882), *The Science of Ethics*, (New York: Putnam's Sons).

Strotz, Robert H. (1955–6), 'Myopia and Inconsistency in Dynamic Utility Maximization', *Review of Economic Studies*, **23**, 165–80.

Winston, Gordon, C. (1982), *The Timing of Economic Activities. Firms, Households, and Markets in Time-Specific Analysis*, (Cambridge: Cambridge University Press).

6   How our economy stands up to scrutiny*

Now, when the shortcomings of socialist state enterprise are widely admitted and most of the world seems to have come around to believing in the superior advantages of democracy and private enterprise, is a good time to ask what exactly it is that the free enterprise market economy accomplishes and what, ideally, it might accomplish.

These questions, of course, have often been dealt with before, but mostly in an incomplete, one-sided way, because welfare economists, whose job it is to raise such questions, are perfectionists. We are very good at showing how perfect competition would accomplish a limited number of market functions to perfection, not so good at judging what the real-world economy's imperfect performance of many more functions adds up to. For several important economic functions happen to be mutually incompatible, in the sense that the perfect accomplishment of one would prevent the accomplishment of another. When we focus on the abstract model of perfect competition, we ignore or abstract from such incompatibilities and so tend to overlook our real economy's great merit, which is that it resolves those incompatibilities by effecting a compromise between them when it performs all functions imperfectly.

For example, we have long realized the difficulty of weighing the conflicting merits of economic efficiency and equity against one another and used to dodge the issue by analysing efficiency in depth, while leaving equity and social justice to be dealt with by philosophers, moralists and politicians.

Similarly, the better to understand the workings of the market economy, we developed the simplified unrealistic model of perfect competition, which was most helpful in clarifying the role of prices in coordinating different people's activities but hid from view the role of monopoly and monopolistic competition in encouraging technical and economic progress, because perfect competition has no room for monopoly and monopolistic competition.[1]

Fortunately, such outstanding economists as Amartya Sen, John Harsanyi and Partha Dasgupta are bringing equity back into the purview of economic theory; and I shall try in what follows to carry on their good work by rounding out the picture of our economy just a little further. I shall try to list some of its neglected and seldom mentioned benefits and stress its worst imperfections.

* This chapter was an acceptance paper for the 1990 Seidman Distinguished Award in Political Economy.

Probably the most important advantage of our economy is a political one: its tolerance of human diversity. It provides people with a livelihood whatever the ideology and opinions they hold or express. I am not saying that it provides a livelihood to everybody; that question I will take up at the end. Nor am I saying that it always provides the same livelihood for the same accomplishment, because there is plenty of discrimination, by race, sex and colour. Indeed, this is one of the many functions our market economy performs imperfectly; but it is valuable nonetheless and as such an essential condition of the freedoms we expect to enjoy in a democracy.

Among the economic merits of free enterprise, the first, perhaps, is its encouragement of technical and economic progress. It finances and rewards innovation, the introduction of new goods and services and of cheaper ways of providing existing goods and services. All this raises the standard of living and usually enhances equity as well, because most innovation consists in making generally available what previously was the privilege of the few.

To create and accomplish things others have not, and have not even thought of, gives people a feeling of superiority whose enjoyment is part of human nature; but the desire for superiority can assume very destructive forms and it takes monopolistic competition to channel it into socially useful innovation. Moreover, to research, develop and put into practice new ideas is usually a lengthy, costly and risky undertaking, which needs financing from the outset; and our economy provides that, mainly out of the profits of monopolistic enterprise.

A related if less spectacular feature of our economy is its rewarding the introduction of every minor improvement, refinement and embellishment of the merchandise offered and the way in which it is offered. That explains our ever-changing fashions, our beautiful shops and shopping centres with their dazzling array of every conceivable good, enticingly displayed and instantly available in all forms, colours, sizes and quantities, offered in an environment so attractive, an atmosphere so polite and friendly that shopping has become many people's favourite pastime. All these amenities result from non-price competition, the favoured form of monopolistic competition.

A parallel but much lesser and slower improvement in the amenities of the workplace has made working conditions safer, cleaner, lighter and healthier, thanks mainly to bargaining by labour unions but also to employers' non-price competition for workers. Note that to secure these benefits requires both competition and monopoly profits. That is not as contradictory as it may sound, because monopolistic competition provides both. To secure them, we only have to combat pure monopoly, being in no danger of competition's ever becoming perfect. Monopolistic competition, of course, comes in many gradations, but we have no way of ascertaining the optimum mix of competition and monopoly profits.

I now come to the traditional subjects of welfare economics. One is competition's tendency to curb profits. Profit has long been a dirty word and still is that for people who think of it as easy gain, obtained by outwitting others or exploiting the advantages of superior wealth, power or knowledge. Adam Smith made profit respectable by showing that competition harnesses its selfish pursuit to serving society's interests and curbing the very profits pursued. 150 years later, Joseph Schumpeter strengthened this point by adding that progress and innovation depend on monopolistic competition and its profits.[2]

But the most remarkable feature of the market economy is its ability to coordinate the independent economic activities of millions of people and thousands of firms more efficiently than any of the attempts at central planning so far made. Coordination in this context means four different things: (1) distributing goods and services according to consumers' differing needs and tastes as well as in proportion to their spending; (2) allocating resources to the production of various goods so that the latter's output will match consumers' demand for them and be produced at minimum cost; (3) guiding people in their choice of what talents and skills to develop, what competencies to acquire, what jobs to accept and undertakings to invest in so as to match those requirements; and (4) persuading consumers to utilize as fully as possible whatever productive capacities and human skills and proficiencies are already in existence.

Markets perform these functions by equating supply and demand and generating prices that show what others pay and charge for various goods and services, thereby making generally known the opportunities that each market offers to potential entrants. Under perfect competition, all markets would be cleared and competitive pressures would compel all the sellers of each item to charge the identical price and all its buyers to pay that same price; and that single price of each product would accurately reflect its equal cost to all its producers and equal worth to all its consumers.

The ideal situation that perfect competition in every market would bring about we call 'Pareto optimality' and visualize as one in which the transactions already concluded in existing markets would leave no unexploited opportunity of making anyone better off without having to make someone else worse off. That is why we infer the inefficiency of centrally planned economies from their having black markets.

Real-world markets, of course, are imperfectly competitive, imperfectly coordinated, and the information their prices convey is only more or less reliable, depending on the competitiveness of the markets that generate them. We cannot measure the extent to which those imperfections detract from the Pareto optimality of perfect competition; but we would not know what degree of efficiency to aim for even if we could. For remember that innovation and progress depend on monopolistic competition and monopoly profits, which perfect competition would eliminate. The perfect economy, therefore, has to be imperfectly competitive and sacrifice some of its coordinating and allocating efficiency for the sake of growth. We may not know where the best compromise between those conflicting goals lies, but the conflict and need for compromise can be reduced by appropriate government policies in the same way that social insurance, social services, low-cost public housing and progressive taxation reduce the conflict between efficiency and equity.

Governments subsidize basic research in universities and research institutes; patent laws encourage innovation by assuring temporary monopoly profits to innovators or their firms; anti-trust legislation, state employment agencies and laws requiring truth in lending and selling and the full disclosure of food ingredients improve the competitiveness of markets. But, while we have no measure of Pareto efficiency, we do know something about how well our markets perform their specific coordinating functions. Statistics of unemployment and capacity utilization show the extent to which resources are utilized, which is one of the economy's most important functions, considering that the unemployment of labour is the greatest and most hurtful form of waste. We have no comparable estimates of the efficiency with which markets allocate resources and distribute goods and jobs; but we know the conditions necessary for their efficiency and, from the way those conditions are fulfilled, we can infer what functions a particular market performs best. We know, for example, that our consumer markets, while imperfectly competitive from the sellers' point of view, are nearly perfect on the buyers' side, because buyers have access to the same shops, face the same prices, which they regard as given, and usually can distil enough useful information from the media and competitive advertising to make intelligent choices. That suggests that our markets distribute consumer goods with reasonable efficiency.

Near perfect competition on the buyers' side of consumer markets also makes goods' prices reflect their worth to buyers fairly accurately, which renders the pattern of prices and purchases a reliable reflection of the public's wants and a good basis for the production and investment plans of producers and would-be producers. At the same time, oligopolistic competition on the sellers' side of the same markets keeps prices from reflecting production costs accurately and so prevents the public's choosing the expenditure pattern that would satisfy its wants at minimum social cost. In addition, monopolistic obstacles to newcomers' entry to some industries prevents minimizing the cost of producing those industries' output.

In labour markets, both sides' good access to market information enables employers to match human aptitudes to the economy's needs and job seekers to choose the jobs that best suit them and decide what occupations to enter and skills to develop. (Today, only very few jobs have restricted entry.) On the other hand, imperfect competition on the employers' side makes both wage and job discrimination possible by colour, race and gender, and keeps wages below what labour's contribution is worth, which creates inequities and is a further obstacle to the minimizing of social costs.

To summarize, the market economy seems to perform all but two of its coordinating functions quite well, the exceptions being failure to minimize the social cost of output and inability to maintain full employment and full utilization of capacity. The first is due to the padding of prices with (and abridgement of wages by) monopoly profits, which also increases the inequality of incomes. But progress, innovation and novelty are encouraged and financed by those monopoly profits, which means that our society pays for its progress by accepting higher than minimal costs of production and inequalities of income.

That brings us to the last and most problematic of the market economy's potential advantages: the clearing of markets and the full employment of human and other resources. For it is one thing to guide people to the occupations that best suit their abilities and to allocate available jobs according to people's abilities; it is quite another thing to provide suitable jobs to all who seek them. In the socialist countries, people's euphoria over the impending reform of their economies is marred by one fear: they look upon unemployment as the inevitable cost of enjoying the advantages of the market economy; and the experience of the West's economies seems to justify that fear. Yet why should the market economy be less good at maintaining full employment than it is at its other coordinating functions? It is pretty good at catering to new or increased demands, because rising prices do cause industries to expand, new ones to be created and new skills to be learned. Why cannot falling prices persuade consumers to make their purchases conform to whatever productive capacities and skills are already available, thereby to keep our workforce employed and equipment utilized? After all, consumers' spending seems just as malleable as the economy's productive capabilities. Why cannot price changes harmonize supply and demand by prompting adjustments in both?

There seem to be two answers to this. First, prices are not nearly as flexible downwards as they are upwards, for reasons I shall deal with presently, which means that they put much less pressure on consumers to buy than on suppliers to produce. However, since flexible prices would only cure pockets of unemployment, localized in particular industries or sectors, a second condition of full employment in market economies is a well-functioning macroeconomic stabilization policy to offset the cumulative changes in aggregate demand created by multiplier processes and self-fulfilling price expectations. Such policies are needed to forestall both recessionary general unemployment and inflationary (or deflationary) wealth redistributions; but they have proved unable to control inflation without also creating unemployment in the process when prices are inflexible downward. In short, prices would have to be more symmetrically flexible, not only for maintaining employment in declining sectors but for the proper functioning of stabilization policies as well.

What, then, keeps prices from being flexible downwards? We know that most sellers are afraid to reduce their list prices lest competitors follow suit and precipitate a general reduction of prices and profits, which is difficult to undo; but that can be (and usually is) guarded against by hidden and implicit price concessions, such as temporary rebates, bonuses, increased recourse to sales, greater use of discount outlets and stepped up non-price competition. The main impediment to flexible prices is price floors that keep prices from falling below a certain level, and as a rule it is the too high price floors of products that create involuntary unemployment.

Let me start, however, with the exception: the government-imposed minimum wage, which constitutes the wage floor of unskilled labour. We have often been told that perfect competition would assure full employment, but no one has ever asserted that it would assure everybody's employment *at a living wage*. The market economy does much for efficiency, much less for equity. Since society also wants equity, government has to intervene to assure a decent living for the poor by providing a safety net and setting a minimum wage to keep unskilled workers from being exploited. But a minimum wage also has an undesired side-effect on those whose work is worth less than the minimum wage: they get fired or fail to get employed. This accounts for most of the shockingly high unemployment rate of black youths and males in our country; and its best, if very difficult, remedy is to reduce the supply of unskilled workers by improving our schools, raising literacy standards and reducing the number of school drop-outs.

Skilled and semi-skilled workers' and professional people's earnings have a higher and very different kind of pay floor. They made an investment in the human capital of their special skills, training and knowledge, on which they expect to get a fair return in the long haul and good annual earnings most of the time. But since every investment is a gamble whose cost is irrevocably sunk, it involves the risk of yielding reduced earnings during recessions or periods of diminished demand for their particular speciality, which they must and usually do accept. They would look for another job only if their present and expected future earnings fell below what they could earn elsewhere, which at times could be quite low, perhaps only what they would earn outside of their speciality, in a semi-skilled or unskilled job. That level of earnings is their pay floor, because below it they would voluntarily quit.

Producers have an investment in their plant and equipment; and they price each of their products by adding to its current out-of-pocket costs a profit-maximizing mark-up, which pays for overhead costs and depreciation, and usually yields a good return on their investment in addition. When business is bad, the profit-maximizing or loss-minimizing mark-up shrinks, to judge by the increased use of sales, rebates, discount outlets and other such hidden price reductions common at such times;[3] and producers accept the reduced return on their investment as the inevitable risk that investment involves. They will not, however, reduce the price of a product below its price floor, which is set by the minimum out-of-pocket expenses they believe necessary to assure the services of their employees and deliveries from the subcontractors and suppliers that provide the product's inputs. They will rather close down its production than reduce its price below that point.

It should now be obvious that, if the price floor of every product were no higher than the sum of the pay floors of its inputs, a fall in demand for a product would not cause the employees providing its inputs to be fired or laid off. Instead, its price, along with the pay of all those who contribute inputs would be reduced, making all of them shoulder part of the loss caused by the fall in demand. Only if worst came to the worst, and the producer decided that the product was not worth producing, would he and all but his unskilled employees (and perhaps some of his subcontractors and their employees) quit voluntarily, because their earnings would reach their respective floors at the same time that the product's price reached its floor.

In our society, however, the necessary conditions for such a situation are seldom fulfilled, first, because producers usually overestimate the pay floors of their inputs; and second, because, to avoid the danger of bankruptcy, the firm's total receipts from all its operations must be sufficient to pay not only the out-of-pocket costs of all its products' inputs but its out-of-pocket overhead costs as well – and those can be high when its bank debts and bonded debt are high.

As to the first, employees, suppliers and subcontractors do not tell the producer what their pay floors are. They do not want him to know their willingness, in worsened circumstances, to continue working for less pay, partly for fear of his abusing that knowledge to exploit them, partly in an attempt to shift their share of the product's eventual loss of revenue onto other people's shoulders. That is why producers tend to set their product's price floor at the level of their *actual* out-of-pocket expenses and, on reaching that, to reduce output rather than price in response to a further fall in demand, creating redundancies and involuntary unemployment.

One may well ask why employers could not rely on factor markets to negotiate an equitable distribution between themselves and their employees of the gains and losses that ever-changing market conditions create. They could if employees and workplaces could be changed as easily as shoppers switch from one store to another in search of the best price or product. But employees, especially professionals, skilled and semi-skilled workers, prefer stable employment, just as employers prefer stable employees, because the firm-specific skill, knowledge and experience that people accumulate in the course of their work are valuable assets that get lost and must be relearned and retaught with every change of worker and workplace, hurting employers and employees alike.[4]

This renders labour contracts very different from sales contracts, making them resemble marriage contracts instead. Just as there, the parties usually expect a fair deal when they sign the contract; but they also commit themselves for better for worse, for richer for poorer times to come; and if circumstances have changed to the worse by then, only the parties' decency, honesty and mutual trust can assure the continued fairness of the contract – qualities rarer in labour relations than in marriage.

How then is the unemployment problem handled? With ease and to mutual satisfaction only when perfect trust and honesty prevail. There are such cases. I have in mind one-man workshops and partnerships of solicitors, public accountants and physicians, where labour, capital and management are merely different hats on the same person's head and inputs of intermediate goods are insignificant. Owners of one-man shops and members of partnerships normally price their services so as to pay for their work and sundry minor expenses and yield a good return on the human capital of their skill or professional education and their investment in premises and equipment.

When demand declines, they lower their fees if they expect that to stimulate demand sufficiently to increase earnings; if not, they accept their lighter workload and reduced income but stay in business as long as earnings cover running expenses and the opportunity cost (pay floor) of their labour. Only in the extreme case of receipts' falling below that minimum would they quit to accept a salaried job or look for another location or occupation. In short, they may fall on lean times but are fairly well protected against unemployment. That is why accumulating enough savings to start a small store or workshop of their own has long been the ambition of all industrial workers in France and many other continental countries as well. They knew that that was the best insurance for old age and unemployment, even if no cure for poverty.

Much the same is also true of small family firms whose members trust one another and probably of all small firms in which employers and employees have close friendly contacts and learn to be fair to one another and trust each other's fairness. Activity levels in such firms tend to be fairly stable because prices fluctuate instead; and the rare incidence of unemployment is due to quitting more than to being laid off.

Bear in mind also that, until the end of the 19th century, a large part of continental Europe's labour force was employed in small family firms. In France, according to the 1906 census, 59 per cent of the non-agricultural working population was its own boss or had jobs in firms with no more than ten employees. Unemployment statistics were non-existent at the time; but that itself is suggestive. Awareness of unemployment as a social problem certainly came hand-in-hand with the emergence of large firms.

Let me also mention a suggestive present-day example. The two fastest developing countries of the postwar period are Taiwan and South Korea, always mentioned together, owing partly to their identical development policies and almost identical growth rates, and partly also to the great similarity of their race, culture, recent history and social, political and economic structure. The one great difference between them was their monetary policies, which in Taiwan kept the average firm and its workforce small, facilitated the establishment of new firms and led to growth mainly through a phenomenally fast, almost 10 per cent annual increase in the number of manufacturing firms. Korean policy, by contrast, encouraged existing firms to expand, often to giant size and on average by an almost 23 per cent annual increase in output, while the number of firms increased by less than 1 per cent annually.[5]

The consequences of these different monetary policies were, first, the ever-increasing disparity in the size of the two countries' firms, and second, the very much higher debt ratios of Korean compared with Taiwanese firms. It should be obvious from the foregoing that both those differences tended to make the price floors of products much closer to their producers' actual out-of-pocket expenses in South Korea than in Taiwan; and that difference showed up strikingly both in Korea's greater inflationary price increases and her higher unemployment rates. During the period considered in my paper, the consumers' price index rose ten-fold in South Korea but only $3^1/2$-fold in Taiwan, whereas the unemployment rate averaged 4.7 per cent in Korea and not quite 1 per cent in Taiwan.

Economies of scale, however, are putting an end to the era of the small firms even in Taiwan, which raises the question as to what happens in large ones that employ much labour and capital, whose relations to management are more or less impersonal. Management can obtain capital either by borrowing, which adds a predetermined cash flow to its out-of-pocket expenses and so detracts from the price flexibility of its products, or by issuing stock, which leaves price flexibilities undiminished but involves relinquishing part of ownership.

Management's position in the labour market is much stronger than in the capital market because, while stockholders have the right to supervise and fire them, it is they who exercise those rights over their employees. But their choice of terms on which they hire labour is similar to that on which they obtain capital. They can hire workers at a fixed wage, which restricts the downward flexibility of their prices and offers workers a stable income (often with merit and seniority increases) at the cost of job security; or they can keep their prices flexible and offer workers job security at the cost of wage stability – or they can offer some compromise between these two.

The general rule in the United States and most other countries has long been to sacrifice employment security for the sake of fixed, pre-set wages. Yet this goes against both parties' interests, because employer and employees alike have an investment in the latter's job-specific skills and experience, which get lost with every change of worker and workplace. Why then has it been the predominant choice? The reason usually given is that it avoids creating ill will and distrust between the parties. For an employer who cites bad business for cutting wages would be suspect, because he could be giving an excuse rather than a reason. But when he uses the same justification for firing workers, he creates no ill will, because the workers fired know that the firm gets no value out of them and so cannot be benefiting at their expense.[6]

In short, employees' distrust of their employer makes both of them prefer a form of contract that is harmful to both – a paradoxical situation that resembles the Prisoner's Dilemma. Only very recently, during the depression of the 1970s, did labour and management begin to realize that both could benefit if they changed their priorities and opted for greater employment stability by settling for more flexible wages and more variable working weeks and working years.

To find a good way of doing that is one of today's most challenging tasks in economics, because substitutes and guarantees for plain honesty and mutual trust are hard to find. But Japan has had much success with the bonus system, which splits workers' remuneration into a fixed and a variable part;[7] in West Germany, codetermination, which is mandatory for firms with 300 or more employees and puts workers on the firm's board of supervisors, is also promising; US firms have successfully experimented with a combination of fixed hourly wages and flexible working weeks;[8] and an eminent economist is working on the economic theory of cooperatives and partnerships, trying to retain their merits while eliminating the shortcomings.[9]

Macroeconomic employment policy must, of course, have primary responsibility for mitigating fluctuations in aggregate demand; but given its severe limitations, more flexible prices and wages would greatly contribute to maintaining stable employment and a stable workforce, along with such concomitant benefits as increased output and faster growth of productivity.

Notes

1. Cf. my 'The benefits of asymmetric markets', *Journal of Economic Perspectives* (1990), **4**, 135–48, for a detailed discussion of why perfect competition is *not* conducive to technical and economic progress.
2. Cf. Joseph Schumpeter, *Theorie der Wirtschaftlichen Entwicklung*, (Munich: Duncker & Humblot, 1926).
3. For a theoretical explanation of why mark-ups shrink, see R.F. Harrod, 'The law of

diminishing elasticity of demand', *The Trade Cycle*, (Oxford: Oxford University Press, 1936), pp. 17–22.

4. Estimates of the employer's investment in his workers' job-specific skills range from one to two months' wages. See my 'Asymmetries in economics', *Scottish Journal of Political Economy* (1978), **25**, 231.

5. Cf. my 'Economic development in Taiwan and South Korea: 1965–81', *Food Research Institute Studies* (1985), **XIX**, 215–64; also in Lawrence J. Lau (ed.), *Models of Development. A Comparative Study of Economic Growth in South Korea and Taiwan*, (San Francisco: ICS Press, 1986), pp. 135–95.

6. Cf. Arthur M. Okun, *Prices & Quantities* (Oxford: Basil Blackwell, 1981), p. 58.

7. Cf. Martin Weitzman, *The Share Economy*, (Cambridge, Mass.: Harvard University Press, 1984), and M. Aoki, *Information, Incentive, and Bargaining in the Japanese Economy*, (Cambridge: Cambridge University Press, 1988).

8. Cf. S.D. Nollen, *New Work Schedules in Practice: Managing Time in a Changing Society*, (New York: Van Nostrand, 1982).

9. Cf. J.E. Meade, *Agathotopia: The Economics of Partnership*, (Aberdeen: Aberdeen University Press, 1989).

7 Growth in the affluent society*

Faith in automatic market forces that push our economy towards full employment requires a hefty amount of optimism. Expressed in professional language, the model of self-adjusting full-employment equilibrium depends on several assumptions whose validity is questionable. The weakness of one of those assumptions, known as Say's Law, has been pointed out by Keynes, who not only exposed its doubtful validity and argued the possibility of underemployment equilibrium but tried to do something about it.

Today, the failure of Keynesian policies to deal with our more complex problems, has, in some mysterious way, restored many economists' faith in the existence of full-employment equilibrium. I have never been able to understand the logic of this. Surely, if Keynesian policies are no longer adequate, the natural thing to conclude would be that different or additional policies are needed. Perhaps Say's Law was not the only unrealistic assumption to have lulled earlier generations of economists into their belief in a self-adjusting full-employment equilibrium.

I am proposing to take a critical look at another one of those questionable assumptions. I have in mind the long-held belief that, when rising labour productivity makes it possible to produce the existing output with less labour, the workers made redundant will always find employment elsewhere, because the employed population will spend more out of its now higher income and its increased spending will raise effective demand sufficiently to cause those workers to be re-employed in the production of the additional output demanded.

Underlying that belief is the implicit assumption that consumers' demand is insatiable, in the sense that, when given more money, they always want to buy more goods and services, however many they may have already. Perhaps that was a reasonable enough assumption to make in past centuries; but is it still justified in today's advanced economies, with their very much higher standards of living?

That the assumption may cease to be justified sooner or later is suggested by the fact that man's basic needs and desires for material comforts are satiable. You only have to look around you at all the people who are dieting and jogging to realize that, with respect to some needs at least, a large part of the advanced countries' populations have not only reached but passed the

* This article is based on the Fred Hirsch Memorial Lecture given in London on 7 October 1986. It first appeared in *Lloyds Bank Review*, no. 163, January 1987.

point of satiety. The early neo-classical economists took for granted the satiability of wants and enshrined it in their law of the diminishing marginal utility of money; but that law got lost when the profession abandoned the assumption of measurable utility.

Marshall and his pupils seem to be just about the only 20th-century economists to have confronted head on the question of satiability of wants. They answered it by classifying man's needs and desires into separate groups, of which the one that related to man's personal needs and comforts they considered the subject of satiable demand; whereas the group that had to do with the social comforts of distinction and superiority they considered the subject of insatiable demand – as if they had sensed that people's demand has to be insatiable for something to keep economic progress going, and believed to have found that something in social comfort. Was that belief justified and, if it was, is it still justified today?

To answer these questions, one must first of all note the ambiguity of the term 'insatiable demand'. Usually, we interpret it to mean *unlimited* demand, which keeps on rising with the rise in incomes; but it could also mean *unfillable* demand for something whose available supply cannot be increased for some reason and is not enough fully to satisfy the demand for it. Note that it is unlimited demand that stimulates the economy and serves as its engine of growth; unfillable demand merely raises prices but does not stimulate the economy. It makes a great deal of difference, therefore, whether people's demand for the sources of social comfort is insatiable in one or the other of those two senses.

To begin with, people's desire for distinction and superior status is unfillable because, to make some people feel superior, there must be others who are inferior to them, which means that not everybody can be superior, although at the bottom of his heart everybody or almost everybody would like to be. Fortunately, the same is not quite and not always true of that other important source of social comfort, the symbols of status. The demand for them may be either unlimited or unfillable, depending on the nature of the particular status symbols people want.

In the poor societies of the past, whose populations often did not have enough to eat and lacked many of the material comforts, the rich and mighty usually made their superior status known by the lavish use of the material goods that others had to go without; and since they tried to outdo one another in the extravagance of their clothes and the magnificence and size of their meals, houses and retinues, there was no limit to the escalation of luxury. If all this seemed outrageously wasteful and morally reprehensible, it did provide employment and livelihood to a lot of people; and it must have been a universal practice, to judge by the many sumptuary laws designed to curb its excesses and enacted by just about every past civilization. Earlier generations of economists therefore had good reason to pin their hopes for sustained economic growth on people's unlimited demand for conspicuous consumption.

Since then, however, the situation has changed. Increased sophistication, the sobering effect of the French Revolution and the rise of puritanism have curbed the extravagance of the rich and made them adopt much less flamboyant status symbols. To appreciate the extent of that change, recall our moral indignation when we learned of the Napoleonic pomp President Bokassa surrounded himself with, or about Michèle Duvalier's truckload of Valentino dresses and Imelda Marcos's 3000 pairs of shoes. Yet their lifestyle was merely a throwback to earlier times when such lavish extravagance was generally taken for granted as part of most rulers' standard behaviour.

What then is the new style and fashion in status symbols? To begin with, a person's income itself has come to be looked upon as a measure of the value that society puts on his services; and that causes him to appreciate a high income for its own sake, quite independently of how much of it he can spend. There is plenty of evidence to show that modern men and women are more anxious to earn money than to spend it and keep accumulating wealth whether or not they have any use for it.

Second, the outward display of high income and wealth has also changed its character. Affluent people today increasingly spend, not so much on more goods as on more exceptional ones, whose outstanding nature matches and symbolizes their own superior status, and with whose eventual donation for public use the very rich can further reassert and advertise their status. For there are many goods even in our mass-production economy that are unique, cannot be duplicated and are limited in supply or at least sufficiently outstanding from similar goods that they can be ranked against them in terms of quality, rarity, beauty or excellence of design, just as people can be ranked according to their status. The public instinctively recognizes that such goods lend distinction to their owners and so are ideally suited for serving as status symbols.

The use of exceptional objects as badges of exceptional status is logical enough; but, by abandoning the flamboyant status symbols of the past in favour of the subdued and sophisticated status symbols of the present, the rich and affluent have also changed the nature of their demand for badges of superiority. That demand was unlimited before; it has become unfillable now. For, just as the availability of superior status is never enough to satisfy all those who want it, so the supply of outstanding and exceptional objects suitable to symbolize high status is also inherently scarce and insufficient fully to satisfy all the demand for them.

The peculiar nature of those goods, their increasing share in the affluent consumers' budget and many of the problems created by the unfillable demand for them have been analysed with great perception by Fred Hirsch, whose memory we celebrate here today. He put all goods and services into one of two groups, which he called the *material* and the *positional* economies. The material economy contains all the goods and services whose supply can be increased either by using more labour and capital or by increasing the productivity of labour and capital. By contrast, the positional economy contains goods and services whose supply is inherently scarce, being limited in some absolute or socially imposed sense and therefore impossible to augment through increased productivity. That is why rising demand for them merely raises their prices or degrades their quality and occasionally raises their costs but does not call forth additional supply. He called these positional goods and services, perhaps because so many of them are used to symbolize their owners' position and rank in society.

Hirsch's favourite example of positional goods was the second houses well-to-do people own, in beautiful country locations, on the seashore, or in the form of picturesque former farmhouses, stately mansions or feudal castles. Indeed, they – along with paintings by dead masters and other antique art objects – are the best examples of positional goods, because their fixed supply is so very evident. A more general and more important example, however, is the distinctive quality of a person's home that transforms it from a mere shelter into a highly visible symbol of his status, which is imparted to it by its good location, its elegance, and by the beauty and rarity of the art objects and furnishings it contains. That distinctive quality, therefore, must be considered the positional component of a house that is added on to its material component represented by its convenience and comfort as a shelter.

Note that, while the Cambridge economists focused on the demand side when they distinguished the public's satiable demand for personal comforts from its insatiable desire for social comforts, Hirsch's two categories constitute a supply-side classification. His positional economy, however, has a large overlap with the sources of social comfort, although not all sources of social comfort are in the positional sector and not all positional goods and services are sources of social comfort. Examples of goods and services contained in the overlap include the examples already mentioned, outstanding objects created by established craftsmen and artists, as well as such things as exotic holidays and the best tables in the most fashionable restaurants.

In the following, I shall mainly focus on that overlap and draw your attention to an important consequence of the public's unfillable demand for positional goods, which Fred Hirsch in his short life had no time to explore.

After that long but necessary digression we can return to the question I started out with. What happens to employment and growth when rising labour productivity reduces the amount of labour needed to produce the pre-existing output and makes idle some of the workers previously employed?

All would be well if the now higher incomes of the employed population generated demand for additional material goods and the equipment needed to produce them in sufficient quantities for their manufacture to re-employ all the workers just made idle. For, in that case, employment would be undiminished and the only effect of the rise in productivity would be the growth of output, real income and the stock of capital. That clearly is the ideal situation.

The necessary condition for that ideal situation to come about is well known from Keynesian economics. Intended saving must equal investment, or intended extra saving must equal additional investment. But that simple Keynesian condition of employment equilibrium must be put a little differently now that we look deeper into the consumer's behaviour and realize that he divides his income, not two ways, between spending and saving, but three ways, between spending on material goods, spending on positional goods and saving. That raises the question: which two of these three uses of income should be bracketed together when stating the condition of employment equilibrium?

One's gut instinct might be to lump together the two kinds of spending and keep them separate from saving; but a moment's reflection shows that that will not do. It is clear that spending on material things elicits output, whose production generates employment and income. It is equally clear that the decision to save calls forth no output and so generates neither employment nor income. But why should the effects of spending on positional goods resemble those of saving rather than those of spending on material goods? That they do follows from the fact that the supply of positional goods and services is limited and cannot be increased, or at least not very much.

If increased spending on positional goods and services cannot lead to the creation of additional input, it cannot generate employment either. What it does instead is to bid up prices until some of the previous owners of the existing stock of positional goods become willing to sell some of their holdings, and some of the previous users of the limited supply of positional services are crowded out by the price increase.

The producers of the services (and of additions to the stock of positional goods) enjoy an increase in rents, the previous owners of the positional goods that they are induced to sell enjoy capital gains and an increase in liquidity. The increase in rents is likely to stimulate spending on material goods, thereby indirectly generating at least some employment; but the main consequence of positional spending, the capital gains and increased liquidity of those selling some of their holdings of positional goods, is unlikely to do even that.

For the sellers of positional goods are typically the old rich. If they still are rich, their need for material comforts is well taken care of; and they will reinvest the proceeds of their sales in financial assets or other positional goods rather than spend even more on material goods. Those of the old rich who are impoverished, and forced to sell some of their cherished and valuable possessions for that reason, are likely either to repay debt out of the proceeds, which is a form of saving, or to use them as a fund out of which to continue maintaining their accustomed level of living into the future, which at least partly constitutes saving.

In short, additional demand for positional goods and services has almost the same economic impact (or lack of impact) as the hoarding of money, except that it also raises the prices of positional goods and shifts the distribution of wealth in favour of the affluent former holders of those goods.

That the demand for positional goods resembles the hoarding of money in its failure to stimulate the economy should come as no surprise. After all, to spend on positional goods is mostly to hoard art objects, antiques, first editions and real estate. Hoarding them and hoarding money or gold are very similar activities, because their objects are so similar. All of them are favoured repositories of wealth owing to their limited supply, which is either absolutely fixed or almost fixed in the sense that their existing stock is large in relation to the limited capacity of adding to it.

Keynes, as many economists before him, looked upon the hoarding of money as something akin to an anti-social act, because its limited supply keeps the demand for it from creating employment. To use Keynes's own words: 'Unemployment develops ... because people want the moon; – men cannot be employed when the object of desire (i.e. money) is something which cannot be produced and the demand for which cannot be readily choked off.'[1] That argument has become well known and well established but was generally believed to apply only to money and gold. All I have done is to generalise it to include also the much broader and larger category of all tangible wealth that appeals to the wealthy, along with a few services that also have a snob appeal. Thereby, I have shifted the sharp dividing line Keynes and others have drawn between money and all else to a new position where it separates money *and* positional goods and services from the material sector.

That dividing line, however, must be not only shifted but softened as well. For, as is usual with classifications in economics, the difference between positional and material goods and services is not as sharp and clear-cut as I, in my desire to simplify the exposition, made it out to be. In reality, the borderline between them is quite fuzzy and gradual. To begin with, the increased rents of the suppliers of positional services and the artists and craftsmen who produce additions to the stock of positional goods do generate some secondary employment, as already mentioned. Second, many goods have both a material and a positional component. Third, excess demand for some positional goods degrades their quality, which often calls for additional

labour or material inputs to prevent or offset their degradation. Finally, demand for such positional goods as made-to-measure clothes and the services
of domestic servants clearly generates employment, although the demand for
these is gradually being choked off by the rise in their costs, which accompanies the rise in labour productivity.

In its impact on output and employment, therefore, the demand for positional
goods and services stands somewhere in between the hoarding of money and
the demand for material goods and services, though perhaps closer to the
former; and it differs from both in having a much greater impact on prices or
costs – causing them to rise the more, the less its impact on output. I conclude, therefore, that the more advanced is an economy, and the larger the
share of positional goods in its total spending,[2] the more will a rise in labour
productivity depress employment and raise the prices and costs of positional
goods.

Those are the bare bones of a mere theory. But how important is it, what
evidence supports it, what are its wider implications and what are the reme-
dial policies it calls for? Statistics of spending on positional goods are as
unavailable as statistics of intended saving – and for the same reason. The
national accounts register spending only when it results in output, not when it
merely increases rents or the turnover and market value of an accumulated
stock of goods. Most positional spending, therefore, the part that elicits no
output, does not enter the national accounts explicitly but is hidden as part of
the residual item: personal saving. (One might say that national accountants,
mindful of the national accounts' main function as a macroeconomic tool,
have properly bracketed positional spending with saving and not with material spending.) Accordingly, the volume of spending on positional goods can
only be gauged by piecing together data on current additions to their stock
and the turnover of the existing stock – and by the indirect evidence of the
rising prices of positional goods relative to the rise in the cost of living.

I cannot present comprehensive estimates, only a couple of examples.
Annual sales of art objects and antiques in the United States are estimated at
around $5 billion – a mere 3 per cent of personal saving. Much more impor-
tant is our expenditure on upgrading, not the contents of our houses, but the
houses themselves. Americans are known to be exceptionally mobile, as
measured by the frequency with which we move from one place to another in
pursuit of a better job. But we are even more mobile and move house almost
twice as often *within the same locality*, in pursuit of a better, more elegant
house that presents a better image. Between 10 and 14 per cent of the owners
of one-family houses move annually within the same town or county, which
means a move every seven to ten years on average. In 1984 (the latest year
for which data are available) 10.4 per cent of American homeowners changed
house within the same vicinity, most of them (7.4 per cent) moving to a more

expensive house than the one they left, presumably because their income had risen and enabled them to move to a house and location more appropriate to their new, higher station in life. Assuming that they paid, on average, 15 per cent more for the house they bought than the price they obtained for the one they sold, the total value of the houses they moved into can be put at $380 billion, with a net expenditure of $50 billion in improving that most visible and expensive symbol of their status. That is about one-third of total personal saving.[3]

I now come to the indirect evidence provided by the rising relative prices of art and housing. According to the Times–Sotheby index and its successor, the more reliable Sotheby index, the prices of paintings, art objects and antique furniture rose, in real terms (that is, corrected for the rise in the cost of living), by slightly over 10 per cent annually during the prosperous 1950s and 1960s, slowing to an annual 6 per cent rise during the past ten years.[4] For earlier times, an unpublished estimate puts the real rate of return on paintings at around 3.6 per cent for the 19th century and at 5.2 per cent for the beginning of the 20th.[5]

Much the same picture emerges also from the American statistics on residential housing. Although housing construction kept pace with the growth of population and the number of families, housing prices nationwide rose annually by almost two percentage points more than the consumer price index between 1918 and today. That figure, of course, is the average of the much faster increase in the market value of positionally favoured housing and the slower increase in that of housing not so favoured. (Indeed, a measure of the *dispersion* of housing prices, were it available, would be a better index of the value of the positional component in housing.) In climatically and culturally favoured San Francisco, the annual rise in the price of single-family houses was 4.7 per cent in real terms over the past 15 years.

Needless to add, the steady, secular and fairly predictable rise in the relative prices of positional goods makes them good investments, which renders them all the more attractive as status symbols but also adds to their tendency to lower employment and impede growth. For not only does spending on positional goods divert income from spending on materials goods, the use of some of them as repositories of accumulated wealth also diverts funds from financial assets, thereby raising the cost of productive investments and slowing capital formation.

Let me now discuss some of the implications. My argument that, in too affluent an economy, rising labour productivity creates unemployment and slows growth reminds one of the stagnation thesis advanced half a century ago by Alvin Hansen. He based his argument on the belief that economic advance would gradually reduce opportunities for profitable investment, thereby reducing capital formation, depressing employment and slowing growth.[6] The profession has largely ignored Hansen's thesis, at first because the long period of postwar prosperity made its gloomy prediction look premature and later, during the period of stagnation, because it could explain the stagnation but not the accompanying inflation. My argument, that people's increasing affluence causes them to spend an ever-larger part of their income in ways that fail to generate employment and raises positional goods prices instead, is altogether different from Hansen's thesis, which it reinforces and improves upon.

For the rising prices of some positional goods and services, along with the worsening quality or increasing cost of others, exert an inflationary pressure on the whole price structure. Especially important and obvious is the inflationary influence of the rise in housing costs mentioned earlier; but Fred Hirsch discussed in some detail also the more subtle inflationary impact of the higher prices, costs or debased quality of *all* positional goods and services.[7]

Accordingly, the increasing importance of positional goods and services in the consumer's budget has not only a *de*flationary effect on output, employment and incomes but at the same time also an *in*flationary effect on the general price level. In short, my argument is not a stagnation but a stagflation thesis. However, I am not presenting my stagflation thesis as anything more than one of many contributing causes of the severe unemployment and high inflation from which we have been suffering for the past decade, and for which the oil shocks of the 1970s and the preceding succession of bad harvests seem to be much more important explanations.

But, however much or little the thesis I am presenting contributes to explaining our past problems, it is a *systemic and chronic cause* of stagflation, whose importance is bound to grow with the growth of our affluence. Accordingly, it should be useful also for identifying the long-run remedies of the chronic component of our economic problems. I shall ignore, therefore, the short run and short-run policies, and focus on possible remedies of our long-run problems, which are long-run also in the sense of threatening to become more serious in the future than they are in the present. The principles of those remedies are simple enough to discuss here; I will not deal with the difficulties of their implementation.

If the argument I presented is valid, then one of the causes of stagflation is the discrepancy between the structure of effective demand and the structure of the availability of supply. Effective demand for material goods and services is insufficient, which causes unemployment and stagnation; effective demand for positional goods and services is excessive, which causes price increases and inflationary pressures.

That problem can be tackled from both the demand and the supply side. On the demand side, reducing inequalities of income would relieve both parts of the problem by simultaneously increasing effective demand in the material sector and diminishing it in the positional sector. For people at the low end of the income scale are far from having their demand for personal comforts saturated, even in the most affluent economies. Given more income, therefore, they would undoubtedly buy more material goods and services, thereby generating more output employment and income; whereas less income in the hands of the affluent would reduce their demand for positional goods and so ease the upward pressure on prices.

The correctness of such a policy is suggested if not proved by the Reagan administration's failure to stimulate the economy through its *opposite* policy of *increasing* inequalities. I have in mind the massive tax concessions given to business during the administration's first term, in the expectation that an increase in retained profits would increase investment and so stimulate the economy. What the increase in retained business profits has done instead is to increase the number of takeovers, which are the business world's equivalent of the consumer's spending on positional goods. As such, they raised share prices but failed to stimulate the economy.

The supply-side remedy would be to relieve unemployment by reducing the supply of labour and to relieve the upward pressure on prices in the positional sector by increasing the supply·of social status; but only the first part of that two-pronged measure seems practicable at this stage.[8] A reduction in the supply of labour is easier to think of as a reduction in the demand for employment. I have in mind to keep people, not from seeking employment but from working for as long a working week, working year and span of working years as they do today. That could greatly diminish unemployment at the cost of a small increase in the employed population's leisure, probably with benefits to both sides. On a small scale and a strictly voluntary basis, the experiment has already been tried in the United States as well as in Europe, in the form of work sharing and job sharing – mostly to the satisfaction of employers and employees alike.[9]

A potentially serious problem connected with a shorter working week is a psychological one. Our civilization trains everybody in the skills and discipline of work, but teaches only to a tiny privileged elite a taste for the constructive use of leisure and the skills and initiative needed to cater to that taste. That is why most people in the United States and the United Kingdom are at a loss and get seriously disturbed when they find themselves with more leisure on their hands than they are used to, and so know what to do with. Such disturbance usually takes quite a violent form in the young and energetic, exemplified by rowdyism and vandalism of the chronically unemployed youths who roam the streets of our large cities. Their behaviour is only partly an angry response to their rejection by society; partly it is also the normal reaction of boredom of energetic young people trained in the discipline and skills of work but left totally unprepared and untrained for leisure. In the aged, the same disturbance usually takes a non-violent but no less severe form, manifest in the disorientation and rapid mental and physical decline of those many retired people who are utterly unprepared for retirement, with not even a hobby or any other constructive activity to keep them busy and fill the emptiness of their suddenly increased free time.

It is hoped, however, that the modest shortening of the working week needed to reduce the chronic unemployment of our time would do more good than harm. The employed population could probably absorb an hour or two of extra leisure per week without ill effects; whereas the millions of jobs created for those at present unemployed would certainly do a lot of good, including the reduction of violence in our streets. In the United States, shortening by just one hour the 36-hour average working week of an employed population of 110 million would create 3 million extra jobs; and even in the United Kingdom, two hours' extra leisure for 20 million employees would re-employ 1 million unemployed. The crude arithmetic of these examples may not be fully realistic, but it gives an idea of the orders of magnitude involved.

It would take a much more drastic reduction of the working week to render acute the psychological problem just outlined; and, in that case, the problem would have to be faced head on, probably requiring a major reform of our excessively work-oriented educational philosophy and school curriculum.[10] But that is not likely to be a problem in our time. Let me end this lecture, therefore, and acknowledge once again my debt for its main ideas to Fred Hirsch.

Notes

1. Cf. J.M. Keynes, *The General Theory of Employment, Interest and Money*, (London: Macmillan, 1936), p. 235. Keynes, incidentally, also noted that 'land resembles money in that its elasticities of production and substitution may be very low' (ibid., p. 241); but as he was concerned with people's demand for liquidity rather than for status symbols, he drew very different conclusions from mine.
2. Note that economic and technical advance comprises the introduction both of new and better products (product innovation) and of superior methods of production (process innovation). The latter raise incomes and are likely to increase the share of positional spending; the former are likely to increase spending on material goods. The two kinds of advance are therefore complementary in their macroeconomic effects.
3. All the data come from the 1986 *Statistical Abstract of the United States*. I have assumed that percentages referred to number of houses apply *pari passu* also to the value of the housing stock; and the 15 per cent difference in price between a house sold and the one bought by the same person is a rough guess.
4. The Sotheby index of art objects and antiques is published weekly in *Barron's*, its detailed description in *Barron's*, 8 November 1981, pp. 4 ff. The now defunct Times–Sotheby index is described in G. Keen, *The Sale of Works of Art: A Study Based on the Times–Sotheby Index*, (London: Nelson, 1971). Unfortunately, there is a six-year gap (1969–75) between the latter's cut-off date and the former's base year.
5. For the source of those estimates and a short general survey of the economic data on the

arts, see R.W. Goldsmith, *Comparative National Balance Sheets: A Study of Twenty Countries, 1688–1978*, (Chicago: University of Chicago Press, 1985), pp. 73–8.

6. Cf. Alvin H. Hansen, *Full Recovery or Stagnation?* (New York: W.W. Norton, 1938), ch. 19; see also A.H. Hansen, 'Economic Progress and Population Growth', *American Economic Review*, (1939), **29**, Proceedings, 1–15.

7. Cf. Fred Hirsch, *Social Limits to Growth*, (Cambridge, Mass.: Harvard University Press, 1976), pp. 172–4. See also F. Hirsch, *The Political Economy of Inflation*, (London: Martin Robertson, 1978), pp. 274–5.

8. The way to increase the supply of social status is to increase the ways or dimensions in which a person can excel over others. In our work- and money- oriented society, a person's income is the main dimension in which his status is measured; but in a more leisure-oriented society, which appreciates excellence in the performance of many activities, irrespective of whether or not they yield income, status would be measured in as many dimensions, with a corresponding increase in its supply.

9. Cf. Stanley D. Nollen, *New Work Schedules in Practice: Managing Time in a Changing Society*, (New York: Van Nostrand, 1982), and the review and short summary of a report of the European Commission on the same subject in *The Economist*, 27 September 1986, p. 69.

10. Cf. R.F. Harrod, 'The possibility of economic satiety', in Committee for Economic Development, *Problems of U.S. Economic Development*, (New York, 1958), pp. 73–4, for a succinct account of the problem and the difficulties of resolving it.

8 Towards a theory of second-hand markets*

My interest in second-hand markets stems from my desire to restate in simpler terms Keynes's revolutionary insight in his *General Theory* that competitive markets no longer maintain our economy's macroequilibrium as Say's Law would have us believe. Keynes was a superb practical economist who could develop the right policies to address the problems of his day almost by instinct and present them in clear, highly convincing language. He was not nearly as good at presenting the theoretical underpinning of the employment policies he recommended, which was his critique and demolition of Say's Law. That is why his *General Theory* made such difficult reading for so many people. It may also explain why today, when Keynes's monetary policies have ceased to be effective, many people, including politicians and even some economists, have not only abandoned his policies but seem also to have forgotten his theoretical insight, as if returning to his predecessors' faith in Say's Law. To my mind, that is not only unjustified in today's complex economy but also dangerous, because it has led too many politicians and the electorate to acquiesce in the US economy's poor performance, in the belief that it will automatically right itself.

That was why I wanted to outdo Keynes by better explaining his important insight. But when I found that my argument hinged on a second-hand market's ability to hamstring the equilibrating force of prices in its related first-hand market, I decided that it will be more persuasive if placed in the wider framework of a more general discussion of the different second-hand markets' very different impacts on the economy.

Let me start by restating Say's Law that supply creates its own demand, meaning that overproduction in the aggregate is impossible, because the economy always keeps aggregate spending equal to the value of total output.[1] That conclusion was based on the realization that productive activity generates output and income in equal values and the assumption that all income not spent on consumption is invested. Flexible prices create a tendency towards microequilibrium, in which every productive activity generates as much income as the spendable income it absorbs; but the macroeconomy cannot suffer, even when the microequilibrium is disrupted. For assume that someone invents a new gadget and starts producing it, hoping it will sell. If it does, the income his productive activity generates exactly offsets the income its sale absorbs; and if it fails to sell, the income its production generates will

* This chapter appeared in *Kyklos*, vol. 47, 1994, pp. 33–51.

create an excess demand for other commodities equal in value to the excess supply he is stuck with, so that aggregate spending will remain equal to the total value of output even then.

It was soon realized, however, that hoarding money would violate the assumption that all income is either consumed or invested and so would invalidate Say's Law. For, by reducing aggregate spending to below the total value of output, it would prompt producers to restrict output and the income it generates, thereby causing spending to be reduced yet further and setting in motion a cumulative downward multiplier process, coming to an end only when the fall in incomes stopped people from hoarding more money. But that seemed to be a merely theoretical, not a practical possibility, because hoarding money was considered irrational and presumed insignificant in modern economies with well-developed banking systems; and what little of it might occur was believed to be easily neutralized by appropriate monetary policy.

That hoarding can be a serious problem, capable of destroying an economy's self-equilibrating capability, became apparent only when Keynes discovered that money was not the only hoardable good: financial assets were just as hoardable and much more hoarded, with a similar but correspondingly much greater depressing impact on the macroeconomy. It is far from obvious, however, why, how and when the hoarding of possessions other than money also reduces spending and has the same depressing effect on the economy. For Keynes did not put it in those terms and may not even have seen the parallelism between hoarding money and hoarding other things, since the way he explained his discovery in the language of financial markets and monetary theory did not make it very clear and was altogether offputting and difficult to follow for most ordinary people (including us ordinary economists) who, unlike Keynes, had no practical, hands-on experience of such markets. That is why some of us accepted Keynes's insight more on faith than on understanding – and faith is easier to lose than understanding.

Yet the problem of hoarding and its disequilibrating impact on the macroeconomy is more general than Keynes realized and more easily and fully understood on the basis of a simple supply and demand analysis of ordinary second-hand markets of the type most of us know from everyday experience. After all, accumulating possessions is a common human passion, especially in our acquisitive society, and is not confined to money and financial assets. Most of us enjoy accumulating some attractive commodity or commodities, one of whose attractions often is their easy salability, which makes them good repositories of wealth. Money is undoubtedly the easiest commodity to sell and some financial assets are good seconds; but every durable good with a large, well-organized second-hand market also fills the bill. I am setting out to show that second-hand markets, if large enough, not only render hoarding attractive but can also disrupt the macroeconomy's equilibrium by obstructing the equilibrating function of the price in their related first-hand market. Moreover, since second-hand markets also facilitate unhoarding, getting rid of unwanted possessions, just as much as they facilitate hoarding, they can disrupt the economy's macroequilibrium also in the opposite direction, by raising its level of activity; and that, too, has to be discussed.

Second-hand markets for durable goods have long been ignored by economists. The classics were so enamoured of the benefits of the division of labour and the invisible hand of competition, which harnessed people's selfish behaviour to serving the common good, that they carefully excluded from their model of the economy every institution and character that made no contribution to their central argument, and so would merely detract attention from it. After all, the sale of a second-hand good by its previous owner made no direct impact on productive activities, which, together with the output they created and the income and employment they generated, were the economists' main concerns. They realized that the purchase of a second-hand commodity diverted demand from a first-hand market and so might depress the economy whose stability depended on total spending on new output equalling the total income its production generated; but they regarded such purchases as mere transfers of the buyer's spendable income to the seller of the used commodity, thereby leaving unchanged the sum total of spending and its stimulus to output, income and employment. They also realized that the prices in the first- and second-hand markets of identical or similar goods were interdependent, meaning that transactions in one of them could have an indirect effect on transactions in the other; but this, too, they neglected, probably in the belief that indirect effects were likely to be much less important than direct effects.

These arguments seem plausible enough at first blush and are probably acceptable approximations to reality whenever second-hand markets are small. But they can become very misleading oversimplifications of reality when second-hand markets are large. For large second-hand markets can have both beneficial and harmful effects. Some stimulate the economy, others depress it; some mitigate the inequalities of capitalism and enable the poor to assert their membership in society, others cater to affluent people's desire to stand out from the crowd or assert their distinctiveness; some accelerate the ups and downs of the business cycle; and the huge second-hand market for financial instruments will be shown to obstruct the automatic workings of the market's invisible hand and call for the deliberate use of a visible one.

Let us begin with the question whether and how second-hand markets detract from or add to the effective demand in their related first-hand markets, where it would contribute to maintaining the economy's macroequilibrium. Note, first, that buying second-hand goods from their previous owners adds, not to the latters' income, but to their liquidity. That makes a great deal of difference if by income one means a more or less stable flow of income over time, and by addition to one's liquidity a once-and-for-all increase in one's holdings of cash. For a rise in income usually leads to a commensurate rise in spending, except in the case of the very rich: whereas an addition to one's liquidity can lead to any or no change in one's spending. A very poor recipient may spend all of it right away; a rich person's spending will not be affected at all, except in the rare case when he sells to invest the proceeds; people in between will often spend it very gradually over their remaining lifetime or spend only its interest; whereas those who sell or trade-in a durable good in order to replace it with a newer one spend instantly not only all, but more than all, the addition to their liquidity.

In short, second-hand markets need not but usually do disrupt the economy's macroequilibrium and can stimulate as well as depress it. Their depressing effect creates the serious problems which will be our main concern; but let us first discuss and get out of the way the stimulating effect.

Second-hand markets for the poor
Durable goods are valued for the useful services they provide and most of them wear out after a while, providing less good or less reliable services and so becoming less valuable with the passage of time. Being bundles of services yielded over time, they are a form of investment goods and can be too expensive for poor people to buy; but these can obtain more cheaply a lesser bundle of those services by buying them second-hand.

Second-hand markets for consumer durables therefore perform the socially valuable service of mitigating the inequalities of income distribution; and in the process they also stimulate the economy, partly by enabling the well-to-do the sooner to replace their worn out or obsolescing durable goods with new ones and thereby *increasing the total demand* for them,[2] partly by generating employment and income for the middlemen who run the second-hand market.

Such second-hand markets are very large and very important in poor countries for mitigating inequalities and stimulating the economy. It is a sign of the United States' high standard of living and better income distribution that all but one of our second-hand markets for consumer durables, including those for used articles of clothing, kitchen utensils, furniture, household appliances, TV sets, radios, hi-fi equipment, computers and even books, are quite small. That is why our census of retail trade lumps them together into the single category of 'Used Merchandise', with their combined gross receipts in 1987 less than a negligible $5.25 billion.[3]

The one exception is the second-hand market for passenger cars, a short account of which gives a good idea of the nature and significance of such markets. Cars are the most expensive and the most coveted consumer durable goods, appreciated not only for their usefulness and the pleasure of driving but – thanks to their second-hand market – also as the most accessible status symbols for demonstrating one's membership in the society to which one belongs or wants to belong. There are 15 000 large and 59 000 small, one man used-car dealerships in the United States, more than two and a half times the 28 300 new-car dealers, all of whom also sell the used cars they acquire as trade-ins for many of the 9 to 11 million new cars they sell annually. Most of those new cars replace the cars scrapped or otherwise retired;[4] only slightly more than one-tenth of them are additions to the over 123 million cars in operation. The number of used cars changing owners annually is around three times the number of new cars bought, a sizable part of which is arranged without dealers' intermediation through classified newspaper advertisements. Even so, dealers' 1990 net receipts (net of what they paid for the cars they sold) of $ 43.7 billion from used-car sales were somewhat higher than dealers' net receipts from new-car sales and eight times as high as all receipts from the sale of all other second-hand consumer durables.

The main benefit of this huge used-car market, in which the average car changes hands three times, is that it extends the range of prices at which cars in running condition are available down to one-tenth of the $7000 price of the cheapest new Ford Fiesta or Hyundai – indeed, even further, since cars needing only minor, inexpensive repairs to bring them to running conditions are supposed to be available for as little as $300 to $350.[5] Thanks to this tremendous price range, 88 per cent of US households own at least one car and 52 per cent own two or more cars.

This extension of the range of prices and its benefits reminds one of a monopolist's price discrimination, since both increase output and the gains from trade; but while the main beneficiary of the monopolist's action is he himself, the second-hand market divides the gain the monopolist would get between manufacturers who make more sales, used-car dealers who earn a mark-up and consumers who gain a future resale value on their cars – not to mention the newspapers, most of whose classified ads offer cars for sale. Further beneficiaries are car repair and service stations, which create twice as much employment as does the manufacture of motor vehicles, their parts and equipment.

Another, not so good impact of the used-car market on the macroeconomy is that it accelerates and reinforces both recessions and recoveries, because consumers often respond to changes in their income by shifting their demand between the dearer new-car and the cheaper used-car market. For example, as the recession deepened from 1988 to 1992, new-car registration in California State fell from 1 461 000 to 1 208 000, while reregistrations of used cars to new owners rose from 4 204 000 to 4 614 000.[6] That must have reduced the industry's gross receipts by around $0.5 billion, while the corresponding rise in used-car sales could not have increased their dealers' value added by even a fifth of that.

As already mentioned, no other consumers' durable has a comparably large second-hand market in the United States for relieving poverty, mostly because only a small proportion of our poor are as deprived of the less expensive essential durables as are the poor of third-world countries; and in some cases because the supply of some used goods available in second-hand markets is limited. Books provide a good example of this latter case.

Books, apart from dictionaries, encyclopaedias, collectables and a few important texts, are not durable goods proper, because the majority of them are consumed in one reading, after which most book buyers keep them as mementoes, interior decoration, symbols of their intellectual interest or out of sheer inertia, being reluctant to throw them out but not finding it worth the trouble to sell them for a fourth or fifth of what they cost. They usually become available for sale only on their owners' death, but by then many have become obsolete and find few readers. That accounts for the limited market availability of used books in the United States, with used-book dealers numbering less than a third of new-book dealers, which explains the need for publicly supported public libraries to cater for the demand of less affluent readers who want books solely for reading.

The housing market in the middle

One of the largest second-hand markets is that for owner-occupied one-family houses, whose annual turnover of over 3 million is approximately three times the sales of new ones, just as in the case of cars. That, however, is just about its only resemblance to the used-car market. For owner-occupied houses depreciate little with age and sell at prices not significantly lower (usually only around 15 per cent lower) than new ones. For the land on which they are built is a natural resource in fixed supply, whose value rises with increasing population density, while the structures themselves are usually long kept in, or restored to, perfect condition at reasonable cost. In 1987, for example, the $54.8 billion total spending on improvements, maintenance and repair to the 58.2 million owner-occupied houses in existence averaged $942 per house.[7]

That is why the second-hand housing market is not much help to the poor. It increases people's mobility and enables them to adjust their housing to both their increasing need as their families and incomes grow larger and their diminishing need as they get old, their children grow up and incomes go down. These are valuable benefits, but the market's impact on the macroeconomy is probably negligible.

As to the poor, it is mainly rental apartments that deteriorate and get cheaper with age, thereby becoming accessible to them; but these cater to only a fraction of poor people in need of housing; and those of them built in choice locations are in danger of being torn down – and their tenants made homeless! – to make room for the building of luxury condominiums on their increasingly valuable land. Hence the need for subsidized public housing even in affluent societies.

Second-hand markets for the rich

We now turn to our main topic, the role of second-hand markets in facilitating affluent people's drive to accumulate valuable possessions and causing it, under certain circumstances, to immobilize part of spendable income, with the same depressing impact on the macroeconomy as the hoarding of money.

As already mentioned, collecting possessions is a source of satisfaction and collections of valuable possessions have the additional advantage of being stores of value. Collectables are works of art and a variety of goods valued and collected for their aesthetic appeal, historic importance, rarity, antiquity or quaintness. They include first editions, authors' copies and special or beautifully illustrated editions of important books, interesting documents, vintage cars, paintings by dead (much less often live) masters, and antique jewellery, ceramics, furniture, clothing, weapons and so on. Most collectables are positional goods, whose supply cannot be augmented, a fundamental feature that gives them scarcity value, their owners status and a feeling of pride, and explains whey increased demand for them cannot increase their supply and raises their price instead. It also explains their availability mainly in second-hand markets.

Purchases of such objects can have almost any impact on economic activity, depending on circumstances. They have no or negligible effect when both buyer and seller are sufficiently affluent for the change in their liquidity to leave unchanged their expenditure on newly produced goods, or when the buyer is a new rich and the seller sells in order to invest in a new venture. When the seller is an impoverished new poor, he will spend the proceeds but mostly only in small instalments, which may depress the economy or stimulate it slightly, depending on whether or not the buyers' spending on other things is affected by his purchase.

In the expanding economies of our time, however, with their growing populations and rising productivities, most buyers are the newly rich who buy valuable works of art, some from the impoverished new poor but mostly out of collections held by the old rich, diverting funds from their own consumption or productive investment but without changing, or only slightly changing, the sellers' lifestyle, thereby depressing the economy.

The outstanding example of this was the fast growing market for paintings by old masters during the long period of postwar prosperity, with its annual turnover believed to have approached \$50 billion by 1989;[8] and with the paintings' prices rising by an average annual 10 per cent above the inflation rate during the first two postwar decades, slowing down to an annual rise of 6 per cent in real terms from the early 1970s until the late 1980s, according to the Sotheby art index.[9]

So spectacular and steady a price increase in a highly organized market with a weekly price index to watch has turned antique paintings, and especially those of the impressionist and post-impressionist periods, into profitable, speculative investments – certainly for art lovers but also for some pension funds and insurance companies. They are, however, not stimulating, but economically depressing investments, because they divert spending from consumption and capital formation and have the same depressing impact on the macroeconomy as the hoarding of money.

The hoarding of art objects is slightly less depressing than the hoarding of money, since it creates commissions for dealers and auction houses and liquidity for sellers; but it is also worse, because the extraordinary rise in art prices may divert speculative funds from more productive uses and also have a slight inflationary effect on the general price level which, added to the depressing impact of hoarding, would turn it into a stagflationary impact.[10] Fortunately, second-hand markets for antiques and other collectables, with the notable exception of the paintings just discussed, are still very small, not large enough for their impact on the macroeconomy to be too serious.

Note that many collectables have no first-hand markets, because only long after having been produced and first sold are they recognized as being worth collecting for their artistic quality, historic importance, rarity value or quaintness. Works of art, like paintings and sculpture, do have a first-hand market, whose prices, however, are usually much lower than those of the second-hand market – the very opposite of the great price gap between new and used cars. For just as some people are reluctant to buy a used car or appliance for fear of getting stuck with a lemon without recourse to manufacturers' guarantees,[11] so many art collectors are leery of contemporary art, whose artistic quality is not yet as firmly and universally established as that of antique art. While that explains the higher prices of antique than of contemporary art, the reason for the inordinately fast increase of the formers' prices is, of course, that an increasing demand confronts a fixed or very inelastic supply.

At the same time, the first-hand market of contemporary art, with its much lower prices, performs much the same function for the less affluent as does the second-hand market for cars. While there is evidence that the work of many artists fashionable in their lifetime appears trite to succeeding generations and becomes unsalable, the creations of some of the more innovative contemporary artists do gain increased appreciation with the passage of time as their revolutionary novelty wears off and later generations coopt them into the inventory of our aesthetic heritage. But that is a slow process and only a few living artists of exceptional talent and longevity are fortunate enough to live to see their own works gain such recognition and benefit from the significant rise in their market value that results from it. Indeed, among the buyers of contemporary art there always are a few shrewd, knowledgeable art dealers and patrons who believe they can recognize the works that future generations will value and buy them on speculation. The fast-rising prices of antique art suggest, however, that the additions the first-hand market of contemporary art makes to the second-hand market's accumulated stock of universally recognized art is insufficient to satisfy the rising demand for collectables and make up for what museums withdraw from the market and wars, terrorism and natural disasters destroy.

The interdependence of first- and second-hand markets

The markets for art objects have many aspects that make them strikingly similar to markets for financial assets, which – quite apart from their intrinsic interest – accounts for their lengthy discussion in the preceding section. After all, an important purpose of this paper is to reformulate Keynes's insight into our economy's lack of self-equilibrating forces in terms of the disequilibrating macroeconomic impact of second-hand markets. An important difference, however, between financial markets and art markets is the much greater substitutability between what the former's first- and second-hand markets deal in and the consequent closer interdependence of their prices. That is the subject matter of this section.

We have already dealt with the destabilizing impact on the overall economy of the second-hand markets for cheaper-than-new consumer durables when we showed how a change in incomes can lead to a transfer of demand between such markets and their related first-hand markets and thereby accelerate and give added impetus to the initiating fall or rise in incomes (see p. 113 above).

Another and more severe destabilizing impact of second-hand markets on the overall economy can be initiated by disruptions of either their or their related first-hand markets' equilibrium. For when the elasticity of substitution between the goods traded in a first- and second-hand market is reasonably high, their prices become interdependent, and a disturbance to either market's equilibrium affects both their prices and pushes them in the same direction. The price change in the market whose equilibrium has been disrupted *narrows the gap* between its demand and supply, the parallel price change in the other market *disrupts its equilibrium*, creating a contrary gap between its supply and demand; and the two prices come to rest at the point where the disturbed market's remaining excess demand (supply) and the other market's emerging excess supply (demand) become equal and thereby offset one another.

This situation, peculiar to commodities with closely related first- and second-hand markets, one is tempted to call a price equilibrium, considering that the two prices, having fully satisfied all the members on both sides of the two markets, have come to rest. On closer inspection, however, it turns out to be only a temporary and partial equilibrium, because prices alone are stabilized, while the remaining gaps between each market's supply and demand continue to generate equilibrating forces – one of them causing prices gradually to move further, the other creating income changes. It is more correct therefore to call that situation not an equilibrium but its very opposite: an impediment that delays and slows the equilibrating movement of prices and thereby prolongs the disequilibrium until the combined effect of those further changes eliminates it.

To see what those changes are, it helps to focus on a specific case and assume that the disequilibrium was created by an excess demand in the first-hand market whose satisfaction out of the second-hand market's stock of supplies led to that temporary 'price equilibrium'. That cannot continue indefinitely, because second-hand markets equate, not flows of supply and demand, but accumulated stocks of supply and their owners' desire to hold them; and, as sales out of those stocks satisfy the first-hand market's excess demand, they get gradually depleted, slowly raising their price, thereby reducing their owners' desire to hold them in step with their depleting stock – and the second-hand market's slowly rising price also pulls up the first-hand market's price.

In short, when the second-hand market satisfies the first-hand market's excess demand, its usually more slowly moving price takes over the equilibrating function, which prolongs the disequilibrium and allows the first-hand market's remaining excess demand to create another equilibrating force that acts *via* income changes. For, while satisfying the first-hand market's excess demand out of the second-hand market's available supply generates no income beyond the second-hand dealers' commission, the diversion of that spendable income from being spent on other goods does prompt their producers to restrict output and the income it generates, which imparts exactly the same negative macroeconomic shock and its multiplier effect to the economy as would the hoarding of money. The reduction in income helps to diminish the excess demand in the commodity's first-hand market which created the disturbance; but as long as that persists, the macroeconomic shock, though diminished, is sustained and continues to push down output, income and employment further still.

To summarize the foregoing, the market equilibrium of a commodity with first- and second-hand markets can be disrupted in either market; and the resulting disequilibrium soon creates a temporary impediment to price movements and equal but smaller disequilibria of opposite signs in the two mar-

kets. The second-hand market's disequilibrium gradually releases the impediment to the equilibrating price movements; the first-hand market's sustained
disequilibrium creates a macroeconomic shock, whose cumulative multiplier
effect in changing aggregate incomes helps to eliminate the disequilibrium.

Which of those two equilibrating forces, price movements or income
changes, will predominate depends on (1) the importances of the commodity's contribution to the economy's total activity and (2) the length of time for
which sales out of its accumulated second-hand stock can satisfy the first-
hand market's excess demand without significantly affecting its price; for
they determine the size and duration of the macroeconomic shock that the
disequilibrium in the commodity's first-hand market imparts to the total
economy.

It may as well be said at the outset that few commodities have an important
enough share in the economy's total activity for a disequilibrium in their
markets to deliver more than a negligible macroeconomic shock; and fewer
are those whose availability in the second-hand market is sufficiently great to
sustain the macroeconomic shock long enough for its cumulative multiplier
effect on incomes to become significant. Indeed, we know only one market,
that for financial assets, where income changes are the predominating equilibrating force and very few others where one would expect both price and
income changes to play an equilibrating role. In the overwhelmingly majority
of markets, prices are the main or only equilibrating force.

For consumers' durable goods, with few exceptions, absorb a very small
fraction of total spending, generate an equally small fraction of total income,
and their excess demand or supply is only a part of that. Therefore, the
macroeconomic shock that they can impart to the economy is negligible.
Moreover, the shock is likely to be not only small but of short duration as
well, because the availability of consumer durables in their second-hand
markets is usually a small fraction of their total accumulated stock, since
second-hand dealers' stocks are mostly small and few consumers will sell off
part of their accumulated possessions just because there is a demand for them
and their prices rise.

Cars and owner-occupied homes are exceptions, to the extent that their
share in the gross domestic product is sizable and seldom falls below 1.5 per
cent of it. Their availability in second-hand markets, however, is limited,
because both of them are necessities, which owners rarely relinquish, while
dealers' inventories of used cars seldom exceed the equivalent of a couple of
months' sales. Vacancy rates of homeowners' housing units vary between 1
and 1.7 per cent of all such homes, the equivalent of between four and seven
months' production of new units; but considering that these figures are national averages and houses are immobile, they must be close to the irreduc-
ible minimum in a country whose population is as mobile as that of the

United States. In short, disequilibrium in these two markets could deliver a sizable macroeconomic shock but probably of too short duration for its multiplier effect noticeably to affect incomes.

Large producers' durables such as aircraft, ships, trucks, non-residential construction and rental housing have as great or almost as great a share in the economy's total income and expenditure as owner-occupied homes and cars; but their availability in their second-hand markets tends to be considerably greater. For they are held for profitability, not their owners' convenience and personal use, which means that whatever is not profitably used becomes available for sale or rent. That is why vacancy rates for rental housing and commercial real estate are a large multiple of that for owner-occupied homes. Disequilibrium in their markets therefore could be expected to have a large enough impact on the overall economy of sufficient duration to have a sizable effect on incomes and employment. There is no way, however, of measuring the macroeconomic impact of any one of those markets on the overall economy, because it is impossible to separate one such impact from the impact of all the other macroeconomic shocks to the economy. Financial assets seem to be the one exception to this rule, because disequilibria in their markets can create shocks whose size and duration are of an altogether higher order of magnitude than those created by any other market.

Financial assets
Financial assets have by far the largest markets. The main part of their first-hand supply consists of the annual $0.5 trillion worth of new bond issues and initial public offerings of equities (IPOs), only a part of which finances capital formation. The accumulated stock of previously issued long-term financial assets is of the order of $20 trillion, about 40 times the value of annual new issues, and a large part of them is actively traded – mostly but not always at higher prices (and hence lower yields) than new issues.[12]

In that respect, previously issued financial assets resemble old paintings. They are more highly valued, because their riskiness, past performance and the reliability of their issuers are graded, the grades regularly published and so much better and more widely known than those of most new issues, just as the aesthetic appeal of dead masters' paintings are better and more universally established than those of most living painters. And just as some of the first owners of living painters' pictures are expert or risk-loving art dealers, art historians and connoisseurs, willing to gamble on the rightness of their instinct or superior expertise, so the people who initially finance capital formation are partly risk-loving, knowledgeable 'angels' and venture capitalists gambling on the success of revolutionary novelties,[13] but mainly established firms investing in replacements, improvements and innovations in their own fields of expertise – although the bulk of the latters' capital formation does not go through financial markets at all, consisting in the reinvestment of their depreciation allowances and undistributed profits, which usually constitute two-thirds to three-quarters of gross private saving. Most personal savers' participation in the first-hand market is largely limited to their purchase of treasury bills and bonds, tax-exempt state and municipal bonds, and to whatever risky investments are made on their behalf by pension funds, insurance companies and managers of open-ended funds. Most of the rest of their saving goes into buying high-grade previously issued bonds, equities and mutual funds.

In short, second-hand markets for financial assets play a much greater role than most other second-hand markets, not only because their size and volume of transactions so greatly exceed those of their first-hand market as well as of all other second- and first-hand markets, but also because they absorb not the overflow but the bulk of personal current saving. This, of course, represents hoarding, just as spending by the new rich on bidding away old paintings from the old rich is hoarding.

But the saving public's buying into the unchanged stock of previously issued assets bids up their prices and depresses their yield, which makes the unchanged, already higher yield of new issues appear that much the more attractive and may persuade some of the holders of the now higher-priced accumulated stock of assets to realize some of their capital gains by shifting part of such holdings into riskier but higher-yielding new issues. Here, therefore, it is the new-issues market that gets the overflow of the second-hand market's demand, whose positive macroeconomic shock may offset, partly, wholly or more than wholly, the depressing effect of the negative macroeconomic shock created by the new savers' bidding away part of the old savers' hoards of previously issued assets.

On the other hand, the expectation of further capital gains, which the rising price of pre-existing securities generates, may slow or prevent that overflow of demand into the first-hand asset market or even divert more current savings from it. In short, owing partly, perhaps largely, to speculation, current saving has very little stimulating influence on current investment.

All that, of course, is just a roundabout way of saying that it is the second-hand market's prices for previously issued financial assets that determine the rate of capital formation in the US economy. Indeed, as the reader must have long realized already, the argument of this and the previous section is new only in wording but not in substance, because it merely spells out in more detail Keynes's theory of liquidity preference that goes back to his 1936 *General Theory of Employment, Interest and Money*. But his argument focused attention on people's desire to hold part of their wealth in cash and its dependence on the yield of financial assets; whereas the same argument is simpler and more natural in saying that the amount of financial assets people want to hold depends on their yield. Accordingly, let me quote here Keynes's statement of the gist of his liquidity preference theory verbatim,[14] except for substituting the words 'financial assets' for his use of the word 'cash':

> The rate of interest is not the 'price' which brings into equilibrium the demand for resources to invest with the readiness to abstain from present consumption. It is the 'price' which equilibrates the desire to hold wealth in the form of financial assets with the available quantity of financial assets....

These one and a half sentences contain the revolutionary core in the *General Theory*, known today as the stock-flow mechanism. As worded above, they assert that, of the two markets whose equilibrating price is the interest rate, the one for previously issued assets predominates, implying that saving and investment are equilibrated by income, not by the rate of interest.

But if my lengthy argument is a mere rewording of Keynes's theory of liquidity preferences published 60 years ago, why burden our minds with it? Apart from such theoretical niceties as helping to integrate the stock-flow mechanism into the theory of markets and explaining what keeps some prices from promptly and continuously equilibrating supply and demand, it makes Keynes's argument more direct and that much the clearer. After all, the Federal Reserve's open market policies raise the price of financial assets not by increasing the money supply but by taking financial assets of equal value out of circulation, thereby raising the scarcity value of the remaining assets and lowering their yields.

The difference is important, because it draws attention to financial assets and their markets whose nature and quantity have changed a great deal since Keynes's time, which largely explains both why his monetary policies have begun to fail and why our present-day recessions seem so much more severe and intractable. An important change to occur was the greatly increased disparity between the volume of financial assets and cash (M_1) in the hands of the public. While the latter (along with the Fed's reserves) increased 25.4 fold between 1939 and 1989, the volume of financial assets rose 65.5 fold – more than two and a half times as fast. Accordingly, while the Federal Reserve's open-market operations can increase the money supply by a given percentage just as easily today as it could half a century ago, the resulting reduction in today's stock of financial assets would be less than 40 per cent of what it would have been then, leading to a correspondingly smaller rise in their prices and reduction in their yields.

Moreover, not only did the accumulated stock of financial assets grow so fast, but the part of it available for sale in the financial markets grew even faster, as shown by the decline of the average holding period for stocks from over seven years to two years between 1960 and today.[15] To make matters worse, the opening up of our financial markets to international transactions acted like a further increase in their size, making it even harder for an isolated national monetary policy to have a significant impact on long-term interest rates.

Another important change has been the great increase in the public debt. Most financial assets finance capital formation, which raises productivity, income and living standards, and with them the public's need and desire to hold financial assets. This is worth stressing, because a parallel increase in the accumulated stock of assets and the desire to hold them would leave their prices and yields more or less unchanged; whereas the fast increase of the federal debt in the 1970s and 1980s added only to the stock of financial assets but without making people better off, and so without also adding to their desire to hold them, thus causing their prices to fall and yields to rise. That was the way in which the federal deficit 'crowded out' productive investment and made it that much the harder to stimulate it.

So far, we have been concerned with the way in which recent changes in financial markets have rendered it more difficult for monetary policy to lower interest rates and stimulate the economy. Another, more important present-day problem of our economy has been people's and firms' increased reluctance to finance or engage in productive and innovative capital formation and the ineffectiveness of lower interest rates to overcome their reluctance. The problem is not new, witness Steindl's classic 1952 book, whose message continues to be valid;[16] but it is receiving much attention in the American economic literature today, usually under the heading of the US industries' increasingly short-term horizon.[17] The evidence is convincing, because the problem takes many forms and probably has several causes; but it is taken up here because the increasing importance and attractiveness of second-hand financial markets is bound to be one of them.

For investment's expected rate of return exceeding the market rate of interest is clearly not sufficient inducement to undertake it. Keynes and Schumpeter, the most distinguished economists of their generation, have both stressed that productive and innovative investments will not be undertaken on the basis of reasonable profit calculations alone. They must, according to Keynes, 'be supported by animal spirits, so that the thought of ultimate loss … is put aside, as a healthy man puts aside the expectation of his death'.[18] Schumpeter spelled out much the same idea by listing such additional requirements as 'the dream and the will to found one's private kingdom'; 'the will to conquer, the impulse to fight, to prove oneself superior to others, to succeed for the sake of success itself; and the joy of creating'.[19]

Such psychological motivations, however, are not likely to change; a more probable explanation is that a safer and simpler, yet no less challenging and fulfilling alternative to productive investment has arisen that tends to crowd it out.

The emergence and preponderance of financiers

The classical economists, who omitted second-hand markets from their models of the economy, also omitted capitalists, in the narrow sense of financiers, from their cast of characters, subsuming their functions under the entrepreneur's functions because, without second-hand financial markets, the job of managing wealth could not be separated from the management and supervision of the enterprises in which that wealth was invested. With the benefit of hindsight, the difficulty of separating those two functions appears to have been an important blessing, because it forced people to invest their savings in productive capital formation.

The early development of second-hand markets in financial assets made possible a limited separation of the two sets of functions, in so far as it enabled part-time capitalists, that is small savers, to benefit as 'free-riders' from the expertise, daring and imagination of the large, full-time capitalists who continued to combine entrepreneurial functions with the management of their wealth, when not as managers then at least by maintaining a long-term controlling interest in the firm or firms of whose stock they owned a substantial share, usually becoming members of the firms' boards and exercising influence over their managements in a supervisory role and participating in their more important decision-making functions. At that stage, therefore, the second-hand financial market performed a socially valuable function, considering that one could hardly expect small savers to acquire adequate information and judgement on what and where the best prospects for capital formation were.

Recently, however, the scope for money management has expanded tremendously thanks to the greatly increased size of second-hand financial markets, their computerization, the proliferation of mutual funds and other secondary (so-called 'non-rated') assets, the freeing of international capital movements and interconnecting of different countries' financial markets, and the great possibilities for currency speculation created by variable and unstable exchange rates. Money management today has something to offer for every taste and temperament, from good protection against risk for those who abhor it, all the way to great challenges to the ingenuity of daring risk-lovers, with dazzlingly large and quick prizes in case of success. No wonder it has gained in allure for many would-be capitalists as well as already established ones, luring their ambition, talents, ingenuity and funds away from entrepreneurial to purely financial activities.

Plenty of evidence shows that that is happening. To begin with, we associate the names of most people who got rich in the last century with the products (such as oil, railroads, cars and newspapers) that made them rich; but that is seldom the case with today's new rich, the likes of Joseph Kennedy, Carl Icahn or George Soros, who became rich as financiers, not as industrialists. Secondly, the substantial shortening of the average holding period of stocks mentioned earlier (p. 122) indicates a notable decline in the number of permanent, large, personal stockholdings of corporations, with owners interested in the corporations' investment policies and able to influence them. The stockholders' abandoning their involvement in and influence over their select firms' long-term prospects for the sake of the purely financial management of their wealth is understandable from their personal point of view but is socially harmful. For their involvement in corporate investment decisions made their judgement and imagination benefit society as well as themselves; whereas their skill in financial management yields them gain at other people's expense – not to mention the depressing effect on the economy that hoarding instead of investing mostly involves.

The place of corporations' personal large stockholders is being taken by such institutional stockholders as insurance companies, pension funds, mutual funds and their agents, most of them looking for short-term income and capital gains, and having portfolios so diverse and holding each stock for so short a time (less than two years on average) that they neither acquire an interest in, nor exercise influence over, the corporations' investment policies. In the few cases where they can and want to exert pressure on corporate managements they usually do so in the interests of raising their firms' short-term productivity by reducing their labour force, especially their white-collar, administrative personnel (for example IBM, General Motors, Westinghouse Electric, American Express and Kodak).

With stockholders' greatly diminished influence on corporate managers, the latter gain a much freer hand for pursuing their own policies; but they, too, tend increasingly to shirk the high risk of innovative capital formation, to underfund such intangible investments as research and development (R&D) and employee training, and to concentrate instead on mergers and takeovers (sometimes even of firms in unrelated industries), which seems less risky and may raise profits but is of course just another form of hoarding and so depresses the economy. Those changing corporate policies are said to reflect and aim to satisfy their new stockholders' myopic concern with short-term capital gains and income; but an important additional explanation is the one proposed in Steindl's book referred to earlier. That explanation, however, has nothing to do with second-hand markets and is beyond the purview of this paper.

Notes

1. That is the usual meaning of Say's Law. To interpret it to mean the economy's tendency to maintain full-employment equilibrium is, according to *The New Palgrave Dictionary of Economics*, Keynes's distortion of its most widely accepted meaning.
2. Cf. W. Kürsten, 'A Theory of Second-hand Markets: the Rapid Depreciation of Consumer

Durables and Product Differentiation Effects', *Journal of Institutional and Theoretical Economics*, (1991), **147**, 459–76.

3. Cf. 1987 Census of Retail Trade, *Special Report Series, Selected Statistics.*
4. All the national data on passenger cars are from *Motor Vehicle Facts and Figures 1991* and the 1987 Census of Retail Trade, *op. cit.*
5. I owe those estimates to Ladislav Dombovic.
6. The California State registration and reregistration figures are unpublished data, kindly made available to me by Steven Krimetz of the Sacramento Office of the Department of Motor Vehicles. The reregistration figures also contain the number of California licence plates issued to their owners moving to California from other states or countries.
7. US Census Bureau, *Current Housing Reports*, Series H-150-87 and *Statistical Abstract of the United States* (1992).
8. Cf. Robert Hughes, 'Art and Money', *Time*, **134**, 27 November 1989, p. 63.
9. Published in the London *Times* in the 1950s and 1960s, currently appearing weekly in *Barron's,*
10. Cf. Tibor Scitovsky, 'Growth in the Affluent Society', *Lloyds Bank Review*, no. 163, January 1987, reprinted in *The Market on Trial, Lloyds Bank Annual Review*, vol. 2; and David Hakes, 'Evidence of Scitovsky Stagflation Thesis', *Review of Radical Political Economics*, 20/4 (1988), 20, (4).
11. Cf. George A. Akerlof, *An Economic Theorist's Book of Tales*, (Cambridge, Mass.: Cambridge University Press, 1984), ch. 2.
12. All the data on financial assets come from the *Annual Statistical Digest 1980–1989* of the Board of Governors of the Federal Reserve System and the *Historical Statistics of the United States – Colonial Times to 1970.*
13. Venture capitalists and venture capital organizations that provide risk equity for funding the establishment and fast growth of innovative new enterprises emerged fairly recently on the American scene: their annual contribution to capital formation has not yet exceeded the very modest sum of $6 billion.
14. Cf. John M. Keynes, *The General Theory of Employment, Interest and Money*, (London: Macmillan, 1936), p. 167.
15. Cf. E. Duttweiler (ed.), *Institutional Investor Factbook 1991.*
16. Cf. Josef Steindl, *Maturity and Stagnation in American Capitalism*, (Oxford: Blackwell, 1952), reprinted by *Monthly Review*, 1976. See also my 'The Political Economy of Josef Steindl', forthcoming in the *Review of Political Economy.*
17. Cf. M. Jacobs, *Short-Term America*, (Boston: Harvard Business School Press, 1991); M.E. Porter, *Capital Choices: Changing the Way America Invests in Industry*, (Boston: Harvard Business School Press, forthcoming).
18. Cf. Keynes, *The General Theory*, p. 161 of the original edition. See also R.C.O. Matthews, 'Animal Spirits', *Proceedings of the British Academy* (1984).
19. Cf. Joseph Schumpeter, *The Theory of Economic Development*, (New York: Harvard University Press, 1934), p. 93.

9   The political economy of Josef Steindl*

I have long known Josef Steindl – more as a dear friend and delightful companion who was also economist, music lover and a man of learning, than as the distinguished economist who also was all those other things. In other words, I liked his writings I was familiar with but learnt fully to appreciate the originality, relevance and broad range of his contributions only as I was preparing myself for this talk. I also discovered that some of his work was above my head; but judging by what I did understand, I have come to realize that he belongs to that distinguished group of imaginative and insightful economists who made lasting contributions to whatever subject caught their attention in almost any branch of economics.

Josef, however, stands out from among that group with his very different approach and way of thinking. His thinking, I imagine, is slow, and therefore deep and thorough. Most economists in the Anglo-Saxon tradition picked out some feature or regularity of the economy, built an imposing formal theory around it and all too often lost touch with reality in the process. By contrast, Steindl studied in careful detail the way in which those features and regularities came about and got established, and so managed to paint a strikingly realistic picture of the way our economy functions. Where Allyn Young explored the consequences of the economies of scale, Steindl studied and wrote about their underlying causes (Steindl, 1945). Where Marshall patterned the firm's life on man's life-cycle and focused attention on the representative or marginal firm, he studied the great differences in the size, cost, profit margin and behaviour of different firms, seeking their causes and consequences and the reasons for the Pareto distribution of firms by size (Steindl, 1965). Where Keynes explored the relation between saving and investment, he distinguished the internal savings of business corporations from personal savings and their internal investment in the expansion and modernization of their productive capacity from other investments; and where most of his contemporaries analysed the behaviour of an idealized system of perfect competition, Steindl observed how actual competition between big and small, efficient and inefficient firms caused the large to grow, the small ones to die, new ones to emerge; and how all that realistic detail helped to explain the overall behaviour of our real-world economy (Steindl, 1952).

Steindl's approach, much more detailed and realistic than everybody else's, explains why many of his writings dealt, and continue to deal, with our

* This chapter appeared in *Review of Political Economy*, 1994.

economy's problems rather than its achievements. In that respect he has been a follower of Keynes as well as of Marx; but one who carried the explanation of underemployment due to insufficient investment much further and into much greater detail than Keynes did and thereby helped to explain the increasing difficulty of applying Keynesian employment policies at the present time. His realistic, revolutionary approach certainly paid off, as those who have read his writings must be well aware; but the very novelty of that approach was also one of the reasons why his work failed to receive the attention and accolade it deserved.

In that respect, his work resembles that of his fellow Austrian, Schumpeter. The two Josefs' personalities could not have been more different: Schumpeter was an aggressive, flamboyant extrovert who sought and loved public exposure, Steindl is the very opposite. The most memorable of their respective books, however, were similar in that both focused on the role of imperfect competition in long-term development; and they did so at a time when the rest of the profession was preoccupied with the optimality of perfect competition and paid little attention to anything else, which explains why the two Josefs' contributions suffered the same fate.

Schumpeter taught neo-classical orthodoxy at Harvard, never his own work; and while his students admired his writings, these made no impact on their economics. As for Steindl, a telephone survey of my Stanford colleagues showed that all but one of them read his *Maturity and Stagnation*, were impressed by its importance and originality, 'but its theoretical core was submerged in their unconscious', to use the words of the one who read it in Japanese translation. Yet Steindl's great work, unlike Schumpeter's *Theory of Economic Development*, has a very important and memorable theoretical core, whose sinking into people's unconscious is harder to explain and probably also due to its manner of presentation having been too much ahead of his time.

I have in mind Steindl's way of presenting his theories along with the facts against which to test their reasonableness and the realism of their underlying assumptions. He was not quite alone in that. Kalecki occasionally referred to facts and Kaldor made a lot of use of what he named 'stylized facts'. Josef, however, meticulously assembled the available statistics, and his presenting and discussing them along with the theory which they might prove or disprove was a precursor of today's econometrics. For example, 45 of the 245 pages of his above-mentioned book are taken up by statistical tables and graphs, and many pages contain modifications and extensions of his basic theoretical argument the better to reconcile it with reality.

At the time, the profession was not prepared for that. Used to having economic theories presented to them in their stark purity, unencumbered by their juxtaposition against the untidy reality, the profession seems to have lost sight of the book's important theoretical core buried under the wealth of documentation and all the modifications and qualifications added in the interest of its better matching with reality. To my shame, the same thing also happened to me.

The theoretical core I have in mind is Steindl's picture of realistic competition, which presents it in a highly favourable light, though with the fatal flaw that in the very long run it gives way to oligopoly and all its unfavourable characteristics. The gist of the book is that, as competitive industries are gradually replaced by oligopolies, progressive and efficient capitalism gives way to stagnation. Steindl's account of a competitive industry and its many social benefits is so convincing and realistic that it ought, to my mind, be included in every textbook on microeconomics and industrial organization. As to the stagnation-inducing effects of oligopoly, they were originally meant to explain the depressed 1930s; but they are relevant also to America's present-day economic problems, as several of Josef's more recent papers make clear (Steindl, 1979, 1989). I should like to say a few words on both those topics.

The central and most interesting part of *Maturity and Stagnation* is Steindl's theory of a competitive industry's long-run equilibrium, which could also be described as a dynamic theory of the secular trend of an industry's growth under imperfect competition. Steindl's theory of competition shows that, under capitalism, industries with low costs of entry will be competitive, and that competition among their member firms has many socially beneficent effects. It encourages innovation, thereby improving product quality and lowering costs; it lowers prices in proportion with the lowering of costs, thereby expanding the market while maintaining unchanged the share of profits and wages in value added; and it brings down the industry's average rate of profit to the level that slows the accumulation of retained profits to what is just sufficient (but no more than sufficient) to finance the industry's capacity expansion in step with the expansion of its market. That assures the industry's equilibrium, which keeps its capacity utilization at its optimum level. An implication of this last is that the availability of jobs in the industry also remains at its optimum.

This long list of social benefits is almost as impressive as the well-known advantages of perfect competition, with the important difference that the former are the real benefits enjoyed by real industries when they are competitive, while the latter are fully achieved only in the idealized never-never land of perfect competition.

Let me now try my hand at imitating Josef's procedure and look at the meaning and sources of the benefits he enumerates. To begin with, why does easy entry render an industry competitive? Competition means expanding sales at competitors' expense; and industries with easy entry usually have many small, high-cost, hardly profitable and highly vulnerable marginal firms, whose markets are easy to encroach upon and which can easily be driven out of the market – something that large, highly profitable, intramarginal firms are likely to do to them, because they can invest in added productive capacity out of retained earnings, which are always the cheapest source of funds, just as such investment is usually the latter's most profitable outlet.

Productivity rises as efficient low-cost firms encroach upon, or take over, the markets of high-cost marginal firms, and also because process innovations 'accompany investment like a shadow', to quote Steindl's words. That observation, which he made as early as 1952, has now become one of the well-documented central ideas of the latest theory of economic growth (Scott, 1989). The rise in productivity lowers costs of production, whereas price reductions and other sales efforts are the competitive weapons with which the large firms drive their weakest competitors out of part or all of their markets. The natural consequence of their use of those competitive weapons is the reduction of the large firms' rate of profit.

As to optimal capacity utilization, unwanted excess capacity is removed as marginal firms are driven out of the market, after which optimal excess capacity and capacity utilization are maintained, because the industry's average rate of profit has been lowered to the level where the accumulation of internal funds is just enough to finance the rate of investment needed to make productive capacity increase in step with, but a step ahead of, market demand.

Bear in mind that Steindl, as a first approximation, makes the realistic assumption that firms use only their internal savings for investment in maintaining, expanding and improving their productive capacity, and finance those investments entirely out of internal funds. When you look at the US National Income and Product Accounts and see that gross business saving tends to be close to three times as large as personal saving, then you realize how sensible Steindl's initial simplifications are; and you also realize that the competition he describes brings about a microeconomic version of Say's Law on the industry level, in the sense of equating each competitive industry's internal saving to the internal investment necessary to keep production abreast of demand.

Indeed, the beauty of Steindl's model is that it integrates micro- and macroeconomic arguments, rendering the passage from the first to the second simple and obvious, since the only modification that the passage to macroeconomics makes to his argument is that it transforms demand from an exogenous datum into an endogenous variable. It shows, for example, that, if all industries were competitive, competition could be relied upon to equate the business sector's full-employment savings to its investment needs for capacity expansion and process innovation, thereby greatly reducing the problem of Keynesian unemployment and easing the task of employment policy.

Another important merit of Steindl's model is that it shows not only the achievements of competition but also its shortcomings. First among these is that it favours the growth of the large firms at the expense of small ones, which are not only the most vulnerable to recessions and competitors' inroads into their markets but the easiest to force completely out of business as well.

This points to the second and much more serious shortcoming of competition: its tendency to destroy itself. For when the large firms' predatory competition has completely driven all the small firms out of the market, it has transformed a competitive industry into a non-competitive oligopoly. That, fortunately, is a slow process because, as long as a competitive industry is in equilibrium, with the growth of its productive capacity matching the growth of its sales, its members lack both the inducement and the capacity to encroach upon their fellow members' markets, which suspends predatory competition. Only when some change or external shock disrupts the equilibrium are the forces of predatory competition set and kept in motion until equilibrium is again restored.

The gradual transformation of competitive into oligopolistic industries and the redistribution of profits from the former to the latter is the basis of Steindl's explanation of the secular slowing of the US economy's rate of growth from the 1880s onwards and its stagnation during the 1930s. For, according to Steindl, oligopolistic industries are non-competitive, because even their marginal, smallest firms are large and profitable enough to give them enough staying power to render the intramarginal firms' expansion at their expense very costly and risky. That inhibits competition and with it the competitive lowering of prices that would expand markets and keep the share of wages up and the share of profits down. With profits and prices undiminished, the high rate of profit of oligopolistic firms leads to a fast accumulation of their retained earnings at the same time that their high prices keep low their scope for investing them in the expansion of productive capacity. That creates an excess of the industry's endogenous savings over its needs for endogenous investment in capacity expansion. Such excess savings, of course, can be used to finance research, development and investment in existing or new firms branching out into the production of new products; but Steindl convincingly explains why that often fails to happen, which leads to stagnation and causes the oligopolistic industries' normal routine of building capacity ahead of demand, to create instead unwanted excess capacity, with its depressing effects on the whole economy.

That is the theoretical skeleton of Steindl's book, which also deals, of course, with personal savings, business debt, debt–equity ratios and many other realistic details besides. But let me leave the book now and say a few words about the way Steindl uses and extends its arguments to explain, first America's long-lasting post-World War II prosperity and then her present-day problems.

Our prolonged postwar prosperity he attributes to such exogenous factors as the Marshall Plan, development aid and generally increased government spending financed partly out of a high corporation profit tax, the increased bargaining power of organized labour, the opening up of international trade, fast technical progress made possible by the great increase in government-financed research and development, and government's taking responsibility for maintaining employment. After all, business firms' excess internal saving creates no problem if offset by innovating investment and employment-generating spending by others.

But most of those exogenous sources of prosperity dried up by the 1970s; and as oligopolistic firms grew larger, their managements became increasingly bureaucratic, hierarchical, overadministered and so more cautious, less willing to finance research and development and to shoulder the risks that the development and introduction of new or innovative products inevitably involves. That is why large firms became more interested in increasing their monopoly power by vertical integration, mergers and takeovers; in short, by the acquisition of already established productive capacity. In other words, their desire to avoid risk made them switch from real investment in innovative products and methods of production to financial investments in existing enterprises and financial assets. That, taken singly, might well have been less risky, but, when many corporations in many oligopolistic industries followed such policies at the same time, their combined effect on the whole economy created worse risks and losses than the sum of the risks that each individual firm tried to avoid. Moreover, to the extent that many of the takeovers were leveraged, financed by debt, the resulting increase in debt-equity ratios rendered those corporations even more vulnerable.

There are two reasons why financial investment fails to create the social benefits of real investment and so injures the economy. First, while real investment is always more or less innovative and so increases productivity and adds to technical know-how, which in turn further stimulates investment, thereby further increasing productivity, financial investment does no such thing. The purchase of existing enterprises may and often does improve the latters' managerial and organizational efficiency, which raises the new owners' rate of profit but seldom favours the firm's workers or customers.

Secondly, financial investment, unlike real investment, usually makes little or no addition to effective demand to stimulate the economy and generate income and employment. For it provides liquidity and often a substantial capital gain for the people and firms whose financial assets or ownership of existing firms or plants are bought or taken over; but they are seldom the people and firms that would use their newly acquired liquid funds either for increased consumption or for real investment. They are more likely to put most or all of those funds into other financial investments, with equally slight or no stimulating effect on the economy.

Those two shortcomings of financial investment, its failure to raise productivity and failure to generate effective demand, are important reasons why the casino society, as Steindl calls our present-day economy, is quite so depressed, manifesting hardly any growth in productivity but plenty of unemployment and unwanted excess capacity. According to Steindl's analysis, therefore, our problem is not insufficient personal saving, for which many economists and politicians blame the American consumer's profligacy, but the predominantly financial use that big business makes of its internal savings, whose impact on the economy is much the same as that of hoarding money. Indeed, one of Steindl's latest papers shows that the US statistics of personal saving are very misleading – and misleading in a way that renders questionable the fashionable argument that the spendthrift American consumer is to blame for our economic troubles (Steindl, 1990a). Let me also add that a joint article by Bhaduri and Steindl (1988) documented the recent shift from industrial to finance capitalism, but only for the United Kingdom.

Perhaps I have focused too narrowly on just one part of Steindl's lifetime work, but it is, to my mind, its most important part and deserves much more recognition than it has received. For the channelling of saving into socially beneficial real investment is still one of the least well understood functions of our economy. Jean-Baptiste Say trusted the invisible hand of market forces to take care of it; Keynes put his faith in businessmen's entrepreneurial animal spirits and believed that aiding them with an appropriate interest rate policy will do the trick. It was left to Steindl's realistic institutional approach to open our eyes to the significance of the fact that three-quarters of private gross saving is performed and controlled by corporations, which could use those savings for productive and innovative investments without need of costly financial intermediation, were it not for their ever-more bureaucratic managements, which have become increasingly risk-averse and lost their entrepreneurial animal spirits.

Yet we are in the midst of a genetic and electronic revolution, with plenty of imaginative people around, willing to gamble on the successful development of their innovative ideas; but they lack the necessary capital, and the annual $4–4.5 billion that the newly emerging venture capital industry manages to generate on their behalf (Harvard Business School, 1988) is insignificant compared to what the large corporations could provide had they not lost their venturesome spirit. The amount of venture capital currently available certainly is woefully inadequate to get us out of a depression in which the proportion of business failures has reached the record levels attained only twice before: during the great depressions of the 1890s and the 1930s. Hence Steindl's conclusion that it is not the lack of savings but the lack of a venturesome spirit in those who control the great bulk of savings that are the root cause of our economic problems.

Unfortunately, too few eyes have seen and recognized the importance of Steindl's work on this critical subject; and I can only hope that the present conference and the publication of its papers will remedy that situation. The importance of Schumpeter's work *is* being recognized now, posthumously. It would help to resolve our economic problems if the importance of Josef Steindl's work was recognized soon, within his and our lifetime.

References

Bhaduri, A. and Steindl, J. (1988), 'The rise of monetarism as a social doctrine', *Thames Papers in Political Economy*, Autumn.

Harvard Business School, (1988), *Venture Capital Conference: September 23–24*.

Scott, M. Fg. (1989), *A New View of Economic Growth*, (Oxford: Clarendon Press).

Steindl, J. (1945), *Small and Big Business: Economic Problems of the Size of Firms*, (Oxford: Basil Blackwell).

—— (1952), *Maturity and Stagnation in American Capitalism*, (Oxford: Basil Blackwell).

—— (1965), *Random Processes and the Growth of Firms: A Study of the Pareto Law*, (London: Griffin).

—— (1979), 'Stagnation theory and stagnation policy', *Cambridge Economic Journal*, 3.

—— (1989), 'From stagnation in the 30s to stagnation in the 70s', in M. Berg (ed.), *Political Economy in the Twentieth Century*, (Oxford: Philip Allan).

—— (1990a), 'Capital gains, pension funds and the low saving ratio in the United States', *Banca Nazionale del Lavoro Quarterly Review*, no. 173.

—— (1990b), *Economic Papers 1941–88*, (London: Macmillan), contains reprints of the above-mentioned 1979 and 1989 papers.

10 Economic development in Taiwan and South Korea: 1965–81*

To help the developing countries develop and the poor to escape poverty was perhaps the noblest and most ambitious aspiration of the postwar world – first voiced by President Truman in his Point Four Program of 1949. His fine words mobilized a lot of resources and effort; unfortunately, however, the outcome of all the development aid, development advice and development policies was mixed and often disappointing. All too often the industrialization of traditional agricultural societies merely transformed their failure fully to utilize man's latent energies – his so-called 'disguised unemployment' – into open, urban unemployment, which is more painful and objectionable in social and human terms. Many of the poorest countries grew more slowly than the advanced countries and so fell further and further behind; and even the fast-developing countries grew in a lopsided way, increasing instead of diminishing the inequality between rich and poor. Indeed, increased inequality of income distribution, both between and within countries, seemed to be an almost inevitable accompaniment of economic development – certainly in its early stages.

But development experiences were vastly different, ranging from retrogression in one Asian and nine African countries, whose populations grew faster than their national income, to almost 7 per cent annual growth in per capita gross domestic product (GDP) over two decades (1960–80) in five Asian countries and city states.[1] Two of those five, South Korea and Taiwan, not only grew very fast but did so without experiencing the customary great and increasing inequalities and the emergence of mass unemployment.[2] Indeed, by the double criterion of growth and equity, they have been the most successful of all the developing countries.

Per capita GNP in real terms grew marginally faster in Taiwan than in Korea, at an average annual rate of 6.9 per cent compared to Korea's 6.7 per cent between 1965 and 1981 (Table 10.1). Taiwan also had slightly less unemployment, an even more egalitarian income distribution, and a much higher standard of living. Taiwan's GDP per capita was US$2.570 by 1981, whereas Korea's was US$1,697. In effect, Taiwan was six years ahead of Korea: Korea's per capita income in 1981 was about the same as Taiwan's in 1975.

* This chapter appeared in *Food Research Institute Studies,* vol. XIX, no. 3, 1985.

Table 10.1   Average annual growth rates in real terms, 1965–81 (per cent)

	Korea	Taiwan
Population	1.9	2.3
Employment	3.4	3.7
Gross national product	8.7	9.4
Gross domestic product	8.6	9.4
Manufacturing output	20.6	15.5
Exports (quantum index)	26.0	18.9
GNP per capita = GDP per capita	6.7	6.9
Labour productivity[a]	5.2	5.4
Real wages in manufacturing	7.9	7.3
Consumers' expenditures per capita	5.5	5.2

[a]   GNP per employed person.

But such international comparisons, based on monetary estimates made in national currencies and then converted into a common currency at current exchange rates, are subject to notoriously wide margins of error. Indeed, two similar estimates, based on different data in slightly different ways, have yielded an eight- and a ten-year gap (Kim and Roemer, 1979, p. 147; Little, 1979, p. 455). Moreover, one must also bear in mind that Korea produces its lower GDP with a greater expenditure of effort. In 1980, the average length of the working week in Korea's manufacturing industries was in excess of 59 hours, 16 per cent longer than Taiwan's 51-hour week. Correcting for that factor makes Taiwan's per capita GDP appear almost twice as high as Korea's. On the other hand, Koreans spend a much higher proportion of their lower GDP on private consumption: two-thirds as compared to Taiwan's one-half. Accordingly, the difference between the two countries' levels of living is not as great as the discrepancy between their per capita GDPs would suggest.

Social indicators are sometimes more useful for assessing differences in levels of living than estimates in money terms. Those available for both countries are listed in Table 10.2; they suggest that Taiwan enjoys a considerably higher level of living than Korea. The only social indicator visible to the naked eye is the number of motorized vehicles (passenger cars and motorcycles) per household. It suggests that in Taiwan just about every household owns such a vehicle, while in Korea only one in 20 households does; the difference shows up strikingly in the contrast between Taiwan's busy country roads and small-town streets and Korea's much quieter countryside.

Table 10.2 Social Indicators

	Korea	Taiwan
Life expectancy at birth (years)	65	72
Infant mortality per 1000 live births	37	25
Daily calorie intake per capita	2 785	2 805
Daily protein intake per capita (grams)	69.6	78
Residential floorspace per capita (m^2)	9.5	15.7
Households with running water (per cent)	54.6	66.8
Households with television sets (per cent)	78.6	100.4
Households with passenger cars and motorcycles (per cent)	5.8	108.4
Electric power consumption per capita (KWH)	914.8	2 131.2

None of the other social indicators is apparent; indeed, the tourist is likely not only not to notice Taiwan's greater prosperity but actually to get the impression that the difference between the two countries goes the other way around. Seoul, certainly, looks more affluent than Taipei, judging by the appearance of its main thoroughfares, the impressiveness of its commercial and office buildings, and the elegance of its stores and shopping areas. The explanation of the conflict between what the tourist sees and what the statistics show derives from the unequal distribution of income and of the things that income buys.

All the social indicators of Table 10.2 are averages and indicate average tendencies, whereas the tourist is shown only the best and his eye instinctively looks for the best. In an egalitarian society, the best is not much better than the average, but they differ greatly in a society with great inequalities.

Income distribution in both Taiwan and Korea is much less unequal than in any other developing or newly industrializing country for which the relevant statistics are available, but it is more egalitarian in Taiwan than in Korea. Inequalities in Korea are much the same as in the advanced industrial countries: somewhat less than in France and Italy, greater than in the United Kingdom and the Scandinavian countries, and just about the same as in the United States and Canada. Taiwan, on the other hand, is the most egalitarian of all capitalist countries if the statistics are to be trusted, a finding that tallies with the very small average size and limited dispersion of the size of Taiwan's business firms, and that also explains the absence of an elite wealthy and large enough to support the elegant shops and finance the imposing office buildings that give Seoul its appearance of affluence. (See Table 10.3).

Table 10.3   Gini index of inequality of income distribution

	1965	1970	1976
Korea	0.344	0.332	0.381
Taiwan	0.322[a]	0.293	0.289
Japan	0.380	0.420[b]	
United States		0.362[c]	
Brazil	0.520[d]	0.630	

Notes:
[a]   1966.
[b]   1971.
[c]   1972.
[d]   1960.

Source: The comparisons are based on Gini indexes of inequality, obtained for Taiwan from Kuo, et al. (1981); for Korea from Park (1980), p. 289; and calculated for other countries from data in World Bank (1982), pp. 158–9.

One more important difference between the two economies has been the much smaller rate of inflation in Taiwan than in Korea. Between 1965 and 1981, the consumer price index rose by a factor of 3.5 in Taiwan and ten fold in Korea, corresponding to average annual price inflation rates of 8 and 15 per cent, respectively. Compared to other countries, Taiwan did about as well, or as badly, as Japan or the United States; Korea had more inflation than any of the industrial countries, but less than the major Latin American economies.

Similarities in tradition and background

Detailed analysis and comparison of the two countries' economic conditions and performance suggest that the similarities are largely due to similarities in their history and traditions. Korea's lag behind Taiwan is more than explained by the later date at which its growth policies began; the other differences are well accounted for by the two countries' divergent economic policies. Unexplained and puzzling is the close similarity in growth rates despite the very different ways in which the two countries went about promoting growth.

To begin with the similarities, both countries – indeed, all five of the high performers – have a common Chinese tradition and Confucian philosophy. That explains, first of all, the great reverence and importance attached to learning in both countries and the very high educational and skill levels of their populations. They started from a very low level at the end of World War II, especially in Korea, where the literacy rate was 13.4 per cent in 1945 (as against Taiwan's 21.3 per cent by 1940) and where there was no large influx of a highly educated middle-class population, such as benefited Taiwan in the late 1940s. Since then, illiteracy has been almost completely eradicated in both countries, and today Taiwan provides nine years and Korea six years of free and compulsory schooling. School enrolment rates at the primary and secondary levels are almost equally high in the two countries and only insignificantly lower than the average in the advanced industrial countries (Table 10.4). That is especially impressive in Korea, whose modernization started later, where compulsory education ends sooner and public expenditure on education is lower (averaging 3.5 per cent of GDP as against Taiwan's 4.5 per cent), but where consumers make up for those disadvantages by paying for the greater part of their children's education out of their own pockets, bringing the total private and public expenditure on education to an astonishingly high 9 per cent of GNP.

*Table 10.4   School enrolment rates**

	Primary school	Secondary school	College and universities
Korea	111	76	12.4
Taiwan	99.7	80.3	10.3
Advanced industrial countries	102	88	37
Italy	102	73	27
Switzerland	86	55	17

* Students enrolled as a percentage of the population in the appropriate age group.

A second condition of those countries' great economic success that can be traced back to their common tradition is the ability and willingness to work hard. Chinese tradition has many tangled strands, but it seems to include a work ethic not unlike the Protestant and Jewish work ethics. The drive and ambition of Korean and Chinese businessmen, as well as their ability to work hard and long hours, are commented on by just about every outside observer of the two economies, and so are the 'untiring concentration and pertinacity' of their workers (Little, 1979, p. 461). One is tempted to add the two countries' very long working week as a further manifestation of the work ethic but, in view of the very limited bargaining strength of their unions, it is hard to tell to what extent those long working hours are voluntary and to what extent they are imposed.

A third factor that probably also contributed to the two countries' economic success is the Chinese tradition in labour relations, which comprises both greater wage flexibility and greater employment stability than in Europe and

America, and which was fully maintained and perhaps even strengthened under Japanese rule. Both countries adhere to the Chinese custom of paying bonuses to workers at major festivals and the end of the year; and even if these constitute a much smaller proportion of the annual wage than they do in Japan, they nevertheless are likely to contribute to the two countries' high personal saving rate and to impart a measure of downward flexibility to wages. Again, relations between employer and employee are more permanent in the two countries than they are in the West, with employers under both moral and governmental pressure to take care of their workers even when business is slow.

Korea and Taiwan are also similar in that both were formerly under Japanese rule, Korea for 35 years and Taiwan (as Formosa) for 50 years; and that fact has also facilitated their subsequent growth in at least two ways. First, the Japanese introduced the new, high-yielding strains of rice, established agricultural research institutes and generally did much to develop the two countries' farm productivity and food production; moreover, they built roads, railways, harbours and whatever beginnings of industry the two countries had, thus providing an excellent start and base for subsequent development. A second and very important consequence of Japanese rule had to do with the confiscation of Japanese property when their rule came to an end. The Japanese acquired a sizable part of the land (21 per cent of all arable land in Taiwan) and built most of the modern manufacturing plants in both countries; and since they owned all the large enterprises and most of the largest landed estates, the confiscation of their property by the liberating armies and its handing over to the new governments drastically reduced the inequality of private wealth holdings in both countries. In Korea, moreover, the Korean War destroyed much physical property and, since most of the loss was borne by the wealthy, that too helped to reduce inequalities of wealth.

Even more important in equalizing the distribution of wealth were the thorough land reforms in both countries, which not only distributed among small tenant farmers the large estates formerly held by the Japanese, but also forced the large indigenous landowners to sell all their land above 3 hectares (except in Korea's upland areas) at prices very much below market values. Taiwan's land reform looks like the putting into practice of Sun Yat-sen's ideal of the equalization of land ownership; but Korea's land reform was identical in almost every detail.[3]

Reduced inequality of wealth is the main reason for the exceptionally equal distribution of income in the two countries. The stability of employment is a lesser contributing cause. Yet another important reason was the rise of farm families' earnings to a par with urban wage-earner families' incomes. In Taiwan, that came about largely through the operation of automatic market forces, aided by favourable circumstances. Impelled by high and rising labour costs in cities, an increasing proportion of new factories and offices were established in rural areas and offered additional employment opportunities to farmers and their families. The poorest farmers especially availed themselves of the opportunity: by 1975, 66 per cent of their total earnings came from jobs off the farm. Nor was the corresponding percentage for all farm families much lower: it was 53.7 per cent in 1975, rising to 72.7 per cent in 1979. That is why, in contrast to most developing countries where mass migration into the cities depletes rural areas, Taiwan's rural population remained fairly stable, with members of farm families commuting or taking part-time jobs in nearby cities during off-peak seasons. The favourable circumstances that aided the process were a small, decentralized country, good roads, a mild climate and a motorcycle in every family.

Korea went out of its way to encourage a similar development, but, perhaps for want of similarly favourable circumstances, had very limited success. It managed nevertheless to equalize rural and urban incomes through the costly expedient of a farm-price support programme combined with subsidized low food prices for consumers.

Thanks to all these equalizing factors and influences, the degree of income inequality had, by the mid-1960s, fallen to just about the same level in the two countries. Since then, inequalities have declined yet further in Taiwan but increased in Korea, which explains why Taiwan is today the more egalitarian country of the two. An explanation for these diverging trends is offered below in the discussion of economic policies.

Two further similarities between the two countries are the exceptionally generous economic aid both have received and the exceptionally heavy burdens of military expenditures they are saddled with: the first an addition to economic resources, the second a drain on them. Both countries have also received substantial military aid from the United States in the form of military equipment, but since much military equipment seems to call for a larger defence establishment, military aid probably encourages domestic defence spending more than reduces it. Defence spending in Taiwan hovers around 10 per cent of GNP; in Korea, thanks to an American military presence, it is 5 to 6 per cent. But even that is much higher than the 3.8 per cent average of industrial countries and the 3 per cent average of newly industrializing countries (World Bank, 1982; Little, 1979, p. 458). The annual aid Taiwan received until 1966 averaged 5.1 per cent of GNP, just enough to finance the above normal part of its defence spending.[4]

Such a simple-minded calculation, of course, leaves out of account that Taiwan would probably have spent as much on defence even if it had received no economic aid, and that aid may well have been crucial in the early 1950s for controlling inflation and securing the survival of the government of the Republic of China on Taiwan. But beyond assuring those initial conditions, aid cannot really be said to have speeded up growth.

Korea's situation is somewhat different. The aid it received exceeded defence expenditures, averaging 8.3 per cent of GNP before 1965 and continuing, at a somewhat lower level, until 1972.[5] The economy, however, was much more devastated by war than Taiwan's; and the aid to rebuild the war-torn country was more comparable to that received by Japan and Western Europe. Unlike Taiwan, where in the early years (1951–3) part of the aid was focused on rebuilding agriculture, in Korea 'the Rhee Government was committed to increasing private and government consumption through the maximization of aid and imports, rather than to the future growth of output'.[6] Later on, of course, aid financed a good part (an average of 10.2 per cent from 1965 to 1981) of total investment and so contributed to growth. The section on sources of investible funds (p. 144) also deals with the contribution of foreign loans, which was sizable in Korea, but zero in Taiwan, during the 1965–81 period.

One more similarity between the two countries worth mentioning here was their very limited imports of entrepreneurial skill and technical know-how in the form of direct foreign investments. In Taiwan, they constituted a mere 6.5 per cent of fixed investment in manufacturing industries between 1967 and 1975; in Korea, they were equally insignificant until 1972, when they rose to about 20 per cent, coming mainly from Japan and going mainly into textiles, electronics, and the hotel business (Krueger, 1979, pp. 145–7; Little, 1981, pp. 37–9). The reasons for their limited need of direct foreign investment are obvious. Perhaps as part of their excellent educational systems and traditions of hard work and untiring application, both countries are well provided with native entrepreneurial skills, drive and ambition. Moreover, they had no need for imported technical knowledge as long as they focused their development on labour-intensive industries in which they had previous experience. That, probably, is why in Korea the increase in foreign direct investment coincided with the decision to shift to more capital-intensive industries. Even at that stage, however, direct foreign investment in Korea was low compared to other developing countries, perhaps owing to the Korean's preference for going it alone. They learned shipbuilding by employing in their shipyards Norwegians from closed-down Norwegian shipyards and their expertise in construction by contracting to do construction work abroad.

These similarities in the two countries' backgrounds help to explain not only their similar economic performances but also the exceptional nature of their success when compared to the record of other developing countries. To explain differences between the two countries themselves, one must look at their differing policies. The effectiveness of those policies and the divergencies between them are discussed in detail below. To introduce the discussion, however, it is useful to look at the general spirit and underlying philosophies that pervaded economic-policy making in the two countries.

The philosophy behind Taiwan's economic policies

Taiwanese officials will occasionally say that their economic policy is to let market forces take their course. That, however, is a highly oversimplified and exaggerated statement. Taiwan has long had and still has plenty of economic controls, which are well used to implement the government's growth policies as set out in a succession of four-year plans; and one could hardly call the country's economy a hands-off, laisser-faire economy. Yet the Taiwanese also know how to press market forces into the service of their economic policies.

In the early 1960s, the 19-Point Economic Financial Reform of the Third Four-Year Plan greatly encouraged investment by private enterprise. In Taiwan today, government does not have the strong ascendancy over private business it still has in Korea, and economic controls tend to be moderate and often make use of the market in a selective and quite sophisticated way. The Taiwanese, like the Koreans, have encouraged exports by creating an essentially free-trade, free-market regime for exports and export production; moreover, unlike the Koreans, they have shown great respect for the strength of market forces, manifest in the careful moderation of their policies when they aim at modifying or deflecting those forces and in the gradual, stepwise fashion in which they change economic controls and policies. Finally, while Korea's development weakened the pull of market forces, Taiwan's strengthened it.

For a market economy to function properly, it must be competitive. Competition depends on the presence of many small firms and the absence of overwhelmingly large ones. In Taiwan, those conditions of competition and the proper functioning of markets are better fulfilled than in most other private enterprise economies, thanks partly to deliberate policies, partly to more or less fortuitous circumstances.

To begin with, heavy industries like steel, shipbuilding and petrochemicals, whose great economies of scale render them natural monopolies in a small country, happen to be publicly owned in Taiwan, probably more for lack of sufficient private resources and interest than for reasons of policy. Privately owned manufacturing firms were usually small in size and few in number in primitive economies, whose forced economic development in the mid-20th century typically took the form of growth in the size rather than in the number of firms, owing partly to economies of scale and partly to its being so much harder for government to facilitate the establishment of new firms than the growth of already established ones.

Astonishingly enough, Taiwan managed to take the opposite route to development. Between 1966 and 1976, the number of manufacturing firms in Taiwan increased 2.5 fold, while the average size of the individual enterprise, as measured by the number of employees, increased by only 29 per cent. In Korea, where development took the more common route, the relation be-

tween those two changes goes the other way around. The number of manufacturing firms increased by a mere 10 per cent, while it is the number of
employees per enterprise that increased even more than 2.5 fold, by 176 per
cent.

The outcome of the two countries' very different routes to development
was the much smaller size of private manufacturing enterprises in Taiwan
and the more competitive spirit that goes with it. Not counting the very small
firms with less than five employees, which in Korea seem too unimportant for
the census to bother with, the average Taiwanese firm in 1976 was only half
as big as the Korean, with 34.6 employees as against 68.8 in Korea. Moreover, the very small firms, ignored by the Korean census, constituted 43 per
cent of all manufacturing firms in Taiwan, bringing the average size of all
Taiwanese firms down to 27 employees. The disparity in firm size between
the two countries seems even greater when one looks at their largest firms. In
1981, the $10 billion gross receipts of Hyundai, Korea's largest conglomer-
ate, were three times as big as the $3.5 billion gross receipts of Taiwan's ten
largest private firms *combined*.

What explains the great difference between the ways in which manufacturing capacity grew in the two countries and the resulting great difference in
firm size between them? While there is one explanation for the faster growth
of Korean firms, at least four account for the faster increase in the number of
Taiwanese firms. One must be the immigration of overseas Chinese, who
brought with them 30 per cent of the total inflow of foreign capital and used it
mostly for establishing independent enterprises of their own. A second is
Taiwan's much higher personal saving rate, which generally makes it easier
to secure the capital for establishing independent businesses, and whose
causes will be discussed below. A third factor is probably the much smaller
size of the average firm, which makes it easier and cheaper for newcomers to
enter the market.

A fourth and possibly the most important factor is Taiwan's policy of
helping people with entrepreneurial inclinations and know-how but insufficient capital to establish themselves as independent businessmen. For the
market to function well, labour, capital and entrepreneurship must be somehow brought together. One usually thinks of the entrepreneur as the initiating
and moving spirit, but real-life capital markets do not lend money to penni-
less entrepreneurs and the capitalist owner of a small firm, as most firms are
in Taiwan, can seldom afford to hire entrepreneurial talent. To remedy that
situation, Taiwan has established 49 industrial parks and districts, some of
them specialized (like the Youth Industrial Parks and the Science-Based
Industrial Park), which not only provide infrastructure facilities but also
enable new investors to rent rather than buy land and buildings, where
generous loans are available, and where the technical skills of scientifically

trained people are accepted as an important part (up to 50 per cent) of their personal investment.

These were the factors facilitating the establishment of new enterprise. Equally important for keeping alive the competitive spirit was the very slow growth of the average enterprise, yet there is no evidence of official policy deliberately aimed at limiting either the size or the rate of growth of private firms. Indeed, Taiwan has many large private industrial groups which, though much smaller in size than those in Korea, are sufficiently large and important to have contributed 30 per cent of the country's total GDP in the 1980s. The explanation therefore of the relatively slow growth of the size of firms lies not in the presence of policies limiting, but in the absence of policies encouraging, their growth.

That brings us to the subject of monetary policy. The crucial difference between the two countries lay in their very different monetary policies. Taiwan's novel monetary policy was all-important for bringing about conditions favourable to the market economy's functioning as it should, although its effect on the size and growth of firms was decidedly an unexpected and unintended side-effect and not among the principal aims of the policy.

The rate of interest, or more correctly the structure of interest rates, is the one price or set of prices whose determination nowhere is nor can be left entirely to the free play of market forces. Different countries pursue different monetary and interest rate policies; yet there is a theoretically definable, though practically very hard to ascertain equilibrium or natural rate of interest, which would equate the demand for investible funds at full employment to the supply of full-employment savings; and Taiwanese monetary policy may be said to have consistently tried to ascertain what the equilibrium interest rate is and to keep actual interest rates close to that equilibrium level. The beginnings of that monetary policy go back to the early 1950s, more than a decade before the period here under review, but since the same policy is still being adhered to today, and since it has profoundly affected and continues to affect many aspects of Taiwan's economy, a short account of it seems to be in order.

At a time when the universally approved and practised policy in developing countries was to keep interest rates low, thereby to encourage capital accumulation and growth, Taiwan, not without some initial hesitation and vacillation, broke new ground and raised the interest rates paid to savers and charged to borrowers to levels then almost unheard of. Originally, the policy was devised, outlined and advocated as a means of curbing China's hyperinflation during the war and civil war, by a Chinese economist, Professor S.C. Tsiang, in two Chinese-language articles published in 1947 in the *Shanghai Economic Review*, and adoption of his policy had much to do with bringing that inflation to a halt.

A high interest rate policy is, of course, a standard remedy for inflation; but totally unexpected was another effect that also followed Taiwan's adoption of the policy: the speeding up of capital accumulation and growth. Savings deposits accumulated very fast following the substantial raising of the interest paid on deposits, presumably because savers found the high interest rate so attractive that they stopped putting their savings into unproductive but price-increasing hoards of goods and real estate and may also have increased their saving as a proportion of income. At the same time, however, that high deposit rates raised both the saving rate and the proportion of savings channelled into bank deposits, lending rates apparently were not high enough to reduce businessmen's demand for investible funds to below the rate at which funds became available. In other words, the high deposit and loan rates instituted in Taiwan came close to but did not exceed the equilibrium rate of interest as defined earlier, which explains why raising interest rates raised the level of investment or capital accumulation.

In addition, the raising of interest rates is also likely to have rendered investment a more efficient and more effective engine of growth. For interest rates held below their natural level create excess demand for investible funds and so force the banks to ration credit. Credit rationing, however, usually favours large firms, the banks' established customers, or those whom government wants to favour, and these are not always the ones who earn the highest rate of return on their investments. Accordingly, credit rationing by bank or government policy is likely to crowd out some high-return investments, which would not be crowded out if the interest rate were the main factor limiting the demand for credit. In other words, rationing credit by interest rates instead of by bank managers and government officials is almost certain to raise the average return on the total volume of investment, thereby further accelerating growth.[7]

Those advantages of a carefully managed interest rate policy in both containing inflation and promoting investment and growth have become well known in the literature of development economics, and the policy has been advocated for and imitated by other countries as well. Indeed, the originator of the policy and Taiwan's pioneering role in developing its application have been all but forgotten, which is the more regrettable because Taiwan's prolonged and consistent adherence to it has also had some further, much less known, but no less important, advantages. One of them is that high interest rates render profitable and encourage the use of labour-intensive methods of production. In developing countries, where labour is plentiful but all else is scarce, that is an important advantage: it increases the employment of labour by creating more job opportunities for any given level of investment and it raises labour's share in the national product. Taiwan is unique among developing countries in that its statistically captured unemployment rate has been consistently and often much below 2 per cent throughout the entire period here under review, and that excellent record must be credited, in large part, to its high interest rate policy. Note that the unemployment so eliminated or minimized is so-called 'Marxian' (or structural) unemployment, whose presence in other developing countries is due to their manufacturing plant and equipment being of such nature and quantity that they cannot provide employment for all those who seek it, however high the effective demand for output. (That is the reason why stimulating demand has never been an effective employment policy in the developing world.)

The high demand for labour consequent upon Taiwan's encouragement and use of labour-intensive methods of production also raised wages and so labour's share in the national product. Indeed, labour's share in Taiwan's national product has steadily risen and property's share fallen over the past one and a half decades and, since wage income is both lower on average and more evenly distributed than property income, this gradual shift in incomes away from capital and in favour of labour has been the main factor in explaining the diminution over time of income inequalities in Taiwan.[8]

Having dealt with the two reasons why the choice of labour-intensive methods of production was an advantage, we can now proceed to discuss another advantage of Taiwan's high interest rate policy, which again has to do with income distribution. Every market transaction gives rise to a gain, and the way that gain is divided between the transacting parties depends on the price at which they effect the transaction. The rate of interest is the price the borrower pays the lender for the loan, and it determines the division between them of the total gain from the loan. The higher the rate of interest, the greater the lender's and the smaller the borrower's share, so that high interest rates favour the lender and limit the borrower's gain.

The man in the street tends instinctively to consider such a state of affairs reprehensible, because the word 'lender' conjures up in his mind's eye a rich capitalist and the word 'borrower' a poor wretch who borrows to stave off starvation. That imagery has its origin in medieval Europe and may still make sense in primitive agricultural communities; but the situation is very different when it comes to bank lending and borrowing in today's newly industrializing economies. There, the typical lender is a small saver, the typical borrower is the corporation, often the large corporation, so that high interest rates favour the low-income saver and limit the profits of business enterprise. Another way of putting this is to say that high interest rates transfer a large part of business profits to small savers in the form of interest on their savings, which supplements their wage and salary income. Accordingly, this is yet another factor that contributes to Taiwan's egalitarian income distribution.

One advantage of having high interest rates on savings deposits has already been dealt with: it encourages small savers to increase both their saving rate and the proportion of their savings which they put into bank deposits and so make available for productive use. Another advantage is that it limits profits, which restrains the rate at which the size of the individual enterprise grows. As already shown, the individual firm's size in Taiwan has grown very slowly and stayed small, and this has helped to maintain competition. Yet another advantage of small firms is that they render the always painful adaptation of the economy to changing circumstances a little more feasible and bearable. Right now, the world economy is going through a major convulsion that calls for the scaling down of some established industries and the creation and expansion of new ones. Examples abound in the United States, Britain, Western Germany and elsewhere of the great and successful resistance large firms can put up to the necessary cutting down of their operations, thereby prolonging the agony but not obviating the necessity of change. High bankruptcy rates in Taiwan suggest that there, too, changes in the pattern and scale of manufacture are called for and painful, but that the small size of the average firm speeds up and facilitates the adjustment process. The subject will be discussed further at the end of this paper.

A final potential advantage of limited profits, mentioned here only for completeness' sake, is their tendency to keep entrepreneurs on their toes and so maintain their efficiency and initiative. Too high and secure profits, whether assured by monopoly advantage or by government protection, can destroy entrepreneurial drive. In America, Europe and Latin America, failure to innovate, inefficiency and generally poor economic performance have often been traced to that factor; but Korean businessmen, thanks perhaps to their Chinese cultural background, seem to be immune. At least, there is no evidence that the large profits and fast accumulation of great fortunes that Korea's economic policies made possible had any unfavourable effects on the drive, stamina and efficiency of Korea's businessmen.

The philosophy behind Korea's economic policies
The main difference between Korea's and Taiwan's economic policies lies neither in their aims nor in their achievements, but in the much more forceful and aggressive spirit with which Korea's policy makers pursued their aims. In a private enterprise economy, of course, profit and self-interest are the main motivations of economic behaviour, and government's main policy tool is the set of incentives and disincentives with whose aid it tries selectively to change the thrust of the profit motive in both Korea and Taiwan, but the difference in the number and nature of inducements used and in the forcefulness with which they are applied is very great.

Just about every industrializing country publishes periodically an economic plan, which sets forth the government's intentions for its own expenditure on infrastructure and other government projects, together with projections of the private sector's future development. Those projections can be anything, from rough guesses to carefully worked out sectoral patterns of compatible and feasible growth, which government hopes for, or expects to occur, or encourages, either by merely announcing it or by the use of more or less effective incentives and disincentives. Accordingly, one cannot tell just by the publication of an economic plan and its wording the extent of government's influence and control over economic affairs. Nor can one tell by the discrepancy between plan and achievement, which was equally great in Taiwan and Korea, and alike also in that achievement almost invariably exceeded the plan by a wide margin.

There is, however, plenty of other evidence to show that, during the period here considered, which largely coincides with the Park regime,[9] government influence over economic affairs was very much greater and more detailed in Korea than in Taiwan. The machinery of economic planning was larger, more elaborate, more centrally and prominently placed in the Korean government's administrative hierarchy, and well provided with channels of communication for consultation with business. The prime minister chaired the Central Economic Committee and the chairman of the Economic Planning Board held the rank of deputy prime minister. A Product Evaluation Board engaged in market research and provided rate-of-return and profitability estimates for the Economic Planning Board, which also acquired an impressively large and competent research arm with the founding of the Korea Development Institute. Close contact between government officials, researchers and private business was maintained in monthly export promotion meetings and specialized working groups. None of this seems to have had a counterpart in Taiwan.

Korean policy makers have, also until recently, made extensive and forceful use of a wide range of incentives, not only of a general but also of a particularistic nature, designed to ensure private industry's close compliance with their plans. The main incentive is differential access to credit and concessionary cost of credit. Both countries have for many years granted credit at lower cost to approved industries, but the criteria that qualify a borrower for low-cost credit tend to be more generally defined in Taiwan than in Korea, and the cost concession is typically twice or even three times greater in Korea than it is in Taiwan. Moreover, in view of Korea's generally lower average interest rates and inflationary climate, the real interest cost of such concessionary loans in Korea has often been zero or even negative. Most of Korea's concessionary loans are given by specialized banks and non-bank financial institutions, many of which are under the direct control of the minister of finance (rather than the Bank of Korea). Furthermore, in Korea, borrowing abroad by private firms also hinges on express authorization by government.

On the disincentive side, firms that fail to do what government wants them to do often find that their loan applications are ignored or their outstanding loans fail to be renewed. These are extremely effective instruments in a country in which business relies on bank credit as heavily as it does in Korea. Over the past ten years, from 1972 to 1981, the sum of the current and fixed liabilities of Korean manufacturing enterprises expressed as a percentage of their net worth was 364 per cent – more than twice as high as in Taiwan and four times as high as in the United States. Moreover, almost two-thirds of that debt was short-term (current liabilities), which makes the profitability, even the very survival, of manufacturing firms depend greatly on interest rates, the banks' willingness to prolong expiring short-term loans, and consequently on the goodwill of government, which owns and controls the banks.

Differences between the two countries' use of tax incentives are very similar. A five-year tax holiday for approved investments, remission of duties on imported inputs into export production and exemption of exports from indirect taxes are standard in both countries, but Korea also provides an assortment of inducements for export and for investment in specified industries in the form of lower rates of profits tax and very generous depreciation allowances and wastage allowances. On the disincentive side, the tax returns of Korean firms that do not toe the line drawn by government are said to be subject to especially careful scrutiny.

In short, the Korean authorities have a very strong control over decision making by private business, because 'it does not take a Korean firm long to learn that it will 'get along' best by 'going along'."[10] Control is greatly facilitated by frequent personal contact between government officials and businessmen, which is made easy because production is concentrated in relatively few firms. Such concentration, in turn, is one of the results of Korea's substantial credit and tax concessions, because they have enabled the firms that went along with the government's economic plans and made the investments called for in those plans to make very large profits, whose accumulation and reinvestment over the years explains their very fast growth.

Mention has already been made of the much larger size of the average firm in Korea than in Taiwan; and Korea, a relatively small country of 38 million people, has conglomerates that are huge by any standard. The 20 largest Korean conglomerates are responsible for producing half the value added in manufacturing; and the four largest (Hyundai, Sam Sung, Daewoo and Lucky) each had an annual gross turnover between US$5 and 10 billion in 1981. Even the smallest of them had a larger turnover than the gross sales of Taiwan's 10 largest companies combined! As remarkable as the size of these companies is the speed with which they have grown from very small beginnings. The oldest and largest, Hyundai, which today employs 150 000 workers, lists 43 overseas offices on five continents and has gross sales of US$10 billion, started out in 1950 as a small construction and car repair shop.

The fast growth of these companies to great size, thanks to government's generous credit and tax incentives, must have played an important part in increasing the inequality of incomes during the 1970s and it has had or could have had other untoward consequences as well. The diminished resilience of an economy when individual firms grow to excessive size has already been alluded to. Another potential danger of the excessively large size of business firms is that they may wield excessive influence over government policy. Observers generally agree, however, that the Korean government definitely has the upper hand, at least as far as determining the direction in which the economy is going. Problems created by large size and insufficient competition in the private sector that may well arise in the future are discussed in the last section of this paper.

Agriculture

Taiwan and Korea are the world's second and third most densely populated countries (after Bangladesh) and both of them have poor soil, of which only a quarter is arable in Taiwan and slightly less (22 per cent) in Korea. Intense cultivation, however, goes a long way in both countries to compensate for the scarcity and poverty of arable land. Furthermore, in Taiwan, the subtropical climate renders double cropping, in the south even triple cropping, possible, thereby considerably increasing the utilization of land, labour, farm machinery and infrastructural facilities. Indeed, the increased practice of multiple cropping has been an important element of agricultural development; and Taiwan's multiple-cropping index had already risen to almost 190 per cent by 1964.[11] In Korea's less favourable climate, double cropping is made possible only by alternating rice with barley (an unpopular food); and the multiple-cropping index has not risen above 140 per cent.

Agricultural experiment research stations, a network of extension offices, the provision of inputs (seed and fertilizer) in kind, lending of equipment, organization of cooperative societies both for marketing and for the distribution of credit and fertilizer, and the building of an infrastructure of roads, railroads and harbours were instituted by the Japanese during the colonial period; and the Japanese seem to have concentrated especially on Taiwan, where the climate was more favourable, colonial rule lasted longer (50 years) and rulers and ruled got along somewhat better than in Korea.

World War II in Taiwan and, more severely, the Korean War in Korea destroyed much of the infrastructure, lowering farm output by 36 per cent in Taiwan and 60 per cent in Korea. Taiwan's agriculture had just about recovered by the time the Korean War ended, while Korea's was still in shambles. From that time onwards, the average annual growth rate of the two countries' farm output was almost the same: 5 per cent until 1965 and 3 per cent subsequently in Korea, 5.1 per cent up to 1965 and 2.8 per cent since then in Taiwan. Accordingly, the two countries were equally successful in rebuilding and expanding their farm output, but Korea had to offset a much greater war devastation and a later start.

That is why Korea had almost but not quite managed to eliminate her large agricultural import surplus even by the end of our period (1981). Taiwan, on the other hand, achieved a sizable export surplus on farm products before 1965, which then declined and changed into a deficit by 1973, owing to a shift in production from rice to livestock, vegetables and fruit. The shift was prompted by the rising dietary standards of an increasingly affluent population and also by the hidden but substantial tax on rice, although that was replaced by a subsidy by the mid-1970s. As a result of that shift, and as a result also of the expanding export market for delicacies like mushrooms and asparagus, rice and other staples make up less than 40 per cent of Taiwan's farm output today, while livestock alone constitutes 36 per cent. Hence the greatly increased demand for imported animal feed, which explains Taiwan's trade deficit on farm products. (Taiwan still has an export surplus in human food; it is imports of fodder and lumber that turn the scales and account for its import surplus in agriculture.) In Korea, on the other hand, livestock is a mere 6 per cent of farm output and food grains still constitute 80 per cent of the national diet.

In short, Taiwan's growing trade deficit in farm products signifies not decline but progress – though more progress in an increasingly affluent public's demand for more sophistication, variety and high quality in its diet than in agriculture's ability to meet that demand, given the limited quantity of land and the competing demands on the agricultural labour force. For, despite the higher value of its farm output, Taiwan employs a much smaller proportion of its labour force on the farm than Korea. Farm families constitute much the same proportion of the population in Taiwan (29.8 per cent) as in Korea (28.4 per cent), but the percentage of the labour force employed on farms is only 19.5 per cent in Taiwan, compared to 34 per cent in Korea. The explanation is that many members of Taiwan's farm families commute on a full-time, part-time or seasonal basis to non-farm jobs in manufacturing, teaching and administration, so that almost three-quarters (72.7 per cent) of the average farm family's income comes from non-farm employment, whereas in Korea, the non-farm income of farm families is only about 20 per cent of their total income.

That situation has come about spontaneously. High urban wages have increasingly persuaded new manufacturing business to locate in rural areas, and short distances, good roads (72 per cent are paved), good public transport and the possession of motorcycles have induced members of farm families to commute to those new jobs rather than to move. An important consequence has been the raising of farm households' incomes to a par with urban incomes. This is an important part of the explanation of Taiwan's good income distribution; and it is something that many countries have striven for but few achieved.

Korea tried to bring about a similar situation by offering tax advantages to firms locating in rural areas, but found it easier to persuade industry to move to the countryside than members of farm households to take employment in those industries. Some workers – including urban workers! – have moved to the vicinity of rural factories but disappointingly few commute to those factories. The reasons for the policy's failure are not fully known: they probably have to do with transport problems in a country more highly centralized than Taiwan, with much poorer roads (only 32 per cent paved), inadequate bus transport, a climate that prevents commuting by motorcycle or bicycle during much of the year and frequent curfews after dark. (The last is an important impediment to rural commuting in a country with a working week almost 60 hours long and a cultural tradition of socializing with fellow workers after work.)[12] Nevertheless, Korea too brought farm-family incomes onto a par with urban wages but in a much more costly way: by paying farmers a high price for rice and barley, which is then resold to consumers at a much lower price. The cost of that subsidy, paid for out of general government revenues, is estimated at about 1.4 per cent of GNP.[13]

While Taiwan enjoys the advantages of a more favourable climate and an earlier start from a higher base, thanks to which she produces proportionately more farm output with the aid of a smaller percentage of her labour force, Korean agriculture accomplished more during the period we are concerned with. Her farm output increased a little (7 per cent) faster than Taiwan's, but her labour productivity in farming increased about twice as fast. Part of that shows up in the employment statistics, according to which farm employment increased somewhat in Taiwan and declined slightly in Korea; but the more detailed studies of the two countries' agriculture show that, at least during the 1965–75 period, the number of man-days worked in farming fell at an average annual rate of 3 per cent in Korea, at not quite two-thirds of 1 per cent in Taiwan. The average annual rise in labour productivity during that period is estimated at 2.78 per cent in Taiwan and at 5.65 per cent in Korea. What accounts for the difference?

In Korea, the great rise in the productivity of farm labour is usually attributed to the great increase in the application of chemical fertilizers, by over 125 per cent between 1965 and 1975. In Taiwan, fertilizer use increased 60 per cent over the same period. Similarly, Korea's stock of fixed capital in farming increased by 183 per cent during that period, compared to an estimated 77 per cent in Taiwan. Finally, the rise in the value of Taiwan's farm output was partly due to Taiwan's shifting production from standard crops to much higher priced (and higher value added!) livestock, vegetables, fruits and mushrooms – all of which are more labour-intensive than rice and other standard crops.[14]

Export promotion

Fast economic growth in both countries began with the 1960s and was what is called 'export-led growth' because its driving force seemed to be the exceptionally fast expansion of the export of manufactures, explained in turn by the adoption of export-promotion policies. However, since those policies consisted of little more than the removal or offsetting of man-made obstacles to international trade, one cannot understand why they were so successful without knowing something about the policies and the situation they replaced.

The classic and almost universally adopted development policy of the immediate postwar years was import substitution: encouragement through import restrictions and tax concessions of the domestic manufacture of goods previously imported. The main aim of that policy was increased self-sufficiency and diminished dependence on the vagaries of world trade, but it was hoped that productivity and total output would also grow in the process. Increased self-sufficiency seemed eminently desirable in the light of the experience of the depressed 1930s, when the prices of the poor countries' primary product exports fell drastically in relation to the prices of their manufactured imports, and perhaps even more desirable during World War II, when the manufactured exports of the advanced countries were simply unavailable.

Self-sufficiency, however, is a very costly and hard-to-achieve luxury, for the simple reason that whatever products a country imports are almost always those in whose manufacture that country has a comparative disadvantage. To overcome that disadvantage has proved so costly and difficult that – apart from the limited success of the simplest forms of (so-called 'primary') import substitution – the policy was a disappointment everywhere. Self-sufficiency made little headway, only little growth accompanied each country's efforts to produce what they had a disadvantage in producing and to overcome their disadvantage; and, for a final blow, what little gain in self-sufficiency they achieved seemed hardly worth having during those years of uninterrupted prosperity, continued trade liberalization and ever-expanding world trade.

The force of that argument was brought home strikingly by the experience of such city states as Singapore and Hong Kong. They were far too small even to try for self-sufficiency and had no choice but to focus on producing what they were good at producing and to exchange that for what they wanted to consume. They then found that the road they had followed for want of any other could not have been bettered. The contrast between their phenomenally fast growth and the import-substituting countries' much slower growth is a measure of the economic gains to be had by exploiting one's comparative advantage and of the costs incurred by trying to overcome one's comparative disadvantage – at least in a period when world trade conditions are favourable to the expansion of exports by new countries and new firms.

Among the large countries that had a choice between alternative policies, Taiwan and Korea were the first to recognize the gains to be had from encouraging the production for export of those products in whose manufacture they had an advantage. Beginning in the early 1960s, both of them engaged in deliberate policies of export promotion, which consisted partly in the dismantling or offsetting of previously instituted protectionist policies that discriminated against exports and partly in measures actively discriminating in favour of exports. The first set of measures comprised the remission of duties on imported inputs into export production and (in Korea) also on imported inputs into domestically produced intermediate goods used in export production; the establishment of export-processing zones and bonded factories, whose main purpose was to cut the red tape involved in the remission of such duties; and the abolition of systems of multiple exchange rates in favour of a single exchange rate which ended that overvaluation of the domestic currency which had been the hallmark of import-substitution regimes.

The second set of measures included cheap bank loans for exporters (in Taiwan about 40 per cent below the interest rate on ordinary bank loans), the remission of indirect taxes on inputs into exports and on the exports themselves, exemption from corporate income tax on a part of export earnings (in Taiwan, total exemption for 'encouraged' products whose export exceeded 50 per cent of total output) and, in Korea, export insurance and discounts on railway freight and electricity rates. The value of these practices to the exporter, expressed as a percentage of gross export receipts, is estimated at 10.7 per cent in Taiwan for 1962–76, at 8.2 per cent in Korea for 1968 (Balassa and Associates, 1982, pp. 240, 314). Roughly speaking, therefore, the effective subsidy to exports was just about the same in the two countries.

In addition, both countries used a variety of further export incentives whose value is more difficult to quantify. They include five-year tax holidays granted to foreign firms establishing manufacturing capacity in export-processing zones, accelerated depreciation on the assets of exporters, Korea's occasional cash subsidies to exporters, citations and cash awards Taiwan gave for exceptional expansion of exports and the development of new exports, the generous wastage allowance in Korea which enabled manufacturers to import duty-free inputs into exportables far in excess of the quantities actually re-exported, and the practice of allowing exporters to use all their export

earnings for the purchase of imports. Other export incentives included quality control, mostly of export goods, by Taiwan's Controls Bureau of Standards and the overseas representation and information gathering for exporters
by such public bodies as consular offices, the foreign branches of the Central
Trust of China, the China External Trade Development Council and the
Korean Trade Promotion Corporation.

Over the period 1965–81, Korea's exports, valued in United States dollars,
rose at an average annual rate of 35 per cent, Taiwan's at 27 per cent; and by
1981, the proportion of the GNP exported had risen to 33.6 per cent in Korea
and 53.5 per cent in Taiwan. Since both countries' exports have a high import
content (40 per cent in Korea, 58 per cent in Taiwan) and also because the
great expansion of exports carried with it the whole economy and rising GNP
and living standards naturally lead to rising imports, the US dollar value of
imports, propelled even further by the rise in oil prices, rose 28.7 per cent
annually in Korea and 25.6 per cent annually in Taiwan to reach, by 1981,
41.3 per cent of GNP in Korea and 52.3 per cent in Taiwan. In short, imports
rose more slowly than exports in both countries, enabling Korea greatly to
reduce her balance-of-payments deficits and Taiwan to achieve full balance-
of-payments equilibrium.

Vulnerability to world depression
Noting those figures, one cannot help asking whether Taiwan had not over-
done – or overachieved – the expansion of its foreign trade. It is natural, of
course, for a small country to be more dependent on foreign trade than for a
large one; but even after allowing for its small size, Taiwan is more dependent on foreign trade than Korea and much more so than the average country.[15]
Needless to say, there are advantages as well as disadvantages to a country's
great involvement in international trade; and I know of no objective standard
by which to weigh the benefits of the gain from trade against vulnerability to
depression abroad. There are, however, means of reducing that vulnerability
without forfeiting the gains from international specialization. One of these is
the simple expedient of spreading the risks by diversifying the nature and
direction of exports. Taiwan has done very well in that respect, having
reduced the commodity concentration of its exports from 56 per cent in 1955
to 23 per cent in 1975 and their geographical concentration from 60 per cent
to 41 per cent (Balassa and Associates, 1982, p. 314, Table 10.13). Korea has
done almost as well, with the commodity concentration of exports at 26 per
cent in 1975 and their geographical concentration at 40.8 per cent.[16]

The other way of reducing a country's exposure to depression abroad
without losing the gains from trade is to combine an open door policy to
international trade with a not-so-open door to international capital movements. That was attempted by Korea in the 1970s, apparently with success.

Most Western European countries also rebelled against having their investment activity, and with it their growth and employment and income levels,
restricted by America's restrictive high interest rate policy of the 1970s and
1980s; but they were impotent because the openness of their capital markets
prevented their pursuing an independent and less restrictive monetary policy.
Exchange control, however, enabled Korea to sustain its economy with the
aid of relatively low interest rates without risking an outflow of capital.
Indeed, Korea managed to engineer an inflow of capital while maintaining
domestic interest rates below their US level by subsidizing foreign borrowing
through the payment of the differential between low domestic and high
foreign interest rates. Taiwan (which also has exchange control) had no such
problems, because it no longer relies on capital inflows, and because its
persistently high interest rates still go hand-in-hand with even higher profit
rates.

The gain from trade and its distribution
The practical and most striking evidence of the gain from trade is the universal success of the policy of export promotion. In a more narrow, strictly static
but also more rigorous sense, the gain from trading a given commodity can
be expressed in dollar terms; and the measure of that gain is proportional to
the difference between its prices in the importing and the exporting country
before trade takes place. The gain is divided between producers, consumers
and the intermediaries between them, in proportions that depend on what the
price elasticities of demand and supply are and on how trade affects the price
of the commodity in the exporting and importing country.

When the exporter is a small country and the importing country or countries large or numerous, trade has little impact on prices in the importing
country, which means that the consumers' share in the gain becomes negligible and most of it is divided between producers and traders. The exporting
country's share in the gain therefore depends on the nationality and domicile
of the traders.

The professional literature has largely ignored or neglected the middle-
man, so we know very little about him and about his share in the gains from
trade. Yet his role is crucial. After all, it is he who discovers the difference in
price between potential export and import markets and ascertains the scope
for profitable trade. He makes potential exporters and importers aware of the
gain to be had from trade, establishes contact between them and makes all the
necessary arrangements, rendered difficult by lack of personal contact, distance, difficult communications and often a language barrier as well. When
the manufacturing firm is small, those arrangements also include the provision of financing, the procurement of inputs, arranging for transport, insurance and dealing with customs (or the remission of customs' duties). Middle-

men also keep abreast of changing prices and market conditions abroad and, by switching trade in response to them, protect domestic exporters or importers. These services require imagination, initiative, knowledge, experience, contacts and familiarity with local conditions in many countries; and all that, being valuable, has to be remunerated accordingly. No wonder if the firms that render these services are often important beneficiaries of international trade and specialization.

In the 18th and 19th centuries, when Britain was the world's main supplier of manufactures, it was Britain's wholesale merchants, not its manufacturers, who attained great wealth and power and even gave their name to the period: merchant capitalism. More recently, Japan's great economic growth and export expansion is, to a large extent, credited to its general trading companies (*sogo shoshas*); and it is they, much more than Japan's manufacturers, that attained great size, wealth and power in the process. Between 1960 and 1973, Japan's ten largest general trading companies handled half (49.9 per cent) of its exports and almost two-thirds (62.8 per cent) of its imports. By that time, however, their role in Japan's foreign trade was very much on the decline, because the large manufacturing firms, such as those in the car and electronic industries, increasingly do their own export marketing and also engage in import trade, often even beyond the importing of their own imported inputs.[17] As a result of their gradual displacement by large manufacturers in the foreign trade of their own country, the Japanese *sogo shoshas* are increasingly trying and managing to get involved in international trade between third countries.

Taiwan and Korea are prominent among those third countries, but Japanese general trading companies are not the only foreigners to handle some of their foreign trade. In Taiwan, Japanese companies are believed to have handled about 60 per cent of textile exports, but, from the late 1960s onwards, they were joined – and to some extent supplanted – by US and European importers, who set up offices in Taipei and dealt directly with local manufacturers, including many small ones. In addition, 'If the manufacturer in Taiwan was a subsidiary of a foreign company, the parent company would generally provide the marketing service. This was true, for example, of many of the electronic companies that would both have their main components supplied by the parent and return the processed and assembled goods to that parent' (Scott, 1979, p. 367).

Unfortunately, no estimates seem to be available of the total involvement of foreign traders in Taiwan's foreign trade, or of the money value of their services; but it is worth noting that the total contribution of domestic wholesale and retail traders to Taiwan's GNP has gradually but steadily declined, from 17 – 18 per cent in the mid-1950s to 12 – 13 per cent by around 1980. Since that proportion tends to be fairly stable in most countries, its secular decline in Taiwan may well be due to the secular increase of foreign trade, which crowds out domestic trade to some extent and itself makes no contribution to Taiwan's GNP when foreign companies handle it.

Korea's experience seems to have been different. Japanese general trading companies are said to have been very important in initiating, financing and arranging Korea's foreign trade in the 1960s: according to an official of one of them (Mitsui), they probably handled about half of Korea's exports. Perhaps for that very reason, the Korean government seemed to be anxious for Koreans to take over also that business and made great efforts to promote the establishment and growth of Korean general trading companies. To engage in the business of importing and exporting required a licence, the granting of which depended on the applicant's exports exceeding a progressively higher minimum value. That requirement practically forced Korean trading companies to grow fast; and it led to mergers when other means of growing failed. As a result, Korea now has ten very large general trading companies, each with many dozens of offices in foreign centres the world over, and most of them with controlling interests, not only in the shipping, insurance and banking companies that handle the ancillary services of the business of foreign trade, but often also in the firms that manufacture the exports themselves, including steel mills, shipyards, construction companies and the largest car factory – in short, most of Korea's large manufacturing plants.

Moreover, Korea's general trading companies, in contrast to Japanese *shoshas*, are heavily involved in exercising quality control and the general supervision of the manufacturing process in the case of the smaller and less reliable Korean manufacturing firms; and they are very much in the habit of ferreting out profitable export opportunities, finding the Korean firms with the appropriate manufacturing capabilities and taking the initiative in persuading and helping those firms to seize hold of such export opportunities. Also, since many of the Korean trading companies control or are closely linked with large construction firms, they are often as ready to build and equip an entire manufacturing plant on a turnkey contract as they are to deliver the products of such a plant. In short, the general trading companies of Korea, again unlike their more specialized Japanese counterparts, are engaged and willing to engage in the export of such a tremendous range of goods and services that they are a powerful force for diversifying the nature and so stabilizing the volume of the country's exports.

Statistics of the value added by Korean general trading companies do not seem to be available; but the national accounts show that the total contribution of wholesale and retail trade to GDP has risen, from the second half of the 1950s to the end of the 1970s by more than five percentage points: from an average of 11.2 per cent to an average of 16.5 per cent of GDP. What part of that substantial increase reflects the transfer of export and import business from foreign to Korean trading companies and what part is due to other factors there is no way of knowing. The subject merits further study, but what scattered information is available suggests strongly that Korea managed to capture for itself a good share of the gain from its foreign trade. Taiwan has also tried to encourage the establishment and growth of indigenous general trading companies, but with very poor success. In 1981, her five largest trading companies transacted a mere 1 per cent of the country's exports and barely 0.25 per cent of its total imports.

Overall growth

So far, export promotion and its successful outcome, export expansion, have been dealt with: how and why expanding exports brought about a not much lesser expansion of the two countries' entire economies as well remain to be seen. It is true that the value of exports had risen to equal half of Taiwan's and a third of Korea's GNP; but those figures refer to gross exports, a large part of which constitutes the re-export of imported inputs. When one subtracts imported inputs from gross exports, one obtains the value of net exports, which turns out to be approximately a fifth of the GNP in each country. The remaining four-fifths of GNP was destined for domestic use, and the question is how and why also that much larger part of total output grew at such an unprecedented rate.

Growth means increased production, due partly to a growing labour force or its increased utilization, partly to the increased productivity of labour. The latter is a more important source of growth, because it is the main basis of the rise in the level of living. Employment was growing in both countries, about twice as fast as population, at an annual rate of 5 per cent in Taiwan, 3.4 per cent in Korea. Labour productivity was growing at an annual rate of 4.2 per cent in Taiwan and 5.1 per cent in Korea. Their combined effect on the real GDP was an average annual growth of 9.4 per cent in Taiwan and 8.6 per cent in Korea, or, on a per capita basis, 6.9 per cent in Taiwan and 6.7 per cent in Korea (see Table 10.1).

Exports increase productivity, because the gain from trade means that labour engaged in producing exports enables the country to obtain in exchange more and better imports than if the same labour were engaged, instead, in producing at home the goods now imported. Accordingly, a parallel expansion of exports and imports increased labour productivity in the general sense of increasing the quantity and quality of goods and services obtained per unit of labour. Labour productivity, however, has also been increasing in the narrower, engineering and technical sense; and there were at least two ways in which export expansion stimulated the rise in labour productivity in that sense too.

First of all, export expansion called for large investments in additional productive capacity in the export industries, which made it possible to reap economies of scale by putting into practice all the new techniques, economical methods of production and better quality control that the export manufacturers learned from their foreign competitors. That benefited not only exports but the domestic consumers of exports as well.

Second, the new techniques, approaches and habits of thought adopted by the export industries were easy to transfer to other industries and economic sectors as soon as their needs for additional productive capacity and investment provided an opportunity to do so. That opportunity was also provided by the expansion of exports because it greatly increased effective demand for domestic output. The booming export industries increased their own demand for intermediate inputs produced by other industries; and the great increase in the income they generated and paid out to their employees, owners and stockholders increased consumers' demand as well. The increase in consumers' demand was especially great owing to the labour-intensive nature of the export industries.

The same high labour intensity of Taiwan's and Korea's rapidly expanding exports also accounts for the two countries' very low and secularly declining unemployment rates – a unique accomplishment among developing countries. Korea, with unemployment rates around 3 to 4 per cent, did less well in that respect than Taiwan, where unemployment fell to 2 per cent and lower, perhaps because of Korea's switch to more capital-intensive industries in the 1970s.

The expansion of the two countries' labour-intensive export industries until the 1970s and Taiwan's also since then had yet another beneficial effect: it increased the earnings of labour and so improved the distribution of income. In Taiwan the statistics show a shift of income from capital to labour among non-farm households and a consequent reduction of inequalities in the overall distribution of income between 1964 and 1978, the period for which the requisite statistics have been collected. In Korea, too, inequalities of income declined from 1965 to 1970, but increased slightly thereafter – probably as the result partly of the switch to capital-intensive industries already mentioned, and partly of the greatly increased inequalities in the distribution of property income, which was closely connected with that change-over.

Equitable income distribution favoured the expansion of effective demand and tended to concentrate it on domestically produced goods. The increase in domestic demand for domestic goods in turn called for investment which not only created additional productive capacity and employment opportunities but, by providing an opportunity for innovation and modernization, led to increasing labour productivity as well.

Investment
The average proportion of GNP devoted to gross domestic capital formation
in Taiwan was, at 28.4 per cent, only a little higher than Korea's 26.5 per
cent; but it may have been considerably more conducive to increasing productivity and productive capacity. Industrialization in Korea was accompanied by a mass migration from rural to urban areas, causing the urban population as a share of the total population to rise from 24 per cent in 1955 to 48
per cent in 1975. To accommodate such mass migration required a lot of
investment in new housing, new schools, new shopping facilities and other
infrastructure, which did not add to productivity and productive capacity.
Taiwan was much more fortunate in that respect: although its manufacturing
sector grew faster than Korea's during the same period, the migration into the
cities added only 75 per cent to their share in the total population,[18] because
new firms and industries, attracted by lower rural wages, increasingly settled
in rural areas. The proportion of workers employed in manufacturing who
lived in rural areas as part of farm households and commuted daily on a
seasonal or full-time basis grew steadily and constituted over half of the
workforce by the mid-1960s. That must have meant substantial savings in
housing and infrastructure investment. Over the 16-year period here considered, government investment, which is largely infrastructure, absorbed only
11.7 per cent and residential construction only 10.4 per cent of gross investment in Taiwan, as against 14.2 per cent and 13.4 per cent in Korea,[19] leaving
a substantially larger part of Taiwan's investible resources for public and
private enterprises to invest in productive capacity.

As already mentioned, Korea also tried, through the offer of tax incentives,
to induce manufacturing enterprises to settle in rural areas, but was more
successful with employers than with their employees. Members of farm
households, rather than stay at home and commute to non-farm jobs, mi-
grated to the cities in much larger numbers than in Taiwan (see above).

Sources of investible funds
Much remains to be said about the different directions into which investible
funds were channelled in the two countries, but it will be better said as part of
a discussion of the way in which funds became available. Taiwan financed its
entire gross domestic capital formation from 1965 to 1981 out of domestic
savings; as a matter of fact, its domestic saving rate, which averaged 28.7 per
cent of GNP, marginally exceeded the investment rate of 28.4 per cent and
even allowed for a small export of capital. Korea, on the other hand, financed
less than two-thirds of its 26.5 per cent average investment out of a domestic
saving rate that averaged only 18.6 per cent: the remainder was financed by
capital imports, of which a third was aid, not quite two-thirds loans and a
negligible proportion foreign direct investment.[20]

Why was domestic saving in Korea so much lower than in Taiwan? Depreciation allowances in Korea, at 7.3 per cent of GNP, were marginally higher than Taiwan's 7.2 per cent; and so was governmental saving: 5.8 per cent in Korea as against 5.6 per cent in Taiwan. On the other hand, net corporate saving of 2.3 per cent in Korea was much lower than Taiwan's 4 per cent; and the discrepancy was even greater between the personal saving rate of households: 5.4 per cent in Korea and 12.1 per cent in Taiwan.

The lower saving rate of Korean corporations seems to be largely explained by the informal pressure government put on firms to pay high dividends in an attempt to develop the stock market, and by the similarly motivated Korean system of taxes that rendered shareholders liable for income tax not only on dividends but also on half of the retained earnings of the corporations in which they held stock.[21] Corporate retained earnings, which averaged 75 per cent of after-tax profits in the first four years of the 1960s, went down to an average of 56 per cent of profits in the 1970s, presumably as a result of those pressures and policies, and that change explains most of the discrepancy between Korea's and Taiwan's corporate savings rate.[22]

In sum, low corporate saving in Korea seems to be the direct result of government's attempt to encourage personal savings by providing and rendering attractive yet another asset, corporate stocks, into which the individual saver can put his earnings. The attempt, however, was unsuccessful. To judge by the value of stocks issued and its relation to GNP, Korea's stock market is even more insignificant as a source of funds than Taiwan's: moreover, household saving, as already noted, is also much lower in Korea.

Household saving
It is customary to express the rate of household saving as a percentage, not of the gross national product, but of consumers' disposable income. The personal saving rate so expressed averaged 7.6 per cent in Korea, 17.6 per cent in Taiwan. The difference between those figures is tremendous; but surprisingly enough, no one seems ever to have tried to explain it. The voluminous literature on Korea's economic performance is full of discussions and explanations of why Korea's saving rate has been so very high in recent years; there is no word anywhere to explain why it has been so very low – yet low it seems when contrasted to the saving rate of Taiwan. Similarly, one will look in vain for an explanation of Taiwan's very high saving rate. The closest one comes are the various explanations offered to account for Japan's comparably high personal saving rate; but they turn out not to be very helpful in explaining the great discrepancy between Taiwan's and Korea's personal saving rates.

According to the standard American theoretical explanation, the so-called 'life-cycle hypothesis', saving is generated by the growth of population and the rise in the standard of living; and net positive saving is proportional to their combined growth rates. The latter is half a percentage point higher in Taiwan than in Korea, which would explain approximately 1.5 percentage points of the 10 percentage points discrepancy between the two countries' personal saving rate.[23] That is very little; and besides, recent empirical research increasingly discredits the theory.

There are more down-to-earth explanations in Japan of the Japanese situation. The two simplest and most often advanced are insufficiency of social security benefits, which forces people to save more for their old age, and the limited availability of consumer credit and mortgage loans, which renders it difficult for people without accumulated savings to dissave. The two arguments apply to Taiwan and to Korea every bit as much as they apply to Japan, but since they apply equally to both countries, they cannot very well explain why their savings rates are so very different.[24]

Equally unhelpful is the next explanation of Japan's high saving rate: the high proportion of older income earners in the population, who, according to the statistics, save a larger percentage of their earnings than others with the same income. It so happens that the age distribution of the employed population is almost identical in Korea and Taiwan, so this factor cannot account for the discrepancy between their saving rates either.

Yet another often cited explanation of Japan's high saving rate is the high proportion of individual proprietorships (unincorporated enterprises) among households. The national account statistics do not separate the savings of unincorporated enterprises from those of wage- and salary-earners; and since the former's saving rate is believed to be quite a bit higher than the latter's, a high proportion of small businessmen among households would explain a high overall household saving rate.

In that respect, there is a difference between Korea and Taiwan. The average Korean manufacturer with more than four employees[25] employs 69 people on average, as compared to 35 in Taiwan, which implies that the number of independent manufacturing establishments in Taiwan is twice as large as it would be if their average size equalled that of Korean establishments. Accordingly, if Taiwan resembled Korea in that respect, it would have only 35 000 independent manufacturing firms instead of the 70 000 it actually has. These 35 000 extra individual proprietorships seem like a large number, but they represent hardly more than 1 per cent of Taiwan's 3 million households. Such a small difference between the two countries in the proportion of households headed by parsimonious businessmen instead of spendthrift employees undoubtedly explains a part, but probably only a small part, of the very great difference between their overall saving rate.[26] It should also be noted that the difference between Taiwan and Korea in the proportion of businessmen households in other sectors of the economy is much smaller (for example, in retailing) or even goes the other way around (in farming)!

Many consider the most important explanation of Japan's high personal saving rate to be the high proportion of temporary income in total income, because people tend to save a higher percentage of temporary than of permanent income. In Japan, half-yearly bonus payments are an important part of total wage and salary payments; they have been steadily increasing in relative importance over the years and by now often amount to one-third of the annual wage or salary.

Taiwan and Korea share Japan's bonus wage system for non-agricultural industries, although their bonus payments are much smaller. The two semi-annual payments together average only two month's wages (or 14.2 per cent) of the total annual wage. Those averages are very similar in the two countries and, at least in Taiwan, where annual data have been available since 1972, show only a very small upward trend. Non-farm employment, however, has increased relative to farm employment in both countries – and more so in Taiwan, where it now comprises 72 per cent of the labour force, as against only 66 per cent in Korea. That may well account for a part of the difference between the two countries' saving rates; but probably only for a very small part. For the rest, other, less conventional, explanations must be sought.

One of these may be the very high expenditure of Korean parents on their children's education, explained partly by the inadequacy of public expenditure on education, which is provided free only up to junior high school level. As a proportion of household income, private expenditures on education averaged 7 per cent in Korea, almost as much as the personal saving rate and more than four times the US percentage. Unfortunately, comparable data seem to be unavailable in Taiwan, but there private expenditure on education is probably much lower.[27]

Another rather simple explanation of the difference in saving rates is that Koreans, being poorer, cannot afford to save as much as the more affluent Taiwanese. That sounds all the more plausible when one considers that the averages of the two countries' saving rates already quoted hide a fairly steady secular increase from about 12 per cent to about 21 per cent in Taiwan, which closely parallels the country's increasing affluence, and in Korea a somewhat faster but very irregular increase, with great ups and downs between a low 0.2 per cent and a high 15 per cent annual saving rate.

Plausible as it sounds, the explanation is distrusted by most economists because they believe that saving is mainly motivated by the need to take care of one's old age, a need just as strong among the poor as it is among the rich: and they can point to the complete lack of evidence of any correlation between saving rates and affluence in the industrial countries, where saving statistics are most reliable. That argument, however, together with the statistical evidence behind it, pertains to modern capitalist societies, in which mature persons are held responsible for their own welfare, both in the present and in their future old age. That was not always so, because in most primitive societies the children (eldest sons according to the Confucian ethic) took care of their parents in their old age. Accordingly, when economic development goes hand-in-hand with social change and the move from extended to nuclear families, it is bound to necessitate personal savings and so to raise the personal saving rate.

Such change, however, does not happen from one year to another, but is bound to be a very slow, very gradual process, and that for two reasons. To begin with, all change in established social institutions and deeply ingrained habits is always a very slow progression, initiated by the most innovating and enterprising classes of society and spreading slowly through different social layers toward the more tradition-bound. Further, to be able to afford to save up for one's and one's wife's old age, one must be either well-to-do or free from financial obligations toward parents and older or disabled relatives who traditionally look to one for support.

In other words, causality runs both ways: personal savings free people from having to rely on their children's or relatives' support in their old age: but they themselves must also be free from old parents and relatives or the obligation to support them in order to be able to afford saving up for their own old age. That circular relationship is a vicious (or virtuous?) circle and makes it very hard to break out of the age-old tradition that views the extended family as the economic and social unit and imposes on its working members a moral obligation to support all those other members who are too young, too old, or too decrepit to earn their living. Accordingly, it requires especially favourable circumstances to initiate and sustain the move from the extended to the nuclear family and the displacement of sons and relatives by accumulated savings as the source of old people's livelihood. Affluence is one such circumstance; institutions that render saving easy, safe and attractive are another.

That brings us to the second unconventional explanation of high personal saving: high real rates of interest on savings deposits. This again is one of those explanations that seem to be simple common sense to the layman, but are distrusted by the economist. And here, again, his distrust is based partly on the lack of empirical evidence of correlation between interest rates and saving rates, and partly on the theoretical idea that, if survival in retirement were the main purpose of people's saving, higher interest rates would lead not to more but less saving, because the higher the interest, the less needs to be saved in order to secure a given sum or annuity for the future.

The fault with this reasoning is once again that it is anchored in the narrow institutional framework of modern capitalist society, which looks upon saving more or saving less as the only alternative ways available in which to provide for one's retirement. In countries like Taiwan and Korea, however, which are in the course of social and economic transformation, the individual's choice is the much broader one between relying on his family and relying on his own accumulated savings as the proper means of taking care of his old age: and a higher real rate of return on savings is bound to influence that choice in favour of saving.

As early as 1950, Taiwan introduced a monetary policy whose key feature was enticingly high real rates of interest on savings deposits, and Taiwan stuck to that policy consistently for over 30 years, with only a single short lapse in 1974. The steady, seven fold rise in the personal saving rate in Taiwan, from 3 per cent of the disposable income in 1952 to 21 per cent in 1980, may well have been due largely to the continued attractiveness of savings deposits as a means of assuring an independent and comfortable old age.

Korea adopted the same monetary policy 15 years later, in 1965 and, because it was hard to reconcile with governmental control over private investment through concessionary loans, which the Korean government was anxious to retain, the monetary policy of 1965 was gradually eroded over the next six years and came to an end by 1971. From then onwards, the real rate of interest on savings deposits fluctuated wildly, alternating between positive levels (in 1973 and 1977/8) and negative levels (in 1974/5 and 1980/81), hovering near zero in-between (in 1972, 1976 and 1979).[28] That was hardly an inducement for the average Korean to abandon his traditional reliance on family and children in favour of the modern way of taking care of his old age through personal savings.

What could well be the main explanation of the great difference between the two countries' personal saving rates has been left to the end, partly because its statistical verification and quantification is ruled out by its very nature: the need for personal savings for making oneself independent by starting one's own business. This is related to but somewhat different from the high propensity to save of already established businessmen; here the concern is with the savings of those who wish to become businessmen.

People start their own business, not only to get a high return on their savings, but also and perhaps mainly because they prefer being their own boss, standing on their own feet and proving their ability by putting to good use their wits, skills, intuition and knowledge of the world and people. In short, running one's own business is also a game of skill and chance, played for high stakes, and self-satisfying quite apart from the expectation of monetary gain. If that assessment of the independent businessman's motivations is right, he will regard his business not only as a good repository of his savings, but also as a good reason to save – and to save more than he would if he had no business to put his savings into!

This motive for saving differentiates very strongly between Taiwan and Korea. As already mentioned, Taiwan's manufacturing sector grew largely as a result of the fast growth in the number of its manufacturing companies. Between 1966 and 1976, 41 808 new manufacturing enterprises were created, adding more than 150 per cent to the number of such enterprises (27 709) already in existence in 1966. That is an average annual increase of 9.6 per cent, which is more than one-half as great as the 17.8 per cent annual increase in total manufacturing production. All that is very different from what happened in Korea, where manufacturing production over the same period increased at an average annual rate of 22.7 per cent, but the number of manufacturing companies rose at the very small annual rate of 0.9 per cent.[29]

The explanation of this striking difference between the two countries' ways of growing is simple. In Taiwan, the small size of the average firm and the large number of very small firms must have made it feasible – and seem feasible! – for newcomers to establish themselves on a modest scale with small initial investments. In Korea, the prevalence of much larger firms must have discouraged newcomers and made it harder for them to enter the market on a very small scale; moreover, the policy of encouraging capital formation through the granting of loans on concessionary terms *to already established firms* actively discriminated in favour of growth through the increasing size (rather than the increasing number) of firms. Accordingly, growth Taiwanese-style kept business firms small and encouraged personal saving by the newly entering or about-to-enter small businessmen; growth Korean-style discouraged new entrants and their saving, and made it easy for established firms to grow without generating their own savings.

The difference between the two countries' very different ways of expanding their manufacturing capacity and output also appears in their statistics. Capital formation financed by bank loans and by bonds issued and sold in financial markets shows up as an increase in indebtedness: the statistics reveal no increase in indebtedness when capital formation is financed by the issuing of stock, out of a firm's own undistributed savings, out of the personal savings of someone starting his own firm, or out of what he borrows in the unorganized capital market. The most widely used index of indebtedness is the debt ratio: the sum of fixed and current liabilities expressed as a percentage of the firm's net worth, reproduced in Figure 10.1 for Korea, Taiwan and the United States. The very low indebtedness of American manufacturing firms is easily explained by the importance of the New York stock market as a source of funds for investment. The stock market is unimportant in Korea and Taiwan, but Taiwanese firms are half as heavily indebted as Koreans, presumably because more than half of their new industrial capacity consists of small firms newly established by individual proprietors and financed out of their and their family's personal

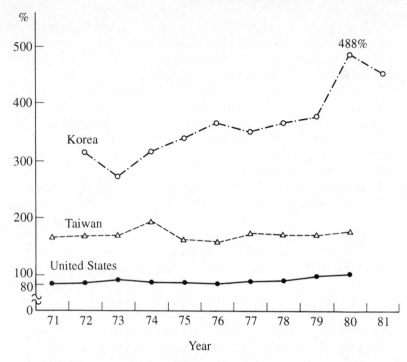

Source: Bank of Korea (1982), pp. 74, 97, 492, 530.

Figure 10.1   *Debt ratios in manufacturing: sum of fixed and current*
liabilities as percentage of net worth

savings, supplemented when necessary by loans from friends and from the
unorganized curb market.

To sum up the arguments of this long section, the much greater importance
of household saving in Taiwan has a number of probable explanations: the
slightly faster growth of Taiwan's GNP; the slightly faster increase in the
proportion of its labour force receiving part of its income in the form of
bonuses; people's lesser spending and need to spend on education; the greater
proportion of people saving up to establish independent businesses; the greater
number of businessmen saving up to enlarge their already established independent businesses; and people's greater willingness to save up for their old
age, owing partly to their greater affluence and partly to the more secure and
higher returns on their accumulated savings.

The above arguments were phrased as explanations of Taiwan's high personal saving rate, but several of them could easily be reworded as explanations of Korea's low personal saving rate. Taiwan's saving rate is the excep-

tional one, being the second highest (after Japan's) in the Western world; on the other hand, Korea would need a much higher personal saving rate in order to continue its high growth rate in the 1980s, with their much less accommodating international financial markets.

Forced investment and growth in Korea

It seemed standard practice of Korean development planners always to project, aim for and actively encourage more investment than seemed feasible on the basis of expected domestic saving and expected foreign capital inflows. The hope behind that policy was that the economy would somehow accommodate itself to those overambitious plans, and that hope was usually fulfilled, very often overfulfilled. In short, the policy worked. It is essential, however, to understand exactly how and why it worked if one wants to understand the causes of Korea's chronic inflation, its disappointing domestic saving rate and its continued dependence on foreign capital.

Once a four-year-plan, or a revision of a four-year-plan, had been agreed upon and established, the Korean government encouraged investment in the desired sectors and industries by every available means, including the offer of tax concessions, credit on specially favourable terms and at specially low interest rates, and a lot of informal pressure. If the inducements set in motion a sufficient volume of investment to conform with (or even exceed) the overambitious investment plans, an excess of effective demand over the available supply was the consequence. In such disequilibrium situations, something has to give in order to restore equality between supply and demand. In the event, three things helped to restore equilibrium, mostly by raising supply, not by restricting demand. They were an increase in domestic supply, an additional inflow of foreign capital and a worsening balance of payments.

Domestic supply can respond to the increase in demand through the increased utilization of existing plant capacity. That seems to have been an important source of additional supply in Korea. Statistics of capacity utilization are unavailable, but a study based on electricity use shows that the utilization rate almost doubled between 1962 and 1971, increasing at an average annual rate of 7.2 per cent (Balassa and Associates, 1982, p. 264). Unfortunately, those estimates do not go beyond 1971, but to judge by the statistics on hours worked in industry, capacity utilization seems to have continued to increase. Korea not only has the world's longest working week (ILO, 1983) but is unique also in that the length of its working week increased, and increased substantially over time, while the working week has become shorter just about everywhere else. The utilization of plant capacity is very likely to have risen parallel to the lengthening of the working week (Figure 10.2).

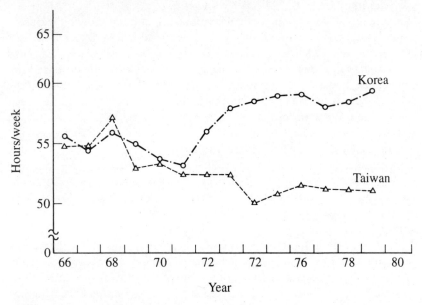

Figure 10.2 Average weekly hours worked

The inflow of foreign capital can also rise more than was originally antici-
pated and finance an additional inflow of imports to meet the excess demand.
Part of that excess demand is generated by the increase in capacity utilization, which increases the need for inputs, including imported inputs. Indeed,
balance-of-payments difficulties are the main reason for the underutilization
of existing capacity in most developing countries. In Korea, however, the
successful export drive not only relieved the foreign exchange shortage, but
increased the country's credit standing as well and so removed that obstacle
to better capacity utilization. In addition, the special inducements, such as tax
concessions, offered to investors probably also increased foreign investment.

 Finally, to the extent that these two sources of additional supply were
insufficient, as they usually were to fill the excess demand, the pressure of the
remaining excess demand raised domestic prices and, by worsening the balance of payments and so raising the price of foreign exchange, raised import
prices as well. These price increases diverted resources from consumption to
investment[30] and whoever allowed them to reduce the real value of his
purchases to below what he had originally hoped and planned for found
himself 'involuntarily financing' some of the investment that was additional
to the investment financed out of voluntary saving and foreign lending.

Korean inflation

Inflation in such a case makes a positive contribution to growth, because it forces the public to reduce its real purchases and so release resources needed for investment. This forced reduction of people's real purchases is best called 'involuntary financing' or 'forced financing', thereby avoiding the once fashionable but misleading 'forced saving'. For the term 'saving' conveys the idea of the saver setting aside something valuable for his own future use, but those whom inflation forces to reduce their real purchases have nothing to show for their sacrifice, no savings they could add to their store of assets and spend at a later date, although they involuntarily financed an investment that benefits society by improving or adding to future productive capacity and adds to some people's net worth. Indeed, the social injustice of the inflationary financing of investment, which causes the latter's benefits to accrue to others than those whose sacrifice financed it, is one of the objections to that policy.

That, in a nutshell, summarizes how an aggressive economic policy causes the economy to perform beyond its apparent capacity and accommodate the excessive demand made upon it by an overambitious investment plan. Considering that in Korea the policy worked and the overambitious projections of investment and growth were not only fulfilled but consistently overfulfilled, one is tempted to applaud and approve of that policy of forced growth. That may well be one's final verdict: but the short summary just given throws more light on the sunny than on the shady side of the picture. For an objective appraisal, one must also weigh all the undesirable side-effects and long-run repercussions of the excessive encouragement of investment and of the consequent inflation.

In addition to the social injustice of inflationary financing just mentioned, another injustice created by inflation is the reduction of the real value of debt for both debtor and creditor, which in effect redistributes real wealth from creditor to debtor – an injustice not without advantages. Another and more important bad effect already mentioned was the very low, often negative real rate of interest on savings deposits brought about by inflation. That greatly reduced the attractiveness of bank deposits to depositors, and if it is true that Korea is now in mid-transition from a traditional to a modern society, then the absence of an attractive and reliable repository for personal savings may well be the main reason for the slowness with which the saving habit is taking root and spreading in Korea.

The low domestic saving rate was an important reason both for Korea's extensive foreign borrowing and for its inflationary policies: and the resulting inflation, in its turn, must have been an important reason for the saving rate failing to rise faster and farther than it did. In short, the policy of supplementing an inadequate supply of investible funds with inflation-induced involuntary financing created a vicious circle, because it perpetuated the situation (the low domestic saving rate) that called for inflationary policies in the first place.

The well-tried and well-proven remedy of preventing the fall in real rates by raising money rates of interest in step with the inflation rate was close to hand and occasionally adopted; but since that amounted, in effect, to abandoning the whole policy of fast growth through forced capital accumulation, it was never kept very long. That alternation of inflationary with restrictive policies explains the great fluctuations in both the inflation rate and the real rate of interest, which, as mentioned earlier, may have been the root cause of the inadequacy of domestic saving.

Another undesirable effect of low and negative real rates of interest can be their supposed tendency to divert the savings of those with already well-established saving habits from more to less constructive uses. In Korea, however, this was probably not too important. The export of domestic savings (illegal in Korea) would be the most obvious form of such diversion and it is believed to have been negligible. Another channel into which savings can be diverted is real estate, whose fast-rising values throughout the period here considered must have rendered land and housing a very attractive inflation hedge. One must remember, however, that one person's spending on real estate is another person's receipt, so saving is misused only if real-estate speculation leads to excessive investment in residential construction. Investment in housing was much greater in Korea than in Taiwan, but so was the need for housing; it is very difficult therefore to assess the extent (if any) to which housing construction was excessive and prompted by people's desire for an inflation-proof repository for their savings.

Better known than the above, owing to the great political scandals connected with it, was the rechannelling of funds from banks into the unorganized credit market. Yet such rechannelling of funds seldom if ever constitutes a diversion of savings from more to less productive investment, although it can be a symptom of inefficient credit allocation in the organized credit market. That was the situation in Korea, where unduly low interest rates on bank deposits and bank loans swelled both the supply and demand for funds in the unorganized market. The reason for the first is obvious. The second happens because cheap bank loans create an excess demand for them, which must be rationed, and such rationing inevitably leads to the accommodation of some projects with low rates of return that crowd out some others with high profitability and forces them into the unorganized market. That is why a large unorganized market can be a sign of inefficiency in the organized market's allocation of investible funds.

It is desirable, of course, that every deserving project crowded out of organized markets by their inefficiency should be accommodated by the unorganized market; but to serve as a safety-valve and so relieve the inefficiency perpetrated by the organized markets is not the only useful function of the curb market. Its other, equally useful, function is to supplement the work of the organized credit market by providing small loans to small businessmen who are creditworthy but whose creditworthiness would be prohibitively expensive for large banks to investigate. Judgements of creditworthiness based on long-term personal contacts among relatives, friends and neighbours, and between small businessmen and equally small lenders or credit brokers who live nearby can be better than those based on an expensive investigation by a bank's loan officer into the credit standing of an unknown applicant. As a retailer of small loans, the unorganized market operates more efficiently and more cheaply than the small-loans window of the most efficient large bank.[31]

Once one becomes aware of the distinction between those two functions of the curb market, one also realizes that the size of the curb market cannot, by itself, indicate the inefficiency of credit allocation in the organized credit market. Only the size of the safety-valve function of the curb market could serve as such an indicator and next to nothing is known about the relative importance of the safety-valve function and the small-loans function of Korea's curb market.

Informed guesses put the share of Korea's curb market at 40 per cent at the most of the total volume of loans processed by the entire financial system. In Taiwan, where the central bank publishes annual estimates of the corresponding percentages, they had fallen from 41 per cent in 1965 to 21 per cent in 1972 and had risen again to 33 per cent by 1979/80. The curb market is no more, or not much more, important in Korea than it is in Taiwan. The function of the curb market, however, is likely to be quite different in the two countries, with the safety-valve function predominating in Korea, the small-loans function predominating in Taiwan. There are three reasons for this assumption. First of all, in Korea there is direct and striking evidence of the inefficient rationing of bank loans, which implies a corresponding need for curb market loans as a safety valve. Export producers in Korea had automatic access, at a concessionary 6 per cent per annum interest cost, to loans much above their needs, a part of which they were able to relend in the curb market at an interest of 24 to 30 per cent per annum, giving export producers a subsidy amounting to 4.5 per cent of the value of their exports.[32]

Secondly, since Taiwan has very many more small firms than Korea, the small-loans function of its curb market is bound to be commensurately more important than the small-loans function of Korea's curb market. Finally, the difference seems to be reflected also by the very different attitude officials in the two countries have to their respective curb markets. While, in Korea, the authorities are making efforts to starve the unorganized market of funds by attracting them into the banking system, in Taiwan their much more matter-of-fact attitude seems to imply recognition of the valuable function performed by that sector of the credit market.

The oil crisis
Social injustice, discouragement of domestic saving, reduced efficiency in the allocation of credit, and greater need of foreign loans were the main side-effects of inflationary finance. For completeness' sake, however, one must add to the list the unfortunate tendency of inflation to engender inflationary expectations and so render inflation harder to contain and the economy more inflation-prone. The oil crises, for example, and the worldwide inflation they created, must have had much the same inflationary impact on Taiwan and Korea: their governments, when they fought inflation, fought it in the same way and with the same weapons, but Taiwan, thanks presumably to its greater past stability, accomplished more, faster and at lower cost.

The first oil price increase led within a year (1974) to a 40 per cent rise in the wholesale price index in both countries. Korea, interested in growth not stability, did nothing about it, allowing prices to rise another 40 per cent the next year, but managing to step up the growth rate of its real GNP from an annual average of 9 per cent in the early 1970s to an average 10.8 per cent from 1975 to 1979.[33] Taiwan, putting stability first, raised interest rates and restricted credit and, while this slowed the growth of real GNP to 1.1 per cent in 1974, it not only eliminated inflation but, by 1975, rolled prices back by 5 per cent. From then on, Taiwan managed to keep inflation within reasonable limits while maintaining a 9.6 per cent annual rate of real GNP growth between 1975 and 1981.

The second oil price increase, coming on top of an already inflationary situation created by devaluation and the investment policy of the late 1970s (see below), again raised Korea's inflation rate to almost 40 per cent by 1979, but by that time (after President Park's assassination) Korea's new government was as stability-minded as Taiwan's and mounted much the same restrictive policies with which Taiwan responded to the first oil price increase. Indeed, Korea raised interest rates by 5 per cent at the beginning of 1980, a more drastic tightening of the monetary screws than Taiwan's 3.5 interest rate increase six years earlier. Moreover, investment in Korea was drastically cut down also by other means (for reasons to be explained), while Taiwan kept total investment up through an accelerated programme of infrastructure investment. That is why real growth in Korea not only slowed, as in Taiwan, but became negative: GNP fell by 6.2 per cent in 1980 and the unemployment rate went up from 3.8 per cent to 5.2 per cent. Nevertheless, the inflation rate came down only very gradually by Taiwanese (though not by Western) standards, to 20 – 25 per cent in 1981 and to around 5 per cent by

1982. Accordingly, if one measures the inflationary impact of the two oil price increases on the two countries by the rise in wholesale prices over the two-year period following each oil shock, Korea's 80 and 65 per cent increases in price levels clearly testify to a larger impact than Taiwan's 35 and 39 per cent price increases.

Changes in the structure of manufacturing output

In the course of development, the structure of manufacturing shifted away from light industries towards heavy industries in both countries, and for much the same reasons (Table 10.5). Real wages were rising, causing light industrial products to become less competitive in world markets and to lose out against developing countries whose unskilled labour was cheaper. Moreover, the developed countries became increasingly protectionist, erecting import barriers, in the beginning primarily against textiles and shoes.

In Taiwan, most of the change in the composition of output came about as the result more of businessmen's reactions to changing prices and market conditions than of governmental policies. (Indeed, it is said that government, foreseeing increasing export difficulties at an early stage, advised the textile industry to reduce or abandon investment plans, but the industry ignored the advice and went ahead expanding capacity anyway.) Exceptions to that rule were the building up of the steel, shipbuilding and petrochemical industries, all of which are state-owned. Hand in hand with the changing structure of Taiwan's manufactured output has gone a change also in the direction of its exports. Taiwan is increasingly exporting to developing countries and, as might be expected, the exports are mainly capital-intensive and skill-intensive manufactured products. It should also be mentioned that, at the end of the 1970s, when the world depression started, investment in manufacturing capacity declined, but total investment and with it employment and the general level of activity continued to rise, thanks to greatly increased public investment in road, railroad and harbour construction, and other infrastructure projects.

In Korea, there was a similar shift toward the chemical and heavy industries, but its timing was different. As is apparent from Table 10.5, the development of heavy industries lagged behind Taiwan's but caught up with a sudden spurt at the end of the period; and the whole development must be attributed to deliberate government policies. For the differential terms of credit and rates of taxes, which the Korean government used for stimulating investment, gave it great power to influence also the direction of investment – and it used that powerfully. Before investigating how and to what purpose it was used, it is well to remember that government is usually distrusted as the maker of investment decisions and to look at the reasons for such distrust.

Table 10.5   *Percentage composition of manufactured output*

Year	Korea	Taiwan	Korea	Taiwan
	Food, beverages and tobacco		Non-metallic mineral products except petroleum and coal	
1960	19.3	44.5	9.2	7.2
1965	26.5	34.8	6.7	6.5
1971	24.6	20.9	6.0	4.5
1975	21.2	18.8	5.6	4.7
1979	16.5	13.0	5.8	3.9
	Textiles, clothing and footwear		Basic metal products	
1960	28.6	14.9	2.4	3.1
1965	19.8	15.0	5.0	2.2
1971	17.5	18.0	4.7	2.9
1975	22.0	15.8	4.7	3.5
1979	19.6	15.5	7.9	6.7
	All light industry (including the above)		Machinery, equipment and fabricated metal products	
1960	70.0	71.2	10.7	8.5
1965	61.8	51.2	11.5	13.3
1971	54.7	50.7	12.2	21.2
1975	51.6	46.7	16.3	23.7
1979	44.7	44.4	24.2	26.0
	Chemicals, petroleum and coal		All heavy industry (sum of the above)	
1960	7.7	10.1	30.0	28.8
1965	15.0	17.4	38.2	39.8
1971	23.5	20.8	45.3	49.3
1975	21.8	21.3	48.4	53.3
1979	17.4	19.0	55.3	55.6

Investment decisions must be based on predictions of future needs and availabilities, and politicians and civil servants need be no worse than businessmen at weighing all the information available for making the best predictions. People in government, however, are seldom affected quite so personally and profoundly by the outcome of their investment decisions as are businessmen, who risk the profitability and often even the survival of their businesses, and who therefore are under greater and more immediate pressure to weigh their investments carefully. Moreover, central planners can too easily overrule and ignore businessmen's dissent, which puts official investment plans in danger of being too monolithic, too narrowly and confidently focused on what seemed best in the planners' judgement, with no or little allowance for mistakes and unforeseen changes in circumstances. By contrast, the sum of the independent investment decisions of many businessmen reflects both differences in judgements and differences in the degree of confidence individuals attach to their judgements, and the outcome of such differences is greater dispersion of investments. It is as if the decisions based on the majority opinion had been cautiously hedged and insured against unexpected mishaps.

In Korean practice, however, potential dangers inherent in too much central control over investment were avoided most of the time, thanks to exceptionally able and intelligent planning. Only at the end of the 1970s did the Korean government make seriously mistaken investment decisions which would probably have been avoided under less tight governmental controls.

The initial Korean emphasis on investment in such light industries as food processing, textiles, clothing and plywood, which were so very successful in expanding exports and providing employment for the unskilled throughout the 1960s, was gradually shifted towards investment in more capital-intensive as well as more skill-intensive products and industries by the end of the decade. Steel, chemicals, shipbuilding and construction, along with electronics and footwear, and the shift, within textiles, to sports clothing and other speciality and high-quality items are the main examples. The reasoning behind the new investment policy seems to have been the desire to exploit Korea's comparative advantage in skilled labour, to defeat US import restrictions by increasing the domestic value-added content in textile exports, to diversify exports, partly by stepping into the void created by Japan's diminishing competitiveness in some sectors and by the advanced countries' own reduced output of certain products for fear of industrial pollution, and to cater to Korea's own increased domestic demand, including the demand of its export industries for intermediate goods. Finally, defence considerations, prompted by the threatened withdrawal of American forces from Korea, also played a part.

Whatever its motivation, the new investment policy was successful. The fast annual growth (10.2 per cent) of real GNP during the initial years (1965–71) of export promotion continued unabated at 10.1 per cent during the next six years (1971–7): and exports, which paid for 53 per cent of imports in 1965 and 60 per cent of them in 1971, had risen fully to equal the value of imports in 1977. That achievement was all the more remarkable in view of the greatly increased price of oil, all of which Korea has to import.

Unfortunately, the gradual and successful shift towards greater capital and skill intensity was suddenly and greatly speeded up in 1977. At the very time when the incipient world depression led cautious businessmen in Taiwan to slow investment in manufacturing capacity, Korea's economic planners also abandoned their original investment plans as laid down in the Fourth Five-Year Plan; but they revised them upwards by crowding into three years (1977–9) 80 per cent of the total investment the plan had projected for five years, and concentrating most of it, also against the plan's original intentions, into the heavy industries. As a result, the share of investment in GNP rose from 29.4 per cent in 1975 to 36.9 per cent in 1977–9, and the combined share of metals, chemicals, intermediate products, machinery, transport equipment and electronics in total investment rose from 48.2 per cent to 78.9 per cent.

To bring about so drastic and sudden a change in a private enterprise economy must have required tremendous governmental pressures and inducements, especially when one considers that most of that investment went into mammoth projects with productive capacities greatly in excess of domestic requirements at a time when export demand was not much in evidence. Today, with the benefit of hindsight, it is hard to understand what possible reasons could have been behind that investment programme, which only led to trouble. For one thing, the great increase in investment activity raised wages and costs, thereby diminishing the competitiveness of Korean exports; for another, the cutting back of projected investments in the light industries created shortages, and the two together largely explain the re-emergence, after 1977, of a trade deficit. Finally, all that investment in heavy industry created large new capacities in steel, shipbuilding, chemicals, automobiles and so on, much of which has remained greatly underutilized ever since. The most extreme example of these overambitious investments was the building of a large complex for the manufacture of atomic, thermo and hydroelectric power-generating equipment, equipped with the most up-to-date computer-controlled machinery, having a capacity that is five times estimated domestic requirements, but with a present utilization rate of only 40 per cent of that capacity.

Yet much of Korea's new heavy industry is highly competitive, thanks to the combination of modern technology and low labour costs. For example, Korea manages (as does Taiwan) to export steel to Japan, although Japan's own steel capacity is greatly underutilized, and both countries' shipyards are busier and have more orders than most other countries' shipyards. Indeed, the underutilization of manufacturing capacity is a worldwide phenomenon in the present global depression: Korea's problem is that many of its newly built plants seem condemned from the outset to indefinite underutilization.

Korea's new economic policy: 1980–81

The mistakes of Korea's investment policy of the late 1970s were fully recognized as such by 1979, and the huge investment programme was stopped in its tracks. In addition, a restrictive policy of high interest rates was instituted in January 1980. As a result, real investment, which had been rising uninterruptedly for 15 years, fell in 1980, leading to a reduction in real GNP – the first since the Korean War – and investment remained low in the following year. Inflation, however, continued, given a further impetus by the second oil crisis and also by the successive devaluations of 1980 with whose aid the authorities tried to restore the competitiveness of exports. The annual rate of inflation reached almost 40 per cent in 1980 and it took two years of restrictive policies to bring it down to around 5 per cent.

The sustained application of these restrictive policies and the policies instituted since the inflation has been brought under control all suggest that the new Korean regime of President Chun is determined to approach economic problems in a new spirit. The new policies include the offer of high real rates of interest on personal bank deposits, the elimination of the interest rate differential between ordinary loans and what used to be concessionary loans, the change in character of the latest (and fifth) five-year-plan from an obligatory to an indicative plan, and various measures (additional to the high interest rate on bank deposits) designed to starve the curb market of funds. They all seem to aim at making greater use of market incentives and the allocating function of market prices, and at relying on the organized financial market to stimulate domestic savings and channel funds to those areas where rates of return are the highest. The government has also announced its intention to denationalize the banks as a means of increasing efficiency and cutting down favouritism in the allocation of loans.

Most of those changes bring Korea's approach to economic problems closer to Taiwan's and they can only be welcomed, although the one last mentioned may create as many problems as it solves. In view of the economy's very great dependence on bank credit, the sale of the banks to private parties, presumably to the large conglomerates, would substantially and dangerously increase the latters' economic power and may merely substitute their favouritism for governmental favouritism – unless the bank debt of manufacturing businesses is substantially reduced and funded first and Korea's stock and bond markets are developed and expanded much beyond their present state.

Present state and future prospects

Until now, the development of most developing countries has hinged on their ability to exploit their comparative advantages and capture the gains from international specialization. World depression, however, breeds a spirit of protectionism, which can stifle international specialization; and that raises the question as to how the developing and newly industrializing countries will fare in today's world. Both Korea and Taiwan are poor in natural resources, but rich in the human resources of labour, labour skills, education and ingenuity. They have no choice, therefore, but to depend heavily on foreign trade also in their further development. Furthermore, Korea has the additional problem of insufficient domestic saving and the need to borrow abroad if it is to continue to grow at a rate anywhere near its past growth rate. The world depression, however, which has brought so many countries to the brink of bankruptcy, is also rendering foreign borrowing more difficult.

The debt problem is easier to discuss and so may well be dealt with first. Korea has accumulated an external debt that, as a proportion of GNP, is not only much higher than Taiwan's, but higher than that of most industrializing countries, and higher even than Mexico's (Table 10.6). Thanks, however, to Korea's very high export earnings, its debt-service ratio (interest payments and repayments of principal as a percentage of export earnings) is about average at 12.2 per cent and considered to be reasonable. It certainly is very much lower than that of Mexico or Brazil. In view of this reasonable debt-service ratio, Korea's ability to borrow has not yet been impaired; but it probably depends crucially on its current and expected future ability to grow and to make its exports grow. Any judgement, therefore, that one may reach concerning Korea's growth prospects will also serve as a judgement concerning Korea's prospective ability to borrow for the purpose of financing such growth.

In that respect, Taiwan has the very great advantage of a high domestic saving rate, which renders continued fast growth independent of foreign

Table 10.6   The burden of foreign public debt in 1980

	Debt outstanding as percentage of GNP	Debt service as percentage of export earnings
Korea	28.8	12.2
Taiwan[a]	12.1	4.2
Mexico	20.6	31.9
Brazil	16.4	34.0
All middle-income oil-importing countries (average)	15.4	11.9

[a]   Data refer to 1979.

borrowing. As to Taiwan's and Korea's dependence on foreign trade, both are small enough and their exports diversified enough for changes in their exports to make no significant impact on world trade. The total exports of each are less than 1 per cent of total world trade, which partly explains why both were able, even during the depressed 1979–81 period, to increase the value of their exports by almost 19 per cent annually.

For the future, both countries are trying, first of all, to limit the growth of their import bill by various energy-conservation methods, by slowing the domestic development of such energy-intensive industries as non-ferrous metal refining, by joint investments in resource-rich countries to secure cheaper raw material supplies (such as aluminium), by off-shore prospecting for oil and gas (Taiwan), by the expansion and modernization of coal mining (Korea) and by greater reliance on nuclear power for electricity generation (Korea).

Furthermore, both countries are trying to expand exports and their efforts are aimed at three targets. One is to recapture, through modernization, automation and improved quality control, the competitiveness of their light industries, which was lost owing to the rise in wages, and the two countries are trying to accomplish that in diametrically opposite ways. The Korean government seems to be repenting its past excessive favouritism towards large firms and is now stressing financial and managerial assistance to small- and medium-sized firms through such agencies as the Small and Medium Industry Promotion Corporation and the Korea Production Technology Service Corporation. Taiwan, on the other hand, is now discovering the benefits to be had from the economies of scale and is encouraging mergers and the growth of very small firms in the interests of greater efficiency.

Textiles is one industry that is receiving a lot of attention; and it is hoped not only to lower costs by modernizing and automating productive methods, but also to improve quality through more sophisticated design and better dyeing techniques. Quality improvement is especially important, because import restrictions are a response mostly to price competition, very seldom to quality competition. Another industry whose exports Korea plans to expand is the one producing nuts, bolts and other machinery parts and components (spare parts). They seem to be superior in quality to American products and Korea hopes to increase their export partly through production in joint US – Korean ventures, again an area where imports are unlikely to be restricted.

Another important aim of both countries is to compensate for the lost comparative advantage of their light industries (once based on cheap manpower) by gaining a comparative advantage in electronics and other emerging industries based on cheap brainpower. In the past, both countries have been heavily engaged in the assembly of consumer electronics: they are now shifting and trying to shift into the production of semiconductors, large-scale integrated circuits, computer terminals, microcomputers, electronic switch-ing systems and telecommunications equipment, much of which they need for automation in their own industries, as well as for export. Electronics being a new industry has the advantage of a rapidly growing market, which is unlikely to be protected by import restriction; but it also has the disadvantage that its established members are reluctant to license their know-how and permit its spread to competitors and foreign countries. Partly to deal with this problem, both Taiwan and Korea are soliciting more direct investment from abroad, with Korea allowing multinational companies to set up wholly-owned subsidiaries; and both countries are increasing public and encouraging pri-vate expenditures on research and development. In that respect, Korea is ahead of Taiwan, thanks principally to the size of many of her manufacturing firms, more than 50 of which already have their own research and develop-ment institutes. Plans are for total research and development expenditures to rise: in Korea by 12 per cent per annum to 2 per cent of GNP in 1986; in Taiwan, by 15 per cent per annum to 1.2 per cent of GNP in 1985. (US expenditures on research and development were 2.3 per cent of GNP in the late 1970s.)

Brainpower in both countries is very cheap. Young electronics engineers earn one-half or less of what their counterparts earn in Japan, who in turn again earn only one-half of what they would get in the United States. The supply is plentiful in both Taiwan and Korea, thanks to the importance they attach to education. Taiwan awards degrees to 50 per cent more engineers in proportion to its population than does the United States, and while most of them used to emigrate to the United States, nowadays they increasingly find challenging and promising jobs at home. Korea's engineers are trained in a number of institutes of science and technology, which are largely manned by a United States-trained faculty paid competitive salaries which they supple-ment by consulting for private industry. Both countries, however, have ambi-tious plans to upgrade their educational systems and put more emphasis on scientific and technical training – especially Korea, which plans to extend compulsory education through senior high school, establish 93 new technical high schools and 20 new junior colleges, and increase public spending on education from 3 per cent of GNP in 1980 to 5 per cent by 1986.[34]

In addition to the two countries' efforts to revive their light exports and establish a comparative advantage in the newly emerging high-technology industries, Korea's new export drive also had a third target in the developing countries' need for intermediate and capital goods, heavy equipment and manufacturing and infrastructural facilities. This part of import demand, far from being restricted by the new protectionism, is enhanced by it. The two countries' cost advantage in heavy industry has been demonstrated by the export successes of their steel and shipbuilding industries, and they are well equipped to cater to demand for heavy equipment from later-developing countries. Korea is especially well placed for capturing such demand with its newly built and still underemployed heavy industries, its large construction industry whose reputation abroad is well established, and the worldwide presence of its trading companies.

The one ingredient Korea lacks for exports of this type is the ability to grant large, long-term export credits on favourable terms, and one of the main uses to which it hopes to put a part (estimated at 12.5 per cent) of the funds it expects to borrow in international credit markets is relending them as export credits to developing countries that become customers.

In this section an attempt has been made to rationalize the two countries' projected and hoped-for export drives, as they are spelled out in Korea's five-year-plan for 1982–6 and Taiwan's four-year-plan for 1982–5. The rates at which they expect their respective GNP and exports to grow are almost identical; they count on their exports to continue expanding as fast as they did during the previous three years (1979–81); and both of them plan to stick with their outward-looking policies and rely on further export expansion to lead the growth of their economies.

Notes

1. The five are Japan, South Korea, Taiwan, Singapore and Hong Kong. The comparison is based on data from World Bank (1982) Appendix Table 1, p. 110, supplemented by the World Bank's unpublished computer printout for Taiwan.
2. For convenience, South Korea is referred to as 'Korea' throughout. The article does not consider economic change in North Korea.
3. The striking similarity of both land reforms to the Japanese land reform carried out under the directive of the Allied Occupation Authorities attests the strong influence of the American expert, the late Wolf Ladejinsky, who served as land reform adviser to all three countries.
4. The average is calculated from Scott (1979), p. 370.
5. This average, quite a bit lower than estimates occasionally quoted elsewhere, is calculated from data given in Krueger (1979), Tables 18 and 30, pp. 67 and 109, respectively.
6. From the review of Krueger's above-cited book by Jayati Datta Mitra (1981), p. 199.
7. See, however, Arndt (1982) for an interesting contrary view.
8. Note that the rise in wages does not discourage the use of labour-intensive methods of production, because it raises the costs both of labour and of goods made with labour (which includes capital goods) in approximately equal proportions. Nor, for that matter, do rising interest rates raise the price of capital goods in relation to other prices. What they do instead is to raise the cost of payments due before production starts in relation to payments made concurrently with production, whatever the nature of the resources so paid for. It is the relative cost of those two kinds of payments that determines the labour or capital intensity of the methods of production chosen; and it, in turn, is determined by the interest rate alone.
9. President Park assumed power in 1961 and was assassinated in 1979.
10. The quotation and much of the argument of this part comes from Mason et al. (1980), ch. 8.
11. The index gives the ratio of acreage harvested to total farmland. The ratio has fallen quite a bit since 1964, probably because of increased livestock feeding and production of perennial crops, especially fruit.

12. I wish to thank Professor Irma Adelman and Yoon Je Cho for information on this subject.

13. I owe this information to Dr Avishay Braverman.

14. The data in this section are from Thorbecke (1979) and Ban et al. (1980).

15. There is a formula according to which it is 'natural' for a smaller country's export and import ratios to exceed a larger country's trade ratios by the fourth root of the ratio in which that country's population exceeds its own (Linnemann, 1966, p. 206; Scott, 1979, p. 350). By that reckoning, Taiwan's exports and imports would have to be around 45 per cent of GNP for its trade dependence to match Korea's, rather than around 50 per cent as they are today.

16. The concentration ratio is the square root of the sum of the squared proportions that each commodity or each country destination forms of a country's total exports and it ranges from 0 to 100 per cent. For example, the 40.8 per cent geographical concentration of Korea's exports shows that 56 per cent of its exports is destined for the United States and Japan and the remainder is well dispersed among other countries. (The concept was introduced by Albert Hirschman. For the formula and its explanation, see the note to Table 10.13 in Balassa and Associates (1982).

17. Honda, for example, imports oranges to Japan, needing their bulky freight for ballast on the return trip of the boats in which it ships its cars for export.

18. The definition of urban areas is different in the two countries, which makes it impossible to compare their degrees of urbanization precisely.

19. Korea's large investment in residential housing may have had another reason as well, which will be presented shortly.

20. Yet another way in which a good export performance also helps the rest of the economy to grow is worth mentioning: it enhances the country's creditworthiness and renders foreign loans easily accessible. Both countries enjoyed that advantage; the interesting question is why Taiwan had no need for it.

21. That tax is additional to the corporate income tax, which both countries levy on the corporation's total net profits.

22. The percentages are calculated from Park (1981), p. 90.

23. The customary simple numerical model of the life cycle hypothesis shows that each percentage point of annual growth in income gives rise to 3 percentage points of positive net saving expressed as a percentage of income. See Modigliani and Brumberg (1954).

24. For an English language summary of the several explanations of Japan's high saving rate, see Shinohara (1982) chap. 10.

25. Korea collects no statistics on manufacturing establishments with four or less employees. The data used are from Taiwan, (1976), Vol. III, Book 1, p. 118, and Korea (1979), p. 155.

26. All of the data used in this paragraph refer to 1976, the year of Taiwan's last industrial census; they come from the sources cited in the previous note.

27. I want to thank Yoon Je Cho for suggesting that explanation for Korea's relatively low household saving rate.

28. Needless to say, the fluctuations in the real rate of interest resulted, not from adjustments in the interest paid on savings deposits, but from failure to adjust it in response to fluctuations in the rate of inflation, which resulted from sudden and drastic changes in economic policies. The personal saving rate also fluctuated, but in no systematic relation to fluctuations in the real rate of interest. Indeed, the fluctuating saving rate is best explained as the result of the public's attempt to maintain its real consumption on a steady course, in the face of great fluctuations in incomes and prices.

29. Although Korean statistics refer only to enterprises employing at least five employees, it is not unreasonable to assume that their rate of increase was more or less same as the rate of increase of *all* enterprises. Note also that the very small increase in the number of companies is a net increase: the difference between the number of new companies established and the number of old companies that have disappeared through merger or something else; and a look at the annual data suggests that the number of mergers must have been quite large. It would be more appropriate to use gross figures, but they are not available. One must bear in mind that the Taiwanese figures are also net and not gross.

30. Resources could have been diverted also from other sources and types of investment, in

which case total investment would not have increased. In Korea, however, to judge by the statistics, that does not seem to have happened to any significant extent.

31. The saving in processing cost, however, benefits the middlemen more than borrower and lender; and that, of course, is the objection to curb markets.

32. The estimate refers to 1968 and is quoted in Mason *et al.* (1980), p. 335.

33. Luck had something to do with that. Alone among the oil-importing countries, Korea saw its balance of payments improve at the time and as a result of the oil price increase, because its construction industry won US$2.5 billion worth of contracts in 1976, mainly from the oil countries. Construction has been Korea's main source of foreign exchange earnings since then, the gross value of foreign contracts averaging US$16 billion annually.

34. Taiwan spent 3.9 per cent of GNP on education in 1980, and the United States 5.2 per cent.

References

Arndt, H.E. (1982), 'Two Kinds of Credit Rationing', *Banca Nazionale del Lavoro Quarterly Review*, no. 143, December.

Balassa, Bela and Associates, (1982), *Development Strategies in Semi-Industrial Economies*, World Bank Research Publication Baltimore, Maryland: (Johns Hopkins University Press).

Ban, S.H., Moon, P.Y. and Perkins, D.H. (1980), *Rural Development: Studies in the Modernization of the Republic of Korea: 1945–1975*, (Cambridge, Mass.: Harvard University Press).

Bank of Korea (1982), *Financial Statements Analysis for 1981*, (Seoul).

International Labour Organization (1983), *International Yearbook of Labour Statistics*, (Geneva).

Kim, Kwang Suk and Roemer, Michael (1979), *Growth and Structural Transformation: Studies in the Modernization of the Republic of Korea: 1945–1975*, (Cambridge, Mass: Harvard University Press).

Korea (various years), *Korea Statistical Yearbooks*, (Seoul).

Krueger, Anne O. (1979), *The Development Role of the Foreign Sector and Aid: Studies in the Modernization of the Republic of Korea: 1945–1975*, (Cambridge, Mass: Harvard University Press).

Kuo, S.W.Y., Ranis, G. and Fei, J.C.H. (1981), *The Taiwan Success Story: Rapid Growth with Improved Distribution in the Republic of China, 1952–1979*, (Boulder, Col: Westview Press).

Linnemann, Hans (1966), *An Economic Study of International Trade Flows*, (Amsterdam: North-Holland Publishing Company).

Little, I.M.D. (1979), 'An Economic Reconnaissance', in W. Galenson (ed.), *Economic Growth and Structural Change in Taiwan*, (Ithaca, New York: Cornell University Press).

— (1981), 'The Experience and Causes of Rapid Labour-Intensive Development in Korea, Taiwan Province, Hong Kong and Singapore; And the Possibilities of Emulation', in Eddy Lee (ed.), *Export-Led Industrialization and Development*, (Singapore: International Labour Office).

Mason, E.S. *et al.* (1980), *The Economic and Social Modernization of the Republic of Korea*, (Cambridge, Mass: Harvard University Press).

Mitra, Jayati Datta (1981), 'Review of Anne O. Krueger, *The Development Role of the Foreign Sector and Aid: Studies in the Modernization of the Republic of Korea: 1945–1975*', *Economic Development and Cultural Change*, **30**.

Modigliani F. and Brumberg, R. (1954), 'Utility Analysis and the Consumption Function: An Interpretation of Cross-Section Data', in K.K. Kurihara, (ed.), *Post Keynesian Economics*, (New Brunswick: Rutgers University Press).

Park, Chon Kee (ed.) (1980), *Human Resources and Social Development in Korea*, (Seoul: Korea Development Institute).

Park, Yung Chul (1981), 'Export-Led Development: The Korean Experience 1960–78', in Eddy Lee (ed.), *Export-Led Industrialization and Development*, (Singapore: International Labour Office).

Scott, M. (1979), *Foreign Trade*, in W. Galenson (ed.), *Economic Growth and Structural Change in Taiwan*, (Ithaca, New York: Cornell University Press).

Shinohara, M. (1982), *Industrial Growth, Trade, and Dynamic Patterns in the Japanese Economy*, (Tokyo: University of Tokyo Press).

Taiwan (1976), *The Report of 1976 Industrial and Commercial Censuses of Taiwan–Fukien District of the Republic of China*, Vol. III, Book I (Taipei).

The Economist (1982), 14–20 August, (London).

Thorbecke, E. (1979), 'Agricultural Development', in W. Galenson (ed.), *Economic Growth and Structural Change in Taiwan*, (Ithaca & London: Cornell University Press).

World Bank, (1982), *World Development Report 1982*, (Washington, DC).

11 Why the US saving rate is low – a conflict between the national accountant's and the individual saver's perceptions*

America's economic troubles are blamed on many causes, among them on the improvidence of the general public. Americans are accused of being spendthrifts and of having become more so in these difficult stagflationary years when, so the argument runs, saving is desperately needed to make possible investment and the rise in productivity, which hinges on investment. The accusation is based on statistical evidence, which indeed shows that personal saving as a proportion of disposable personal income in the United States has fallen to its lowest level in 30 years during the late 1970s and has been for a long time quite a bit lower than it is in most Western European countries. During the 1960–78 period, for example, the US saving rate averaged 6.9 per cent, which is just about the same as Sweden's 6.8 per cent average for the corresponding period and Great Britain's 6.9 per cent, but significantly lower than Western Germany's 11.9 per cent. France's 13.2 per cent and the Netherland's 14.7 per cent average.

These differences in saving rates may, of course, have many explanations besides the alleged greater improvidence of the American public. Better social security provisions and/or better social services could be one explanation, and that might also account for Sweden's and Great Britain's low saving rates; the much greater availability of instalment credit in the United States than anywhere else may be another. A third explanation could be the US slower rate of growth. According to the well-known Modigliani–Brumberg life cycle hypothesis, if people saved exclusively in order to accumulate a nest egg on which to live in retirement, so that they would dissave in old age everything they saved when young, the public's total net saving would still be positive in a growing economy and higher, the faster the rate of growth. According to Modigliani and Brumberg, each percentage point of annual rate of growth, whether in population or in per capita income, would lead to a rise of about 3 per cent in disposable income saved. The average annual growth rates of the countries just mentioned over the 1960–78 period were 3.6 per cent in the United States, 3.1 per cent in Sweden, 2.6 per cent in Great

---

* This chapter appeared in J. Cohen and G. Harcourt (eds), *International Monetary Problems and Supply-Side Economics*, (London: Macmillan, 1986).

Britain, 3.8 per cent in Western Germany, 4.8 per cent in France and 4.5 per cent in the Netherlands.

Yet another explanation of these divergent saving rates, and the one to be explored here, has to do with that peculiarly American way of saving: the purchase of a home. Almost two-thirds of US households own the houses and apartments they live in, compared to 31 per cent in Sweden, 37 per cent in Western Germany, 40 per cent in France and 54 per cent in Britain. Those differences in home ownership also contribute to national differences in saving rates, partly because they make the same saving behaviour look slightly different in the statistics, given the particular way in which the statistics are presented, and partly also because the homeowner's perception of his own saving differs from what the national accounts estimate his saving to be; and that too can influence saving behaviour.

As is well known, the US national income and product accounts treat home ownership in a peculiar way. They split the personality of every homeowner into tenant and landlord, and add the imaginary transactions between each homeowner's two personalities onto the actual market transactions entered on the two sides of the national accounts. The tenant's notional rent payments to his landlord-self are included in Personal Consumption Expenditure; the landlord's notional rental income from his tenant-self is added onto Disposable Personal Income.

The reasons for this procedure are not entirely clear. It does keep the secular rise in home ownership, which is considered a good thing, from showing up in the national accounts as a *fall* in income and product. That, clearly, is an advantage, though to single out home ownership for such special treatment seems somewhat arbitrary. After all, it is not the only change that would show up in the national accounts in such a paradoxical fashion. The increasingly widespread ownership of safety razors and household appliances also has the effect of simultaneously raising human welfare and lowering national income by lowering the income of barbers, laundries and domestic servants, yet the national accounts ignore the notional payments made for the use of those appliances and their owners' notional earnings from allowing them to be used. Another important reason for the special treatment of home ownership must be that the purchase of a home is clearly an investment, whose management fits in better with a professional landlord's business practice than with household behaviour. Unfortunately, however, the treatment of home owners in the national accounts as if they were landlords creates at least as many problems as it solves. The nature of those problems will appear in the following.

The current practice of adding the homeowner's notional rent payments to his out-of-pocket expenditures and his notional rental income to his into-pocket income would seem innocent enough if rent payments and rental income were equal. Even then, however, adding the same figure to both into-pocket income and out-of-pocket expenditure would make the unchanged level of saving *look smaller* when expressed in the form of a saving rate, as a percentage of the now seemingly higher level of disposable income. The point may be minor but is not negligible, considering the importance of rent in most people's budgets.

The two notional items, however, are far from being equal; and that makes matters worse. Interest, taxes and the provision for capital consumption must be subtracted from notional *gross* rent payments to obtain the notional *net* rental income; and the latter's addition to disposable income, while the much larger notional rent payments are added to consumption expenditure, reduces the *level* of personal saving by the amount of the three items which are subtracted from notional rent payments. That is the present practice. The question is, how far is it justified, and how far is that reduction in the level of saving a real reduction?

To begin with the simplest item, mortgage interest is clearly part of the homeowner's housing costs, so it is right and proper that it should reduce personal saving, the difference between disposable income and consumption expenditure. The second item, real-estate taxes on owner-occupied homes, looks similar but is slightly different. Taxes are an expense, so they too diminish saving; but real-estate taxes are no different from income or social security taxes and therefore should be deducted from personal income when disposable income is calculated, instead of being added, as they now are, to consumption expenditure. The *level* of saving is the same, of course, whether real-estate taxes are deducted from income or added to expenditure, but the saving rate, expressed as a percentage of disposable income, is higher in the first case, lower in the second. So here again, the practice of splitting home-owners' personalities lowers the apparent saving rate.

The third item brings us to substantive and much more important issues. The provision for capital consumption is not an out-of-pocket expense but part of the landlord's gross saving. Why, then, is it added onto consumption expenditure and so made to reduce personal saving? The answer is that in the national accounts of most industrial countries, personal income and personal saving are *net* concepts. That explains why only the notional *net* rental income of the homeowner's landlord-self can be and is included in personal income, and why his capital consumption allowances, which are *gross* saving, cannot be and are not included in personal saving. Instead, they are included, for want of a better place and somewhat confusingly, as part of the similar allowances and provisions of unincorporated businesses. The procedure is logical, consistent and unassailable if one accepts the present definitions of the categories of the national accounts. I question, however, the usefulness of defining and presenting personal income and personal saving in a conceptual form that differs from the one in which most people think of their own income and saving; and I propose to show that by that criterion *gross* personal income and *gross* personal saving are the most useful concepts.

Net income is certainly the operational concept of businessmen and business firms, and that includes the landlord who lives on the rents he collects from his tenants. Indeed, the landlord has long been regarded as the quintessential capitalist, who aims at maintaining his capital intact as a source of undiminished future income and feels free to dispose only of the net income that remains to him after he has made full provision for the maintenance and depreciation of his wealth. The use of the net income concept therefore is very much in order for representing the yield of the activities of any capitalist enterprise, including the landlord's.

But the homeowner is not that kind of landlord. To begin with, unlike the professional landlord, he has no financial inducement to go to the trouble of estimating the depreciation of his home and his income net of depreciation. For the typical homeowner is not particularly interested in keeping the value of his home intact. He spends most of his active life paying off his mortgage, the repayment part of which he considers saving; and he looks forward to having no or only negligible housing costs thereafter. Since the life expectancy of houses usually exceeds that of their owners, he is not likely to budget for the replacement of his home as he budgets for the replacement of his car. Secondly, even those anxious to leave their real property undiminished to their heirs are not likely to provide for its depreciation, because, in our world of growing population, people usually expect the real value of land to rise in the long run and to offset more or less the depreciation of the building that stands on it. In short, there are several reasons why homeowners very seldom think of their homes as depreciating property, for whose depreciation they should make allowance and build up a depreciation fund.

So far, we have been focusing on depreciation, or the capital consumption allowance, which businessmen, including professional landlords, are allowed to deduct in estimating their *taxable* net income, and which the national accounts subtract also from homeowners' notional rental income in order to arrive at net personal income and net personal saving, but which the homeowners themselves ignore and do not even think of when they assess what their own income is and decide how much to save out of that income. We now come to our last item, the provision for inflation, where the contrast between the picture that the national income accounts paint of the homeowner's situation and the idea the homeowner himself forms of his own situation happens to be the greatest.

The capital consumption allowance businessmen are allowed to deduct in estimating their net income for tax purposes is based on historical costs of the depreciating property and so takes no account of the inflationary rise in its replacement costs. To adjust for that rise when estimating *true* net income (as against taxable net income), the national income accounts contain a further deduction, known as the capital consumption adjustment. The annual capital consumption adjustment is the annual rise in the replacement cost, not only of that year's depreciation allowance, but of the entire depreciable property. In the case of corporations, the capital consumption adjustment is mostly a small addition to the capital consumption allowance: even in the very inflationary late 1970s, it was hardly more than a 10 per cent addition. For residential housing, however, the capital consumption adjustment tends to be relatively large: in the late 1970s, it was 35 per cent larger than the capital consumption allowance itself.

The reason for the very large capital consumption adjustment on housing is, of course, the exceptionally fast rise in the cost of residential construction. We all know about the very fast rise in the market value of existing houses; and construction costs have been rising more or less parallel with the prices of existing houses. Indeed, the annual capital consumption adjustment on homes happens to be a pretty good measure of the homeowners' annual capital gain – or at least of that part of it which accrues to them on the house itself. (The capital gain on the land is additional.) The only but crucial difference is that, while a capital gain is thought of as an *addition* to income, the capital consumption adjustment is an addition to a depreciation allowance and so a *deduction* from net income.

If I was right in arguing that homeowners seldom if ever set aside depreciation allowances into a fund earmarked for financing the eventual replacement of their homes, then they are equally unlikely to make, or even to think of making, additional provision for the rising replacement cost of their homes. At the same time, homeowners are usually well aware of their capital gains due to the rising market prices of their homes, which are real gains when, as has recently happened, real-estate prices rise faster than the consumer price index. A capital gain on one's home is, of course, an unrealizable gain as long as one needs a home and chooses to live in the same or a similar one; nevertheless it is a gain, because if necessary one can move to a smaller home or a cheaper location and so realize at least part of the gain. The feeling therefore that one is better off, better provided for the future, is justified.

One would hardly expect such improvement in homeowners' welfare to show up as a rise in personal income in the national accounts, which are known explicitly to exclude capital gains. But it comes as a shock to find the homeowner's capital gain – or at least an item closely related to it – showing up in the statistics with a contrary sign as a *reduction* in personal income! I am referring, of course, to the diminution of net personal income through the deduction from it of the capital consumption adjustment. Such divergence in sign and direction between the way in which people view the change in their own economic well-being and the way in which the national accounts reflect that change is more serious than the apparent and quantitative differences we have dealt with so far and needs to be looked at more carefully.

We have seen that inflation leads to a parallel rise in housing prices and construction costs, which have quantitatively similar but contrary effects on the economic situation of homeowners. The paradox just mentioned arises because both homeowners and national income accountants register only one of those effects and ignore the other; but the effect one of them registers is the one that the other ignores and *vice versa*. Homeowners, on the one hand, are well aware of their gain from the rising price of their homes but ignore the loss due to the rise in replacement costs, because their horizon is bounded by their life expectancy, which is finite and shorter than their homes' life expectancy. National income accountants, on the other hand, fully enter into their accounts the homeowner's loss from rising replacement costs, because they look upon the homeowner as if he were a capitalist landlord, bent on maintaining capital intact and averse to disposing of any funds beyond his net income; and they exclude capital gains (especially unrealized capital gains) from consideration, mainly on the ground that the estimating of those gains is subject to greater difficulties and wider margins of error than the estimation of income proper.

I have stated already my objections to treating homeowners as if they were capitalists, with the capitalist's instincts, when most of them hardly have any capital and do not even own their homes as unencumbered property. But how about the exclusion of capital gains from the national accounts? Most of us accept the argument that the estimation of capital gains is so much more unreliable than the estimation of income, and the equating of unrealized capital gains to income so questionable, that they are better excluded. Yet is it not inconsistent to exclude from income the gains due to the rising market price of assets, and at the same time to include, as a deduction from income, the capital consumption adjustment, which measures the loss due to the rising replacement cost of those same assets?

Surprisingly enough, there is little or no inconsistency as a rule, because capital gains due to rising market prices would be an addition to incomes; whereas losses due to rising replacement costs are an addition to depreciation charges, which themselves are a conventional and very rough approximation to *true* capital consumption, which is generally considered unmeasurable. It seems perfectly admissible to add a crudely measured capital consumption adjustment to an equally crudely measured capital consumption allowance, because estimates of capital consumption are mostly kept separate from the other estimates, and because users of the national accounts know and expect those estimates to be much less reliable and meaningful than are the other estimates. That, after all, is an important reason why most macroeconomic models and arguments operate with gross concepts.

But the capital consumption of homeowners' homes is the exception to that rule, because it enters personal income which, along with personal saving, is among the very few estimates presented on a net basis. In that case, therefore, there is an inconsistency between the inclusion of the loss due to rising replacement costs and the exclusion of the gains due to rising housing prices; and the best way, to my mind, of removing the inconsistency is to present personal income and personal saving on a gross basis also.[1]

The argument, however, in favour of presenting series of gross personal income and gross personal saving in the national accounts is not merely that it removes the just-mentioned inconsistency. A general and more important advantage would be that national economic statistics are more meaningful and intelligible to the general public when they represent the true summation of what each individual regards as his own personal income, take-home pay (disposable income) and saving, defined as he himself defines and thinks of them.

The extent to which that is *not* true today is best illustrated by a simple numerical example. Take a family with a family income of $57 000 and a disposable income that, after payment of income and social security taxes, amounts to $40 000. Of that they save 15 per cent, or $6 000. They live in a home they could hardly afford today but which they bought a few years ago for $90 000, with the lot valued at $30 000, the building at $60 000. They regard as their annual housing cost the interest they pay on the mortgage and forgo on the downpayment, together with tax, insurance and maintenance expenses; but national income accountants add to those costs $2800 annual capital consumption, the sum of a $1200 capital consumption allowance estimated on a 50-year-life basis ($60 000/50) and a $1600 capital consumption adjustment, estimated during the past four years to equal 135 per cent of the capital consumption allowance. The family's *net* saving therefore turns out to be, not $6000, but only $3200, not 15 per cent but only 8 per cent of their disposable income. That is a tremendous difference; yet the example is not unrealistic and quite conservative in its assumptions.

We are now ready to look at the difference in the national aggregates. The wonderfully clear and detailed presentation of the revised national income and product estimates just published makes it easy to revise the estimates as there presented and make them conform to the conceptual framework here proposed. What I want to do is to omit the imaginary transactions between the tenant and the landlord-selves of homeowners, transfer real-estate taxes from consumption expenditure to personal tax and non-tax payments, and transfer back homeowners' provision for capital consumption into personal saving. Those three changes put personal income and personal saving onto a gross basis and turn them into true sums of what individual persons regard as their personal income and personal saving.

Table 11.1

Year	(1) Gross personal disposable income $ billion	(2) Gross personal saving $ billion	(3) Gross saving rate (2)/(1) × 100 %	(4) Net saving rate %
1980	1 782.0	145.6	8.2	5.6
1979	1 603.7	125.5	7.8	5.2
1978	1 427.0	109.9	7.7	5.2
1977	1 276.9	103.3	8.1	5.6
1976	1 160.7	107.1	9.2	6.9
1975	1 064.2	116.5	10.9	8.6
1974	968.4	105.0	10.8	8.5
1973	885.4	96.2	10.9	8.6
1972	782.5	68.1	8.7	6.5
1971	724.9	74.1	10.2	8.1
1970	670.1	67.9	10.1	8.0
1969	615.2	51.9	8.4	6.9
1968	571.2	51.9	9.1	7.1
1967	526.6	53.4	10.1	8.1
1966	493.9	44.5	9.0	7.0
1965	457.3	41.6	9.1	7.1
1964	423.2	37.1	8.8	6.7
1963	389.3	29.0	7.4	5.4
1962	371.4	30.2	8.1	6.0
1961	351.5	29.6	8.4	6.3
1960	338.6	26.0	7.7	5.6
1959	326.3	27.2	8.3	6.2
1958	307.9	29.5	9.6	7.4
1957	298.3	27.8	9.3	7.2
1956	283.3	26.4	9.3	7.3
1955	266.0	21.1	7.9	6.0
1954	248.7	21.8	8.6	6.6
1953	245.0	22.6	9.2	7.3
1952	231.8	21.3	9.2	7.3
1951	221.2	19.7	8.9	7.1
1950	202.4	15.0	7.4	5.8
1949	184.4	10.3	5.6	4.0
1948	185.2	13.7	7.4	5.9
1947	166.1	7.5	4.5	3.1
1946	156.0	15.5	9.9	8.6

Table 11.1 shows the series of gross disposable personal income, gross personal saving, the latter as a percentage of the former or the gross saving rate, and, for a standard of comparison, the net saving rate as published. Gross personal saving is 30 per cent higher on average than net personal saving; gross disposable personal income is 3 per cent lower than its net equivalent;[2] and the saving rate is a third (32 per cent) higher in gross than in net terms. That last discrepancy is the average of an almost 50 per cent excess of gross over net saving in recent years and a much smaller one before that. Indeed, the much discussed decline in the saving rate of the late 1970s no longer seems exceptionally great on a gross basis: it is slightly smaller than that of the early 1960s and much smaller than that of the immediate postwar years. A more detailed inspection of the data shows that much of the recent dip in the net saving rate is explained by the large increase in the capital consumption adjustment of those years, due to the inflation.

As to the overall rise in the saving rate, that would be meaningful only in comparison to other countries' saving rates similarly amended and presented on a gross basis. Other countries, however, do not publish their national accounts in anywhere near the same detail as the United States, so I was unable to construct comparable gross series for them. But because home ownership is so much less widespread in Europe, it is reasonable to assume that the discrepancy between the gross and the net saving rate would be very much smaller in the European countries than it is in the United States.

Notes

1. I learned after writing this paper that the UK national accounts define and present those items in such a manner, despite the contrary recommendations of the UN.
2. The apparent paradox is due to the exclusion of imputed rental income and real-estate taxes from the gross and their inclusion in the net series.

12 The meaning, nature and source of value in economics*

The values economists are mainly concerned with are the subjective values people attribute to the sources of their satisfactions and dissatisfactions. Those value judgements show what people want and how badly they want it. We have no objective unit of measurement for denoting the extent of satisfaction; the subjective value people attach to sources of their satisfactions are always relative and express the value of one satisfaction in terms of the equivalent value of another. That is why money, which is general purchasing power over many things, turns out to be the best available measure of subjective value. Our not having a unit in which to measure satisfaction also prevents us from comparing one person's satisfaction and ability to experience it with another person's. The commonsense notion that two people in similar situations would enjoy the same satisfaction in equal measure has been rejected as not proven by present-day economists.

Our interest in the public's subjective value judgements is due to our concern with the economy's ability to allocate resources, coordinate production and distribute products, so that the public should be provided with the goods and services they want, in the quantities they want them, and in a way that creates the greatest benefit at the least cost *as those benefits and costs are evaluated by the people who experience them.*

To accomplish all this fully, it would be necessary first to aggregate different people's subjective preferences into society's global preferences, which, for some sources of satisfaction, can be a very difficult undertaking. Indeed, Kenneth Arrow was awarded a Nobel Prize for proving that in the general case and for *the entire range* of human needs and desires, it is impossible to carry out such aggregation in a meaningful and reasonable way (Arrow, 1987).

For the greater part of that range, however, the problem of aggregating individual preferences and making the economy cater to them in the way just described can be, and more or less is, resolved by competitive markets. The range in question comprises all the needs and desires that consumer goods and services can satisfy. Difficulties arise only in the case of collective and related goods and services. I shall deal with those at length later, but let me first say a few words on how markets resolve the problem for consumer goods.

* This chapter appeared in M. Hechter *et al.* (eds), *The Origin of Values*, (New York: De Gruyter, 1993).

These are the goods and services that are separable and salable piecemeal to individuals through consumer markets. Competitive markets establish a single price for each good and service, of which consumers can buy at that price as much or as little as they want and each finds it worth buying whatever quantity renders the value he or she attaches to the last unit bought equal to its market price. As a result, every consumer's marginal valuation of each good he or she buys becomes equal to its marginal valuation by all its other consumers who face the same price, with differences in their needs, tastes and budgets showing up, not in the values they attribute to them, but in the quantities in which they buy them.

In other words, competitive consumer markets perform three simultaneous functions: (1) they enable everybody to buy a different basket of goods according to what they want and can afford; (2) they bring about a consensus among buyers with respect to the marginal value they attribute to the goods they consume; and (3) they provide the important convenience of making the market-clearing price of each good reflect its identical valuation by all its consumers. If you then add that those prices are the signals that enable a perfectly competitive economy to utilize and allocate resources and productive methods in best conformity to consumers' preferences, then you have listed all the much-touted advantages of the market economy.

We economists are justly proud of our ability to deal with values in such quantitative terms, but our ability to do this is subject to three limitations. First, we can measure the values people attach to the sources of their pains and pleasures only when these are reflected by market prices, which means that we can measure the value only of those satisfactions whose sources reach their beneficiaries through consumer markets and only of those pains for which the people who suffer them are compensated through labour markets. Second, market prices reflect individuals' subjective valuations accurately only when competition among them is perfect. Third, the values reflected in market prices are not what value means in common parlance but marginal or incremental values: the lowest value buyers attribute to the benefit they get from a single unit of what they buy and the highest value sellers place on the cost to them of rendering one unit of their services or of producing one unit of the goods they sell.

The last mentioned is not a serious limitation, because marginal values are the only ones that matter in economics: they contain all the information that has to be transmitted from one economic agent to another to enable markets to perform their coordinating functions. For it is by equalizing the *marginal* valuation of each resource and product by all its sellers and buyers that perfectly competitive markets minimize costs of production, maximize the worth to buyers of the total output and ensure the best allocation of resources among different industries and producers.

The first two limitations did not, in the beginning, seem too serious either: the first because, as recently as 60 years ago, nine-tenths or more of the gross national product consisted of consumer goods and services and the investment needed to produce them; the second because competition seemed more pervasive and more nearly perfect to earlier generations of economists than to today's.

Gradually, however, all that has changed. The state's role in the US economy has more than doubled, which has reduced the scope of consumer markets correspondingly; and the limitations and shortcomings of markets as well as interdependencies between costs and satisfactions that go and do not go through markets have become both greater and more apparent. Since all these detract from the perfect functioning of the ideal of a perfectly competitive market economy, they are known as market failures, which, no less than the market's accomplishments, are of concern to economists, who, after all, have to develop and advise on policies designed to correct or supplement the functioning of markets. In that connection, we often have to estimate values not reflected or incorrectly reflected by market prices. Some of the time that proves a hopelessly difficult task; but it is not the less important for that. A short discussion of the nature of that task is best introduced by a list of market failures.

To begin with, most markets are imperfectly competitive, though in the all-important consumer markets, at least one side is perfectly competitive, causing prices correctly to reflect buyers' but to overstate sellers' marginal valuations. Second, many important economic goods and services do not reach their beneficiaries through consumer markets, which means that their worth to those whom they benefit or are supposed to benefit are not reflected in market prices. Third, consumers' valuation of their own satisfactions are sometimes unreliable and therefore need overruling or correcting. Fourth, the production and/or consumption of some goods generate favourable or unfavourable side-effects, which do not go through the market but which nevertheless must or ought to be estimated and taken into account. I shall say a few words about each of these problems.

Collective goods
Many goods and services are not separable and cannot be sold piecemeal in quantities appropriate to each consumer's different tastes and budget. National defence, police protection, public parks, roads and city streets, and radio and television programmes on the air are some of the more obvious examples of these so-called 'collective' or public goods (Sadmo, 1987). They are available to everybody in their entirety (that is, in the same quantity) which causes different people with their differing tastes and incomes to put different values on them. Market exchange between rational individuals can-

not, as a rule, ensure the provision of these goods and services in a satisfactory way without agreement among the beneficiaries, owing to a prisoner's dilemma type of problem. That is why most collective goods are made available 'free', usually by the state at taxpayers' expense, but with some provided and financed by private firms that benefit indirectly from providing them to prospective customers.

It is convenient to deal with these latter first. Under imperfect competition, sellers set their prices above the marginal cost to them of the goods and services they sell, which renders it profitable for them to engage in non-price competition, in the form of advertising the availability and advantages of their wares and offering prospective buyers various services and conveniences as means of creating goodwill and increasing sales. Examples, in addition to television and radio programmes already mentioned, are artistically arranged shop windows, elegantly furnished stores, colourful shopping malls, department stores and the many other attractions that have made shopping and window-shopping many people's favourite pastime in the advanced market economies. The general public clearly appreciates all these amenities; but there is no way of quantifying the value it puts on them. Suffice it to say that their free provision indemnifies the public to some extent for the profit mark-up added to the cost of its purchases and compensates for the market's loss of efficiency created by prices that overstate marginal costs. Moreover the fact that most people prefer to do their shopping in elegant but expensive stores rather than in cheap but unattractive discount houses is clear evidence that they consider those amenities worth their cost.

More important, more valuable, and much more numerous than the privately provided collective services just discussed are those provided by government and paid for out of taxes. The political process gives taxpayers an indirect influence over the nature and quantity of public services provided; but that is very tenuous, which is why economists have always looked for some way of ascertaining the public's value judgements of collective goods similar to those reflected by market prices in consumer markets.

In principle, the worth to the public of a collective good such as national defence could be ascertained if citizens could be prevailed on to state truthfully how much each of them would be willing to contribute to maintaining their country's actual level of national defence. By summing the amounts so named and comparing their sum to the actual level of defence spending, one could tell whether that is insufficient, excessive or just adequate, and tell it by the same standard that determines the supply of the goods and services sold in consumer markets. (Note the parallelism between the sum of quantities sold at a given price and the sum of contributions offered for a given quantity.) Moreover, the different figures named by different people would be a good guide also for an equitable distribution of the tax burden that national defence imposes.

Needless to say, however, that is not a practical proposition, not only because the public is not well enough informed for its opinion on so complex a subject to have much use, but also because people could not be trusted to reveal the true value they put on defence. They would be tempted to *overstate* it if the survey were known to be designed merely as a guide to help determine the proper level of defence spending; whereas they would be sure to *understate* it if the survey were also to be used for determining each taxpayer's tax assessment. Much thought has gone into trying to find a reliable method for ascertaining what expenditure on collective goods would best conform to what the public wants and believes it can afford, but a practical way of doing this is still in the offing.

Equity
A special kind of collective good that deserves special mention is the distribution of income. This is a collective good because rich and poor alike share the same income distribution; and it is rather special because one's judgement of it is a moral one; and people's moral judgements are bound to be much more nearly uniform than their judgements of personal gratifications and their sources. After all, to judge the ethical value of an income distribution, one must abstract from one's own position in that distribution and, when people do that, differences in their judgements as to the most desirable distribution may not be all that great. Most of us are fair-minded and compassionate enough to attach value to an equitable distribution, but few would opt for complete equality of incomes, for two reasons. First, because everybody considers economic inducement to seek work and to accept its discomforts preferable to forced labour, and that necessitates some income inequality; second, because superior status, including superior economic status, is an important source of satisfaction, which most people want to be able to aspire to, and that too is incompatible with income equality.

Our society seems to resolve the conflict between these value judgements by limiting its desire for equality to equality of opportunity and focusing its concern for an equitable distribution of income on the lower end of the income scale. Free education, scholarships and free or below-cost access to the necessities of life for the needy ensure the former, whereas the last-mentioned, together with relief payments and old age and unemployment insurance, is also designed to keep people above the poverty line. Only very few of the most advanced countries attack the problem of inequality also at the upper end of the income scale with progressive tax structures. (The present US tax structure is regressive, because the slight progressivity of the income tax is more than offset by the regressivity of the sales and various excise taxes.)

Merit goods

Many people believe that the value of some important goods is not, or not fully, recognized by a part of the public, owing to ignorance, lack of foresight or both. Accordingly, they consider it desirable to encourage the purchase and consumption of such goods, called merit goods, by making it compulsory (old age and unemployment insurance), free (health services in many countries) or subsidized (the performing arts). The provision of a part of poor relief in kind (food, foodstamps, free housing or Medicaid) rather than in money is also due to these being considered merit goods (Musgrave, 1987).

Yet another type of merit goods is those whose availability is valued even by people who make no use of them. Hospitals and public transport are examples, because even those who never use them want to have them available for emergencies, on a standby basis.

External economies and diseconomies

Many goods and services affect the well-being not only of their producers and consumers but of third parties as well. These side-effects can be favourable or unfavourable and, since they do not go through the market, they do not show up in market prices, which is why the market forces that coordinate economic decisions fail to take them into account (Bohm, 1987). It remains for policy makers, therefore, to correct or supplement market prices whenever external effects arise and are important.

Health services and education are examples of services that generate external economies: the former because they reduce the spread of contagious diseases and the latter because other people benefit from consorting with and having access to the educated. That is another important reason for providing health care and education free.

Most external effects, however, are unfavourable, for reasons to be discussed later. Think of pollution, degradation of the environment and the many dangers to health that the modern economy creates. The ideal way of dealing with diseconomies would be to internalize their costs by imposing on their originators a tax or fine that equals the diseconomy's cost to those hurt by them. That would induce them to prevent or offset the diseconomies generated by their activity to the level that maximizes the excess of benefits over costs if preventing or offsetting the diseconomies is impractical or too expensive. That, however, is easier said than done, partly because enforcement can be difficult and expensive and partly also because estimating the social cost of a diseconomy can be a difficult or near impossible undertaking. The subject will be taken up again when we deal with the genesis of diseconomies.

Internal economies and diseconomies

Similar to those external effects on third parties are internal side-effects that the production and/or the enjoyment of goods and services can have on the transacting parties themselves. Production for the market often has favourable or unfavourable effects on the producer, additional to the disutility of the effort involved and the compensation paid for it, just as the consumption of some goods imposes non-monetary costs on the consumer, which is additional to the market price he or she pays for them. Examples of goods that create the latter are narcotics and other addictive substances and foods harmful to health. Since these non-monetary costs are usually delayed, not always recognized, and their incidence is often uncertain, many people ignore or discount them, which is why informed opinion favours discouraging their use. Indeed, they could be called demerit goods, since they are the counterpart and exact opposite of merit goods.

To come now to the non-monetary side-effects of work, they can be both negative and positive. The delayed damage to health of many kinds of work has long been ignored or unsuspected, but now that it and its remedies are becoming generally known and much discussed, little remains to be said about it. The best-known examples are exposure to radioactivity and the mining, processing and use of asbestos.

Equally ignored and overlooked are and have long been the positive side-effects of work: the challenge of interesting, difficult, responsible or dangerous work, and the satisfaction and sense of accomplishment that people get out of successfully accomplishing it. One bad effect of overlooking the intrinsic satisfaction of productive work is the overemphasis on its monetary incentive, which can militate against equity. Keynes and Schumpeter, the two most distinguished economists of the previous generation, both warned against exaggerating the role of profit as the motive force of investment and growth, arguing that investments whose financial returns are drawn out over many years to come are far too risky to be prompted solely by even the best estimates of their expected profits. To use Keynes's words: 'If human nature felt no temptation to take a chance, no intrinsic satisfaction (profit apart) in constructing a factory, a railway, a mine or farm, there might not be much investment as a result of cold calculation' (Keynes, 1936, p. 150).

A good illustration of what is wrong with exaggerating the role of the profit incentive is the Reagan administration's failure to promote innovation, increase productivity and stimulate the economy by means of tax policies favouring profits. All that increased profits have accomplished is to encourage takeovers instead of investment and growth and to worsen the distribution of income.

Ignoring the intrinsic satisfaction of work has also made us overlook an important negative aspect of technical and economic progress. Most innovations in manufacturing methods of the past century have rendered work more fragmented, more monotonous, less responsible, less creative and therefore less satisfying to the worker. Karl Marx drew attention to all this a long time ago when he warned against the alienation of workers from their work (Catephores, 1987), but employers and economists alike ignored his warning. Only now, a century later, is worker dissatisfaction generally recognized as a negative side-effect of technical progress, which lowers labour productivity, and which is not too difficult to guard against once its existence and importance are recognized.

Scarcity values

Having surveyed some of the values that market prices fail to reflect but that economists must somehow estimate and take into account, let me take up one of the central concerns of economics, value created by scarcity; and I shall focus on the creation of scarcity by economic growth.

An economy grows when technical progress or a growing labour force increases the capacity to produce and effective demand increases along with it. That condition is usually fulfilled, because the income generated by production always equals the sales value of what is produced, so that growth always creates enough additional purchasing power to pay for the additional output produced. Nevertheless, growth creates problems, because, while additional demand usually extends fairly evenly over the whole range of goods and services, additions to supply and productive capacity are usually spotty and uneven. The resulting problems are resolved by price changes, which harmonize the structure of demand and the structure of supply. Some of these price changes are random and more or less cancel and offset one another in the long run; but the prices of those goods and resources that are in fixed supply always and only rise, because they become forever scarcer relative to the increased demand for them.

The simplest and most conspicuous examples of goods in fixed supply are paintings by dead masters and homes in choice locations or of historical value. The demand for them as status symbols is steadily increasing in our increasingly affluent society, which accounts for the rise in their prices relative to other prices in the economy (Hirsch, 1976).

More important are the consequences of the world's ever-growing population and its ever-growing demand confronting the fixed supply of natural resources. Land is the classic example of a natural resource in fixed supply and, in its case, secularly rising land prices have registered its increasing scarcity in relation to the rising demand for it. In this country, the inflation-corrected price of land has risen approximately in proportion with the increase in population during the first half of this century; and its rise is likely to accelerate. Bear in mind that, in Japan, whose present population density is

12.5 times that of the United States, the average price of land has risen to almost 50 times what it is in the United States.

The serious consequences that may result as the world's growing population presses against the limits that the fixed quantity of land imposes on the food supply were pointed out 200 years ago by Malthus; but so far, the great scientific and technical advances in agriculture have postponed the day of worldwide starvation he predicted (Weir, 1987).

Greater, I believe, are the dangers inherent in our ever-increasing demand on the fixed supply of such other natural resources as the purity of our air and fresh water supply and the ozone layer in the stratosphere, because they share the characteristics of collective goods of having no market prices whose rising level would reflect their increasing scarcity and serve as an early warning system to remind us of the need to do something about it.

For the supply of land, together with the depletable mineral resources of the soil, is not only fixed but also separable and salable piecemeal, in the process of which they acquire market prices that rise as they become scarcer, thereby giving timely and fair warning of the ever-increasing necessity to economize their use. By contrast, the many ingredients of a safe, healthy, pleasant and beautiful environment are *collective* resources, which means that they do not go through the market, do not acquire a market price, and their husbanding, when necessary, cannot be left to the market but must be undertaken collectively, by the state.

All this created no problem as long as their fixed supply was more than sufficient for our needs, which meant that their marginal value was zero and there was no need to restrict their use. Now, however, when population growth and global economic development make ever-greater demands on our environmental resources, these have become scarce, which calls for restricting their use; but their scarcity, instead of imposing a price to measure and warn us of that scarcity, has degraded their quality. That, unfortunately, is the wrong signal in our type of economy, where people look on a change in price as a call for action and for changing their behaviour but tend to be helpless and remain inert in the face of a decline in quality.

To illustrate what I mean, compare the husbanding of parking space with that of clean air. Parking space was once a free good; but when increased city traffic made it scarce and put a price on it, that harmonized supply and demand by both encouraging the creation of parking lots and garages and discouraging city driving. Air pollution, by contrast, for lack of a market to put a price on the privilege to pollute, degraded the quality of the air, which left the polluters unmoved and caused the general public to suffer in silence.

The authorities did nothing against mere unpleasantness and unsightliness and waited for years before worsening morbidity and mortality statistics made them realize the need for legislation to limit pollution, and even then acted half-heartedly. The measures so far enacted against air, water and soil pollution in the United States are costing about 2.5 to 3 per cent of the GNP and are woefully inadequate and poorly enforced, with the nuclear defence industry and the Defense and Energy Departments the main transgressors of the regulations; and we have done very little as yet about the more global and serious problems of the greenhouse effect and the diminishing ozone layer in the stratosphere.

You will have noticed that the problems of our deteriorating environment have already been mentioned under the name of external diseconomies. Also presented was a theoretically correct solution: monetizing and internalizing external diseconomies by estimating their costs to those hurt by them and imposing those costs in the form of a fine or tax on those whose activity generates the diseconomies. That would be the correct solution, because it would cause the polluters to develop and employ methods capable of eliminating or offsetting the diseconomy or reducing it to the point where the excess of the benefits from the polluting activity over its costs to the public is maximized.

Unfortunately, that is easier said than done, not only because enforcement is difficult and expensive, but mainly because estimating the social cost of a diseconomy can be an extremely difficult undertaking even in the best of circumstances, and utterly hopeless in some cases. How is one to estimate the cost to mankind of a rise in the temperature of the earth's surface due to the greenhouse effect, or of the additional ultraviolet radiation due to depletion of the ozone layer, when we are still uncertain about their exact effects? We only know that, whatever the effects, they may affect millions, even billions of people and generations to come.

Welfare and growth

I explored in detail the preceding grim subject as a preparation for my next and last topic. Given the central position that economists in their theories accord price as a measure of the value that consumers attribute to individual goods, the idea naturally arose to add together the market value of all the goods and services produced, and use the figure obtained as a measure of the economy's overall performance and the consuming public's welfare. That was the purpose of national product and national income estimates, two seemingly different concepts that nevertheless measure the same thing, considering that every penny spent on what is produced and sold becomes the income of someone who contributed to its production or sale.

Those estimates have become the economist's best-known tools and are extremely useful for the first purpose mentioned. Their popular use as an indicator of a nation's welfare is fraught with many pitfalls, which is why economists have never ceased warning against putting them to that use. Let me mention some of them.

First, the satisfaction we get out of consuming goods and services depends on their quantity and quality, not on their prices. Prices must be used only as weights when adding up physical quantities or dissimilar objects; but changes in prices must be corrected for when comparing the national product of different dates and when one wants to measure the change in the *real* national product. A similar, but more complex correction for price differences is also needed when comparing different countries' levels of well-being (Kravis, 1987).

Second, a country's real national product must rise in proportion with its population to keep people's welfare unchanged. To show changes in the average person's economic welfare, one needs estimates of the real national product *per capita of population*.

The last step is to weigh changes in the national product against the costs incurred in producing it. Of the many such costs, some are measurable, others not. The most obvious cost is an increase in labour input, which implies a loss of leisure. A larger output per capita of population may result from increased participation of women and others in the labour force, from people's working longer hours, having more working days, or from any combination of those three factors, since they all encroach on leisure. To correct for such costs, one would have to express the national product per annual work hours; but that has seldom been done until a recent book documented the great loss of leisure the US working population has suffered over the past 20 years (Schor, 1991).

Labour, however, is not the only factor of production: capital equipment is another, and the output produced by society's labour input can temporarily be increased by failing to maintain and allowing to deteriorate the country's capital equipment and infrastructure. In time of war, most countries tend to increase their production of war material by letting their capital equipment run down; and the Reagan administration in the United States managed to give an exaggerated impression of economic prosperity through the non-maintenance of the country's highway network, bridges and other infrastructure.

These are some of the measurable costs to allow for when interpreting the effect on welfare of a rise in the national product; potentially more important are the unmeasurable costs. One of these is the inequity in the distribution of income and in people's access to the necessities of life. For example, our economic performance over the past decade or so has been accompanied by increased inequality in the distribution of income and also by poor people's diminished access to such necessities of life as housing and medical care. We have statistics of the extent of those changes, though no way of numerically expressing the loss of national welfare they represent; but at least we know that appropriate social and economic policies could, if adopted, nullify those costs.

Much less manageable and reversible, and possibly much more serious, are the environmental costs of our economic activity; but these have already been discussed in some detail and with ample stress on the difficulty, and in some cases the utter impossibility, of quantifying them. Let me close, therefore, by just repeating that national product and income estimates are a very incomplete measure of our welfare, which depends on so many other economic and non-economic factors as well.

References

Arrow, K.J. (1987), 'Arrow's Theorem', in J. Eatwell, M. Milgate and P. Newman (eds), *The New Palgrave: A Dictionary of Economics*, (London: Macmillan), Vol. 1, pp. 124–6.

Bohm, P. (1987), 'External Economies', in *The New Palgrave*, Vol. 2, pp. 261–3.

Catephores, G. (1987), 'Alienation', in *The New Palgrave*, Vol. 1, pp. 76–8.

Hirsch, F. (1976), *Social Limits to Growth*, (Cambridge, Mass.:/London: Harvard University Press).

Keynes, J.M. (1936), *The General Theory of Employment, Interest and Money*, (London: Macmillan).

Kravis, I.B. (1987), 'International Income Comparisons', in *The New Palgrave*, Vol. 2, pp. 906–9.

Musgrave, R.A. (1987), 'Merit Goods', in *The New Palgrave*, Vol. 3, pp. 452–3.

Sadmo, A. (1987), 'Public Goods', in *The New Palgrave*, Vol. 3, pp. 1061–6.

Schor, J.B. (1991), *The Overworked American: The unexpected decline of leisure*, (New York: Basic Books).

Weir, D.R. (1987), 'Malthus's Theory of Population', in *The New Palgrave*, Vol. 3, pp. 290–93.

13 What ails the United States of America

Today, when leaders of the East European communist countries have declared the failure of their own economies, the United States, the leading capitalist country, is facing an ever-growing number of increasingly intractable problems of its own. The US economy's growth rate is lagging behind; the business cycle, which Keynes taught us to alleviate, has become more stubborn and seems to be superimposed on a secularly rising level of unemployment; in addition, income inequalities are becoming greater, both within and between different professions; finally, and most important, crime, violence, drug use and dishonest dealing on just about every level of the social scale have reached frightening proportions.

People familiar with some of the writings on the cost of progress (Scitovsky, 1959; de Jouvenel, 1960; Mishan, 1967) will not be surprised to learn that many of these problems are partly or wholly the unfortunate and often unavoidable side-effects of the economic, technical and social progress benefiting our society. I cannot deal with so broad a subject in a short account, but will try to give at least a survey of it by focusing on some of the by-products of the division of labour, the liberation of women, the communication revolution and the increased efficiency of our financial markets.

The division of labour

Let me start with the division of labour. We owe to it the tremendous rise in our standard of living, because specialization has added to our understanding of the world around us and greatly improved our mental and manual skills in dealing with whatever problem and performing whatever task we specialized in. But the tremendous increase in society's collective knowledge, skills and understanding has been achieved at the cost of the fragmentation of that knowledge and skill. For human beings' mental and menial capacities are limited, which means that we pay for our better and deeper command of our own speciality with our increasing ignorance and helplessness in dealing with all the other specialities.

In the United States, our puritan tradition has further exaggerated the contrast between our specialized knowledge and general ignorance, because our educational philosophy focuses on imparting the discipline and the rather specialized knowledge and skills necessary to prepare us for a life of work, while playing down and neglecting to provide us with enough general knowledge of the tremendous scope of human endeavours, interests, achievements and history to enable us to enjoy not only comfort in our leisure but also the stimulation of all the art, music, literature and the great diversity of the world around us that people have created for their own and our enjoyment. Consumerism is the usual term for a surfeit of comfort and insufficient stimulus, and our narrow specialization to the detriment of general culture has very much to do with it.

That side-effect of the division of labour has two further unfortunate consequences. First, it makes us exaggerate our faith in the knowledge and infallibility of specialists in fields alien to us, forgetting that they too are human and can make mistakes and that knowledge in no field is perfect. That partly accounts for what has become known as the litigation explosion in our society. For most people find it hard to distinguish the consequences of incompetence and negligence from unavoidable accidents or the limited availability of knowledge in fields other than their own, which is why they believe all mishaps inexcusable; and that belief of plaintiffs is often shared by judge and jury.

Second, and no less important, the entire functioning of our economy suffers from the fragmentation of knowledge. For the market economy is based on every participant's selfish interest being limited by the conflicting and competing selfish interests of the same market's other participants; and for those mutually limiting interests to allocate resources and distribute products efficiently, and promote the improvement of existing and creation of new products, three conditions have to be fulfilled: (1) buyers must know what is good for them and know about the quality and availability of everything the market has to offer in order to choose intelligently; (2) they must be personally liable to pay for their purchases, thereby to keep their own demand within reasonable limits; and (3) sellers must be honest in stating their offers and fulfilling their side of the bargain.

The fragmentation of knowledge makes it ever harder for consumers to satisfy the first condition, because they have to choose in dozens of markets from among hundreds and thousands of goods and services, whose ever-increasing variety and complexity makes informed choices very difficult.

Let me begin by mentioning two extreme examples of markets in which consumers' choice is exceptionally difficult and where the two other conditions of the proper functioning of markets are also imperfectly satisfied. They are those for medical services and legal assistance. Given the tremendous advance of medical knowledge, most people know little about what health services they need and are at a loss when it comes to choosing their physicians and judging the soundness of their advice and the necessity of the tests and treatments they prescribe. Yet physicians often prescribe too many and too expensive ones, partly for fear of being sued for negligence but also because all too many of them have a financial interest in the labs and hospitals that perform those tests and treatments. Moreover, patients themselves can also be guilty of overusing doctors' time when they do not have to pay out of their own pocket, on a fee for service basis, at least part of the cost of each visit and test performed. No wonder that, compared to most other professional services as well as to other countries' health facilities, US medical services are greatly overused and overpriced, and US physicians overpaid, which today renders them unaffordably expensive for well over 30 million members of the population.

Things work out somewhat better when general practitioners (GPs) deal with simple ailments, make the first diagnosis, know what specialist to send the patient to, and make or help make the judgement as to what treatment, if any, is advisable. Unfortunately, we have a shortage of GPs and a surfeit of specialists, for reasons which again are worth noting. When consumers lack the knowledge by which to judge the goods and services available to them, they judge them by their reputations; and in the case of physicians, specialists tend to acquire reputations much sooner and more easily than do GPs. That enables reputable specialists to attract more patients and charge higher, often much higher, fees, which emboldens their less reputable specialist colleagues also to charge higher fees than GPs do. That accounts for the very great disparity between specialists' and GPs' earnings, which in turn explains why too few medical students opt for general practice and far too many for surgery and other specialities instead. Hence our great shortage of GPs, which is especially hard on rural populations, whose only accessible doctor used to be a GP and many of whom are now stranded with no doctor at all.

Very similar are the reasons for the malfunctioning of the market for legal services, where again clients tend to be ignorant about the subject, and the system of contingency fees enables unscrupulous lawyers to lure clients into excessive litigation. What that means will be apparent to anybody who has ever had a minor traffic accident with no bodily or psychic harm but who was then besieged by dozens of phone calls from lawyers offering to litigate on their behalf and to give them the names of doctors willing to diagnose and testify to more serious harm than that actually suffered. That, then, is a second reason for the tremendous increase in litigation and the number of lawyers in our society. Also, here again, just as in the case of physicians, most clients judge lawyers by their reputations, which again leads to great disparities between the earnings of general practitioners and specialists in the law.

Most of our other markets, however, have functioned pretty well so far, thanks to an altogether different kind of division of labour that has eliminated the fragmentation of knowledge where knowledge is crucial: among consumers. I am referring to the traditional European and US division of labour between husbands and wives that made the former into specialists the better to earn the family's income and the latter into generalists to enable them to attend to all the other ingredients of their family's welfare. While men's jobs called for narrow specialization in whatever knowledge and skill their occupation or profession required, wives had to become all-rounders, knowledgeable enough to deal with all the market transactions involved in housekeeping, creating a home, taking care of the family's health, entertainment, social life and so on, and to attend to religion, culture, relations with the wider family and the children's education and upbringing into upright and disciplined grown-ups.

For women to do all that and do it well requires and imparts more judgement and a much broader knowledge of markets and the world around them than do most men's specialities, which explains why the materfamilias, the wife and mother of the family, enjoys the highest regard and greatest authority in the countries of Southern Europe, such as Italy, Spain, Portugal or Greece, as the upholder of moral and aesthetic standards and the repository of general education and worldly wisdom.

In short, that sexist division of labour enabled the family to maintain, teach and perpetuate honesty, decency and civilization in our society as well as enabling most markets of the private enterprise economy to function reasonably well. But it ensured those important benefits at the very high cost of depriving women of independence, making them depend on marriage for a decent livelihood and status in society, thus making them subservient to men and putting them in an inferior position. The position of women was especially burdensome in the United States, which had half as many, or even fewer, domestic servants per family than other countries, owing mainly to the shortage and high cost of US labour, but also to the puritan tradition that frowned upon domestic service as the most flagrant manifestation of the class society.

The liberation of women
The extra heavy burden housekeeping imposed on American wives may explain why the US feminist movement was one of the earliest to start, declaring its demand for voting rights, full legal equality and equal educational and occupational opportunity as early as 1848, and why it cast its net so much wider than feminism elsewhere. Catherine Beecher (1841) and Beecher and Stowe (1869) exposed the exploitation of cheap female labour by the textile mills' 14-hour working days, deplored wealthy, educated, unmarried women's suffering from inactivity, demanded schooling in 'domestic economy' to give women self-assurance for their task of creating and organizing a harmonious, cooperative family essential for the education of children and, to make that possible, showed how the drudgery of housekeeping can be eased by applying to it the same principles of scientific management that Frank Gilbreth and later Frederick Taylor brought to manufacturing.

Indeed, Beecher and Stowe's book first proposed the redesigning of kitchens to eliminate the cook's unnecessary walking and stooping; Christine Frederick's book (1926) published the motion studies she made of kitchen work and housekeeping; and these two books, by drawing attention to the great scope for increasing the efficiency of housekeeping, sparked off America's virtual monopoly in the development, and primacy in the general adoption, of every conceivable household and kitchen appliance, from the simple egg-beater, carpet-cleaner and electric iron to washing and drying machines, dishwashers, vacuum cleaners, refrigerators, garbage disposers and the thermostatic control of household heating and cooking in electric kitchens. A good index of the American household's mechanization is its tremendously increased consumption of electric power. While lighting was the main use of electricity in the home 100 years ago, today's households, which consume 35 per cent of all the electric power generated, use more than nine-tenths of that for purposes other than lighting (see Schurr *et al.*, 1990).

Mechanizing the household worked wonders in stimulating America's technical ingenuity and industry and has rendered most household chores much less strenuous, fatiguing and unpleasant; but it has not lightened much the burden on the American housewife, because it hardly diminished the time she spent in housekeeping. Originally prompted by a shortage of domestic servants, the easing burden of householding led, in turn, to further reductions in paid household help, while much of the unpaid help of maiden aunts and unmarried daughters in the extended families of earlier days has also disappeared as they opted for independence by taking paid jobs and moving to homes of their own. As a result, 'the middle-class American housewife's managerial functions diminished and she increasingly became instead the family's chauffeur, charwoman and short-order cook' (Cowan, 1976).

Economic independence, however, the principal aim of the women's liberation movement, is being achieved through their increased entry into the labour force. Their participation in the US labour force rose from 18.2 per cent of all adult women in 1890 to 31.8 per cent in 1947 and to 57.8 per cent in 1992, by which time it was less than 18 percentage points below the male participation rate of 75.6 per cent. That is a revolutionary change; but it has been an incomplete and lopsided revolution, in two respects. To begin with, women's liberation in the United States remains way behind most other civilized countries in not yet having secured women's control over their own bodies which medical advance in birth control has made possible. That incomplete and lopsided liberation of American women is creating some of the most severe problems in US society and economy.

For coeducation in schools and women's increased participation in the labour force have led to many more, closer and friendlier contacts between men and women, which inevitably also increased their sexual contacts. That created no problems in Scandinavia, Britain, France, Italy, the ex-communist world and other countries where women enjoy easy access to birth-control information and medication, and free or affordable abortion. In the United States, however, where that is still far from being the case, the sexes' closer relations have led and continue to lead to many unwanted children. We do not know their number, but we know the number of births to never married mothers. Some of these are wanted, mostly because all too many single women are so poor and lonely that they want a child just to relieve their loneliness. Their children, unfortunately, are born into poverty and destined for a life no better than unwanted ones, which is why the fate of most illegitimate children can be discussed together.

Illegitimate births as a proportion of total live births in the United States have risen eightfold between 1940 and 1990, from 3.5 to 28 per cent of total live births. In numbers that is an increase from 90 000 to 1 165 000 annual illegitimate births, of which 30 per cent (348 000) were births to girls of 18 years or younger. By 1992, 15.4 million children, a quarter of all US children under the age of 18, were members of the 12.6 million fatherless families; and while divorced or widowed mothers headed a little more than half of these, the remaining 5.5 million fatherless families were headed by never married mothers or mothers abandoned by their children's fathers. Since 5.8 million of all fatherless families were below the poverty line, it is reasonable to assume that these included most of the 5.5 million families headed by unmarried or abandoned mothers.

The fate of the children in these families is that most of them go hungry, which in early life is known to reduce cognitive abilities and to lead to poor performance in school (see Maital and Morgan, 1992); few get health care and the parental attention and education so essential for a proper upbringing; and boys with no father figure in the home to imitate look for him in the street and too often find him in the leaders of the gangs they join. In short, most of these children are born into poverty, often to mothers unprepared for them and children themselves; they grow up with inadequate schooling, often as drop-outs; and few avoid contributing to the crime, violence, drug trade and addiction rampant in our midst.

The other respect in which women's increased labour force participation is 'a stalled revolution is that neither the workplace nor men have caught up with the dramatic changes in the lives of women who both work and raise a family. Workplaces have done little to become more flexible in the face of the changing needs of workers with families, and fathers whose wives work full-time come nowhere near to equally sharing either household or childrearing responsibilities' (Weal, 1994.) In families where both parents are working, and in one-parent families, children return from school to their empty home, where they are alone for hours until a parent comes home from work; and studies show that these 'latchkey children', as they are called, 'are more depressed, more likely to use alcohol, cigarettes and marijuana and get lower grades than their supervised counterparts'. The Children's Hospital of the Stanford Medical School is experimenting with KidCall, a non-crisis phone programme for children who are alone after school, which answers questions, gives advice, reads stories for children and helps with their homework, but this is a very partial solution of the problem.

Middle-class parents, in both one- and two-parent families, often try to compensate for this by hiring baby-sitters; but that helps only at a very young age and is an imperfect substitute for parental guidance even then, considering that most baby-sitters are either too young or from a different culture. The children's lesser guidance and supervision in such families is not nearly as fatal as that of children without any guidance and illegitimate children born into poverty: but it still inflicts a cost on society. For few of the baby-sitters in the United States can be compared to the nannies who brought up the British aristocracy's children, who often knew more about parenting than the parents themselves, were considered members of the family and guardians of its conscience, often for two generations running. They are, however, a dying-out breed, even in England.

Finally, a less important but still noteworthy by-product of women's market work is their becoming less knowledgeable shoppers, being too busy to keep up with changing fashions and learn about new market opportunities, improvements and innovating products. That is why they increasingly turn to such 'specialized generalists' as real-estate brokers for choosing the best mortgage for their home, interior designers for choosing its furnishings, car brokers to choose their new car and publications like Consumer Reports. The advice of such intermediaries is much better than nothing; but the economy suffers when consumers abdicate their sovereignty and deprive producers of direct information as to their preferences, which in the past have pointed the way in which buyers wanted the economy to move.

The information highway
Xerox, fax, cellular phones, computer networks, fibre-optic and satellite communication for telephone and television are all parts of a new information and communication highway, the latest step in our technical progress, which is yet to be completed. Its benefits are self-evident; but it too has its undesirable side-effects. The first of them, pointed out by the artistically-minded French, is the expected increasing uniformity of the world around us. The fascinating variety of art, architecture, fashions, culinary traditions and exotic atmosphere of foreign lands is gradually being displaced by dull uniformity as the whole world submits to the same influences by listening to the identical tunes and watching the identical movies and television programmes.

Travel will become less interesting, exciting and worthwhile, not only because we can experience the same thing at home from a comfortable armchair in front of a television screen, but also, and mainly, because the sight and sound of other places will lose much of their stimulating strangeness, exotic quality and novelty.

That, however, is still in the far distant future. More immediate and much more serious are the social effects. From the informational point of view, the entire globe is becoming a single village; and since our minds' ability to process information is limited, the media single out from the masses of available information only what is sensational and likely to attract the public's attention; and, as is well known, four-fifths of that consists of crime, violence, murder, rape, kidnapping, terrorism and the devastation of war. Until the past few years, those horrors were still relatively rare in our immediate vicinity; but they happened all the time in various other parts of the globe; and our television screens provided us with a continuous spectacle of them, culled from wherever and however far away they happened, to provide us with our daily ration of slaughter and similar sensations.

All this made us grown-ups depressed, giving us the illusion that we lived in an exceptionally cruel and uncivilized age, although we may merely have been better informed about all the cruelty committed in the world than were our forefathers, whose blissful ignorance of happenings on other continents, in other countries, perhaps even in other cities, assured their peaceful and cheerful existence.

Many of our children, however, were seriously damaged by the miracle of witnessing the spectacle of the entire world's cruelty in their living-room as vividly as if it had happened next door. For young children have no conception yet of the globe's magnitude and the tremendous distances from which many of the events reported on TV news programmes come. To them, all the violence they saw on TV news and in horror films may well have appeared as the normal daily routine of the adult life that awaited them and for which they had to prepare.

The past tense of the last two paragraphs is explained by the worst byproduct of our communication highway, which is that, sooner or later, it turns the illusion it creates into reality. For the children who grow up watching the world's worst horrors compressed into daily 30-minute television news programmes are in danger of turning into adults who at best are inured to all that violence and at worst join its perpetrators – especially when brought up in poverty, without adequate schooling, supervision and a respectable father figure to imitate. The United States seems to have reached that stage already. Terrorism, gang warfare and the senseless killing of innocent people and children are rapidly becoming almost as common in our immediate neighbourhoods as they were, and unfortunately still are, in what used to be known as darkest Africa. The problem may even be worse in US society than in primitive societies, because too many children in the United States are not only victims of all that violence but also among its practitioners, growing up without ever learning the difference between right and wrong.

The creation and storage of wealth

An important benefit of the US economy's rising productivity and the resulting rise in incomes has been people's ability to save up a nest-egg for a dignified and comfortable old age, which frees them from dependence on their children's charity. They cannot, of course, accumulate and store in kind the food, medical care and other amenities they will need in old age; instead, they accumulate financial assets that can later be exchanged for goods and services as the need arises. That imposes no burden on their children if, and only if, their accumulating those assets does not diminish total spending, which would depress the economy, and if it either adds productive capacity or improves existing capacity, thereby enabling the economy to cater to the increased demand that their exchanging those assets into goods and services will generate.

In short, saving is beneficial only if it finances investment, otherwise it not only fails to create productive capacity but also depresses the economy. That was recognized more than a century ago by John Stuart Mill, because he argued that the hoarding of cash creates a general glut and so depresses the economy; but only Keynes realized, much later, that putting savings into previously issued financial assets can also fail to generate investment and create a general glut, just as can the hoarding of cash.

That such a seemingly obvious generalization from the hoarding of cash to the hoarding of pre-existing assets should have taken so long and even then required the genius of Keynes to recognize may be due to economists' never paying any attention to second-hand markets. The probable reason for that was the belief that buyers in such markets merely transfer part of their income to the sellers, whose spending of it offsets the buyers' hoarding, thereby keeping second-hand transactions from having an impact on the economy. That was a reasonable inference to make as long as the volume of transactions in the accumulated stock of existing assets was small relatively to the issue and sale of new assets. But with the continuing accumulation of financial assets into an ever-larger stock, second-hand transactions in those assets became a multiple of the issue of new assets, which made the above inference invalid and led to Keynes's realization that the rate of interest has ceased to be the price which brings into equilibrium the demand for resources to invest with the readiness to abstain from present consumption and has become instead the price that equilibrates the desire to hold wealth in the form of financial assets with the available quantity of financial assets.

Realizing that automatic market forces could no longer be relied on to ensure full-employment equilibrium, Keynes advocated the use of deliberate monetary and fiscal policies, which were successful in maintaining stable, high levels of employment in the immediate postwar period. Since then, however, the further great accumulation of the stock of financial assets, the proliferation of secondary (so-called 'non-rated') assets, the new technology for the automatic buying and selling of assets in response to their changing prices, together with the integration of financial markets across national frontiers, have made speculation and the purely financial management of wealth very much easier, more efficient and therefore much more attractive. As a result, the rich, who used to be on the boards of the companies in which they had a controlling interest and in whose planning for development and innovative investments they participated, tend increasingly to relinquish such functions in favour of the purely financial management of their wealth. Similarly, corporate managers are diverting their corporations' savings from risky innovative investments to mergers with or takeovers of existing companies, and sometimes to speculative purchases of financial assets. Both those trends could be expected to turn what used to be the positive-sum game of innovative capital formation into the zero- or negative-sum game of speculation; and, to judge by our high, chronic and hard-to-remedy unemployment, that seems to be what has happened. (A detailed and rigorous exposition of this paragraph's topic is contained in Chapter 8 above.)

A cure-all?
Having dealt with that long and disheartening list of social and economic problems, it seems fitting to conclude with some discussion of what might be done about them – the more so because there exists a cure-all, neither perfect nor easy to establish, but one that would alleviate many of the above-mentioned problems. I have in mind turning the unemployment of the relatively few into added leisure for the many by creating jobs for the unemployed through shortening the working week of the employed, while keeping it unchanged for their employers. The objections employers and employees alike might have to such a change are not insurmountable and its social and economic benefits are likely to exceed, perhaps even greatly to exceed, its costs to businesses and their workers. The difficult problem is how to redistribute those benefits so as to make the change acceptable to its opponents by compensating them for their costs.

Let me start by enumerating the benefits. Diminished unemployment and the consequent reduction in poverty are the most obvious ones. Less obvious but amply documented (see also the examples quoted below) is the increase in labour productivity that seems always to result from shortening the working week. All the other benefits are the social benefits that would stem from workers having more time to spend with their spouses and children, making family ties stronger and family life happier, reducing divorce rates, increasing parenting, decreasing the number of latchkey children and school dropouts, improving school performance and diminishing truancy and all the crime, violence, drug addiction and juvenile gang warfare that result from poverty and parents' lack of time to supervise, teach, discipline and just spend with their children.

All these benefits are not only very important and valuable in themselves, they would also save billions of dollars of public expenditure on unemployment compensation, poverty relief, Medicaid, police protection, maintaining and building prisons and the fight against drugs. Government could use these savings partly to relieve employers of the extra cost to them of needing more workers to perform the same work that fewer working a longer week performed before, and partly also to enable them to pay an undiminished or only slightly diminished weekly wage for the shorter working week.

Labour's fight for a shorter working week against employers' hostility to the idea has a long history in the United States. The fight for the 40-hour week was won thanks to Henry Ford's initiative in granting it and President Woodrow Wilson's intervention; but the campaign for a 30-hour working week during the Great Depression of the 1930s when unemployment rose to one-quarter of the labour force was unsuccessful (Schor, 1991). Today, some labour unions are advocating shorter working weeks; a bill introduced in the House of Representatives in the autumn of 1993 called for a government-mandated 30-hour working week but had little support, and employers seem to be unanimously against it.

Employers' hostility to employing more workers to make up for a shorter working week is mainly due to the cost to them of the additional contributions to social insurance and pension, health and welfare funds payable on behalf of the additional workers. For those payments increase not only with wages but also with the number of workers; and they are quite substantial, at present amounting to more than 20 per cent of wages paid. Also, employers' bargaining power in the labour market is weakened and their difficulty in finding extra workers increased without an excess supply of labour, which may add to their hostility to a shorter working week. Labour, on the other hand, would be reluctant to accept a shorter week if it involved a corresponding reduction in wages.

However, the subject is receiving a lot of attention in Europe, especially in Germany and France, where the unemployment rate is much higher and more chronic than in the United States, although their social problems are not nearly as bad. In Germany, whose present 37-hour working week is already three hours shorter than the 40 hours worked in the United States, many firms are experimenting with shortening it further as a substitute for dismissing workers. One of the best-known examples is provided by the Volkswagen company, whose two-year contract for 1994 and 1995 agreed with its unions to cut the working week to 28¹/₂ hours for all workers and office employees in their Wolfsburg, Hannover and Salzgitter plants and, with the exception of Wolfsburg workers, to shift from five to four days. Another German car company, BMW, adopted a four-day working week in 1990, *with no cut in wages*, because the resulting rise in their workers' productivity more than offset the cost of hiring more people.

Many such experiments have also been made by French manufacturers, including the French subsidiaries of two American electronic firms, Hewlett Packard and Digital Equipment. The latter, for example, trying to avoid having to reduce its workforce, polled its 4000 employees to find out how many of them would like to reduce their five-day (36³/₄-hour) week to a four- or three-day week. Almost 15 per cent (590) of them voted in favour, mostly of a four-day week, most of them in order to have more time to spend with their children, others to take up a hobby or prepare themselves for more advanced work. These employees signed two-year contracts for four-day working weeks at 84 per cent of their previous salary plus periodic lump-sum payments that brought their actual pay up to 92.7 per cent of what they earned for a four-day week. The 20 per cent reduction in these employees' worktime has, to their own surprise, hardly diminished their output, and the productivity and profitability of the company's French subsidiary has not suffered (I owe all this information to Robin Ashmore of Digital Equipment Corporation).

But the French, given their almost 13 per cent unemployment rate, compared with Western Germany (8.3 per cent) and the United States (6 per cent), are considering a much more ambitious plan (nationwide and compulsory) that would shorten the country's working week; and such a plan, specific and very detailed, developed and published by M. Larrouturou (1994), has been much discussed in parliament, President Mitterrand's office, the administration, on television and among businessmen and labour unions.

To illustrate the effects that such a plan might have in the United States, it is worth looking at some of the detail of the French plan. It proposes to reduce France's present five-day, 39-hour working week by 15 per cent to a four-day, 33-hour working week. To make up fully for the worktime lost, firms would have to increase their workforce by 18 per cent. To enable them to pay for this additional workforce, the plan suggests reducing the weekly wage by an average 5 per cent (the lowest wage by 3 per cent, the highest by 8 per cent) and relieving employers from paying the present 8.8 per cent payroll tax, which contributes part of the cost of unemployment insurance. These two changes, together with the 5 per cent increase in productivity the shorter working week is estimated to bring about, would take care of the full cost to the firm of its additional workforce.

A questionnaire survey of workers showed that 87 per cent of them would willingly accept a 5 per cent reduction in wages in exchange for a 15 per cent reduction in their working week; as to the public purse, its loss of the revenue from the payroll tax would be more than fully offset by the reduced cost of unemployment compensation, provided that M. Larrouturou's estimate that his plan would re-employ two million workers is to be trusted.

The social benefits of the plan, which from our point of view are the most interesting, would stem from the way in which it envisages the transition to the four-day week. For enterprises would maintain the traditional five-day working week, but let each worker choose one of the five working days as an additional free day for him- or herself. Childless couples or those with grown children would presumably choose the same additional day to spend their leisure together; but those with small children would choose to be free on different workdays and, by coordinating their own choices of free days with those of three other working parents of their acquaintance, could ensure *parenting for all their children on every day of the week.*

In the United States, with its severe social problems, this last benefit and its long-run effects would be more important than the relief of unemployment and poverty; and to obtain it would not even require a universal nationwide switch to a shorter working week, which the French are discussing. It would be sufficient merely to require employers to give some of their workers *the option to switch* to the four-day week, somewhat along the lines discussed in the example of the Digital Equipment Corporation. The logistics of the workplace, in which the same job is not performed by the same person every day, receives detailed attention in the Larrouturou plan; but that would be much simpler if only a part of the workforce opted for a four-day week and worked side-by-side with colleagues on the five-day working week.

The main problems would be how to compensate employers for the additional contributions for social insurance health and pension plans they would have to pay when hiring additional workers to make up for their existing workers' shorter hours and for sweetening the workers' pill by not reducing their pay or reducing it in lesser proportion than the reduction in their worktime.

I suspect that both problems could be resolved by financing them out of the savings on government's expenditures created by reform, as not only unemployment and poverty but also crime, violence and drug use would diminish in a saner and less unruly society. Unfortunately, however, the most important of those benefits may take years to materialize, whereas the reform to bring them about and the funds to finance it would be needed right away. That might not have been too great an obstacle had not our federal debt and annual federal deficit risen five fold over the past one and a half decades. That has been the cumulative effect of the US government's bad economic policies over those years, and it is severely limiting the country's ability to use money to deal with economic problems, domestic and external alike. That is yet another of the United States' ills, and one of the most important.

References

Beecher, Catherine E. (1841), *Treatise on Domestic Economy*, (Boston: Marsh, Capon, Lyon & Webb).
—— and Stowe, Harriet B. (1869), *The American Woman's Home*, (New York: Ford).
Cowan, R.S. (1976), 'The industrial revolution in the home', *Technology & Culture*, **17**, January, 22.
De Jouvenel, Bertrand (1960), 'Efficiency and Amenity', 40th Earl Grey Memorial Lecture, King's College, Newcastle-upon-Tyne.
Frederick, Christine (1926), *Household Engineering: Scientific Management in the Home*, (Chicago: American School of Home Economics).
Larrouturou, Pierre (1994), *Combattre radicalement le chômage*, (Paris: Édition du Seuil); Excerpt from the same author's and publisher's *Non, ça ne peut plus durer: 12 propositions pour une société plus humaine* (forthcoming).
Maital, Shlomo and Morgan, K.L. (1992), 'Hungry children are bad business', *Challenge*, July/ August.
Mishan, E.J. (1967), *The Costs of Economic Growth*, (London: Staples).
Schor, Juliet B. (1991), *The Overworked American*, (New York: Basic Books).
Schurr, S.H., Burwell, C.C., Devine W.D. Jr. and Sonenblum, S. (1990), *Electricity in the American Economy*, Historical Statistics of the Electric Utility Industry, (New York: Greenwood), p. 251.
Scitovsky, Tibor (1959), 'What Price Economic Progress?' *Yale Review*, Autumn.
Weal, E. (1994), 'My Life as a Mother', in *San Francisco Peninsula Parent*, May.

14 Hindsight economics*

Many years ago, when asked to write my recollections as an economist, I demurred, believing that the work I was then doing was more valuable and interesting than my recollections could possibly be. But now, at 80, my writings are seldom more than variations on or postscripts to work I originally failed fully to develop or bring to fruition; and I discovered a common thread connecting much of my earlier work, which gave me a new insight into the subconscious workings of my mind. That was something new, which seemed worth spelling out; and that is what I am proposing to do in the following.

As an overprotected, privately tutored, only and lonely child, I became an avid reader and do-it-yourselfer, with my parents' chauffeur as my only friend. Chauffeurs in those days were skilled mechanics who had to spend much of their time attending to the many problems with the early cars; and I soon became our chauffeur's apprentice garage mechanic. As such, I owe to him my knowledge of things mechanical, love for exercising my manual dexterity on home repairs and, since he was a socialist, also my acquaintance with socialism and first introduction to economics through reading the first volume of Marx's *Das Kapital*.

In the semi-feudal Hungary of those days, all upper middle-class youths with no special talents or vocation studied law; and I too followed that course. But since I was able to do most of the reading and preparation for the exams during summer vacations, I concurrently spent five terms at Cambridge where, on exhausting the university's meagre offerings in international law, I switched to economics, more or less as a hobby. I did not study very seriously at that stage but learned enough to return to the subject later and to enable me even then to come up with the most valuable economic advice I have given in my entire career. For when I returned home from Cambridge in the spring of 1931, my father asked what if anything I had learned that would be useful in those difficult days to someone like him (he was then president of Hungary's largest bank). I mentioned Britain's declaring bank holidays in past financial crises; he listened carefully and soon thereafter prevailed upon the government to proclaim the bank holiday that helped Hungary weather the Great Depression somewhat better than did neighbouring Austria, the closing down of whose largest bank, the Kredit Anstalt, was a landmark of the depression.

* This chapter appeared in Banca Nazionale del Lavoro, *Quarterly Review*, no. 178, September 1991.

I learned economics in earnest only years later, when I became anxious to emigrate and found myself woefully unprepared to make my own way in the West. I enrolled at the London School of Economics (LSE) in 1935, more or less by chance, and that turned out to have been an excellent choice, because the School exposed one to many conflicting ideas and ideologies, forcing one to compare, judge, reconcile and choose. At that time, many of the students and the non-economic faculty were Marxists, whereas the Economics Department, save for one or two junior members, was very conservative, with Hayek its leading light and young Nicholas Kaldor still his ardent admirer and follower. Apparently fearful of becoming a poor man's Oxbridge, the Department spurned Cambridge economics, hardly even mentioned Alfred Marshall and relied on texts by Wicksteed, Taussig, Frank Knight, Mises, Hayek, Gustav Cassell (Walras's popularizer), and Knut Wicksell.

Like many of my fellow students, I was seduced by the elegant logic of what we were taught and the utopian picture it presented, but also disturbed by its unreality and apparent uselessness. In the London of the depressed 1930s, we witnessed plenty of misery and unemployment, labour demonstrations were frequent, and we were disappointed by the economics profession's failure to come up with a remedy. Young economists increasingly studied the socialist alternative; and Hayek edited a volume of essays that argued the pros and cons of *Collective Economic Planning*, concluding in his 'Summary of the Debate' that the nays had it. He was the only one in the LSE faculty to diagnose the pressing economic problem of the time in his *Theory of the Trade Cycle*; but his diagnosis was too involved and his remedy (curbing the preceding prosperity) too ascetic to attract many followers.

Some of us students felt that there must be something seriously wrong with an economic theory that leaves its practitioners quite so helpless in the face of severe economic problems. We often discussed the need for reforming the theory or adopting a completely new approach that would expose rather than hide the economy's shortcomings and point the way to remedying them; but we had no idea how to go about it. I had a vague feeling that the concepts of conflict and exploitation, eliminated in the model of perfect competition, ought somehow to be reintroduced into a more realistic general model of markets and the economy; but, not knowing where to start, I merely worked very hard, reading and studying way beyond what was required and recommended, discovering the existence of national income estimates and generally hoping to find clues to a better approach and trying to prepare myself for an active role in bringing about the reform that the discipline needed.

Then, a year after my arrival, Keynes' *General Theory of Employment* appeared and put an end to all those thoughts. I remember persuading the manager of the School's bookshop to let me have a copy the day before its publication and staying up half the night to read it. For it was like a breath of fresh air, making all our texts look stale and stuffy. It seemed to have accomplished much of the reform of economic theory we were hoping for; and the angry, passionate strife it brought into the Economics Department soon filled our lives. Lionel Robbins' Monday seminars became the scene of heated arguments between the solidly anti-Keynesian senior faculty (Hayek and Robbins) and the Keynesian young instructors (Kaldor and Lerner), foreign visitors (Kalecki and Lange) and some of us students. Witnessing and participating in those weekly battles became the main excitement of our lives; and for those of us preparing for exams and writing dissertations, it was excellent training as well. For anxious both to get good grades and to be honest to ourselves, we tried not just to give the answers expected or the ones we believed right but to state our beliefs *and* defend them against, or reconcile them with, our examiners' conflicting beliefs. That was a difficult but rewarding task and made me feel that I had acquitted myself reasonably well. One day, however, when Kaldor paid me the compliment of suggesting that I submit a paper for publication in the forthcoming but not yet complete issue of the *Review of Economic Studies*, I shamefacedly had to admit to having nothing on paper or in mind that would be fit to print.

I learned to write economics only much later when, after two minor temporary jobs, a travelling fellowship from the University of London took me to the United States and World War II stranded me there, with no job in sight and not a printed page to my name. I tried in vain to have my fellowship extended when a well-meant but unavailing telegram I received in that connection turned me into a suspect and unwelcome alien. It came when German submarine attacks on British merchant shipping were at their height and the campaign was supposed to be aided by information sent from and via the United States by spies, masquerading as refugees. The cable said: RE FELLOWSHIP CONTACT KALDOR BURNT CLOSE GRANTCHESTER NEAR CAMBRIDGE. My first reaction to reading it was a feeling of unease, thinking that an alert censor, seeing the syllables SHIP and BURNT in a seemingly cryptic text, might smell a rat. Indeed, many years later, a friendly FBI agent confirmed that I had been put under surveillance as a result of that telegram.

Being on a student visa, I could not accept Paul Samuelson's offer of a research assistantship, nor could I leave; so my only hope of saving my career lay in establishing a reputation by publishing as much as possible. With the words 'publish or perish' constantly ringing in my ears, I made the rounds of Columbia, Chicago and Harvard, spending agonizing months in their libraries, chewing my pencil and waiting for inspiration that was awfully slow in coming. I was obsessed with the idea that I must be able to explain how and why Keynesian unemployment fitted or failed to fit into classical economics, which I believed Hicks's 'Keynes and the Classics' and Lange's almost identical article had failed to do.[1] I suspected that the answer lay in some prices' failing to clear their markets; the question was which prices and why.

That started me on a lifelong preoccupation with the way prices were determined. I pored over a shelf full of T.N.E.C. reports, Gardiner Means's *The Structure of the American Economy* and several other American studies of the frequency and magnitude of price changes; but my work on all that became bogged down and bore fruit only years later, when after my military and civil service I started teaching and teaching duties forced me to focus on microeconomics.

In the interim, my first published article explained involuntary unemployment by showing that interest rates failed to equate the flow of new capital formation to what the flow of saving would be at full employment, because they also had to equilibrate people's desire to hold previously issued financial assets against their accumulated stock; and the same price could not simultaneously perform both tasks, equating instead one market's excess demand to the other's excess supply. I still believe that to have been one of my best papers, because it uncovered an important gap left by the classical economists.[2]

The classics' great achievement was to recognize the advantages of the division of labour and the contribution markets make to it by enabling people to specialize. That was well brought out by their simple model of the economy with its small cast of characters and all attention focused on the market transactions necessitated by the division of labour: trades between people cast in different characters, such as workers and managers, producers and merchants, merchants and consumers.

I was dimly aware of the incompleteness of that cast of characters; and it gradually dawned on me that, by confining their analysis to only those markets that facilitate the flow of resources and products, the classics might have overlooked other markets the transactions in which inhibit that flow, which would explain their uncritical acceptance of Say's Law. The main missing character was the capitalist, whose role was the financial management of his wealth (I misnamed him 'speculator' at the time); the overlooked markets were the single-character markets where capitalists trade with other capitalists in the accumulated stock of financial and tangible assets.

The classics could hardly be faulted for these omissions. In their day, financial markets, instruments and information were not yet good enough to enable people efficiently to separate the financial management of their wealth from the physical management of the equipment and other tangible assets in which it was embodied, so there was no need to distinguish capitalists from entrepreneurs.

As to the markets in which the holders of the accumulated stock of assets traded them among themselves, they must have seemed unimportant at the time, because the prices they generated performed no function beyond reflecting the owners' marginal valuations of their possessions. Those prices could, of course, influence the prices of the newly created counterparts of those goods and assets in the parallel first-hand markets; but that influence was negligible as long as either the second-hand markets and their transactions were negligible or contacts between the two sets of markets were slight.

Only gradually have the accumulating stocks of assets and goods and the increasing volume of transactions in those stocks increased their influence on the prices that governed the rate at which new assets were issued or goods produced. Producers of durable goods, however, managed to differentiate the first- and second-hand markets for their products through frequent improvements and design changes that made the used specimens seem obsolete substitutes for the new ones and so kept their sale from depressing the latter's price.

Very different was and is the case of financial assets. Unlike physical assets, they neither depreciate nor go out of fashion, which is why they have no separate first- and second-hand markets. Moreover, the volume of transactions in previously issued financial assets has, by now, far outstripped the rate at which new issues and new savings come onto asset markets, which explains why, today, the cost of raising capital by issuing financial assets is mainly determined by the price at which previously issued similar assets change hands and is no longer that which equates saving and investment, except by accident.

It appeared therefore that the stickiness of market prices was not the only obstacle to their equating the flow of demand and supply; another obstacle was their dependence also, and mainly, on prices in the related markets in which the accumulated stocks of similar assets were traded.

That was the gist of my first paper. It seemed to have been read by no one and did nothing to help me emerge from obscurity – owing perhaps to its publication at a time (August 1940) when even the most cloistered academics were preoccupied with the far more important events of Dunkirk and the fall of France. Anyhow, my paper's failure to attract attention changed the direction of my work. It stopped me writing on the subject until almost half a century later, when I explored the macroeconomic impact of affluent people's increasing demand for positional goods.[3]

Also it made me abandon all thought of a major contribution. Instead, I started writing short papers and notes on a great variety of subjects, because I read a lot and, being a slow reader, slow at absorbing new ideas, became pretty good at spotting and clearing up mistakes, ambiguities and obscurities overlooked by others. These were noticed and later helped me overcome the handicap of my late start on an academic career; and they also gave me a foothold in several branches of economics, because many of them proved to be a germ I was able to develop much further.

My work on those papers was interrupted, however, by my being called up for military service. I welcomed that, because it allayed my bad conscience for not taking part in the war and also because it prevented my appearing at my deportation hearing (scheduled for a few days after my having to report for duty) and possible deportation. Basic training compared favourably with my Hungarian military service and was my true initiation to America and the kindness of Americans. My subsequent training was for combat intelligence and propaganda; I shipped to Europe in a mobile radio broadcasting company, where my fellow NCOs were Joseph Wechsberg of *The New Yorker*, Igor Cassini, the then Hollywood gossip columnist, Perkins, the *New York Herald Tribune* music critic with a double first in classics from Cambridge University, who always carried a volume of Greek plays in his hip pocket, and others of that ilk. Being in the company's French section, I was made redundant by the speedy liberation of France and I volunteered for a truck-driving job where I remained until a chance encounter with a young Harvard economist turned intelligence officer (Paul Sweezy) led to my becoming one of the first three members of the US Strategic Bombing Survey (USSBS).

That was an interesting assignment from both the human and the economist's point of view. It took me to just-liberated Paris and Brussels for long enough to witness the inhabitants' adjustment to their newly won freedom, gave me a glimpse of the fighting in Cologne and provided a chance to interrogate one of the impressive technocrats in charge of Germany's war production just before his capture.

At the beginning of my new assignment, two colleagues and I did the initial thinking, planning, information gathering and recruiting of economists for USSBS, which soon became a mammoth, 1000-man organization. By luck, sheer force of numbers and thanks also to my lecturing the incoming staff on the organization of Germany's Economics and War Production ministries and the names of their top officials, we tracked down most of these from Albert Speer downwards and managed to find and assemble all the statistical data worth having. (I am still proud of having discovered Germany's national inventory of machine tools on punch cards, evacuated from Berlin to Jena in the Russian zone, and spiriting away punch cards, Hollerith machines, their operators and the latters' families from under the Russians' noses, convoying them to USSBS headquarters in the American zone one day before the Russians arrived.)

The main conclusions, however, of our shelf full of reports were very simple. They were that the levelling of German cities by indiscriminate night bombing was counterproductive, because it strengthened the Germans' resolve to fight on rather than lower their morale; and that precision raids on key industries failed to reduce war production because the Germans were much better equipped with machine tools and other productive equipment than we and the British were (and believed *they* were). All their industries worked on a single shift and could easily compensate for damage to part of their equipment by lengthening the working week or introducing a second shift.

A colleague and I were the last members of USSBS to leave Europe, writing the final version of its main report in London.[4] On my discharge from the army, I spent some time in the Department of Commerce but then obtained a permanent appointment at Stanford University. As soon as I started teaching there, I returned to the question of how prices were determined. For I had two problems in teaching microeconomics to graduate students. One stemmed from the very literal-minded cast of my thinking: I could not comprehend how prices come about in competitive markets, when no one is supposed to have a conscious influence on them. How was I to explain to students something I failed to understand myself? Walras seems to have shared my difficulty, because he resolved it by introducing the character of the auctioneer; but I did not like his solution, because it presupposed the existence of perfect markets, whose rare emergence, I felt, ought itself to be explained along with how prices are determined. My other problem was how to introduce the concept of market power, not only in the limiting case of pure monopoly but into the general model of competition as well.

I resolved these problems by introducing another new character, the price maker, who sets the price and other features of the market offers that confront the price takers facing him; and I postulated the two necessary conditions for him to do that: (1) his better knowledge of market-relevant information than the price takers' to give him a bargaining advantage, and (2) sufficient disparity in numbers between the two sides to make it profitable for price makers to exploit that advantage by making their offers on a take-it-or-leave-it basis.[5]

Looking back at it now, I believe that to have been my main contribution to economics. For my two postulates were not only realistic but turned out to be unavoidable features of most markets in every advanced economy, considering that specialization and the division of labour go hand-in-hand with the specialization and division also of the underlying knowledge and depend crucially on the existence of markets in which a few well-informed specialists confront many not-so-well informed non-specialists. That is why the pedagogical device I introduced to explain how market prices came about was instantly and universally accepted, although more as an obvious description of reality than as an analytical model.

Yet, focusing analysis on the asymmetric market relations between price makers and price takers has raised, and pointed the way to answering, a great number of important questions. For one thing, it suggested that, while competition can, to some degree, restrain the price maker's power to exploit the price takers facing him, perfectly competitive markets only emerge in those rare cases where special circumstances account for the two sides' equal expertise.

For another, once the persons responsible for setting prices were identified, the question naturally arose how long they would keep unchanged a price once set, which immediately led to the discovery and study of transaction costs, costs of change (nowadays called menu costs), the time lags with which price takers respond to price changes and price makers' offers respond to changes in turnover. In short, the character of the price maker had to be introduced to open the way to studying the speed with which and extent to which prices clear markets.

Yet another advantage of modelling the asymmetric market and adding the price maker to the cast of characters was to bring to the fore non-price competition, previously known only as an alternative competitive weapon; although it is also a means to secure a monopoly position, a source of various marketing amenities and valuable services benefiting price takers and, most important of all, the motivation for innovation, growth and the ongoing adaptation of products to fit consumers' convenience and changing tastes. To my shame, I recognized these valuable social benefits of non-price (and so of imperfect) competition only decades later,[6] and most of the profession ignores them still, to judge by the article on non-price competition in *The New Palgrave Dictionary*.

The model of the asymmetric market also has its uses in macroeconomics and explains, for example, excess claims (cost-push) inflation, the most common type, which we live with most of the time. That is the kind of inflation which coexists with underemployment and underproduction, because the claims are not to output but to rates of remuneration; and they are excessive in relation not to the volume but to the price of output, in the sense that the sum of the wages and prices the suppliers of the inputs demand plus the price maker's own mark-up exceed the price previously set on the product whose inputs they are. The sellers in the factor markets must be price makers or good at bargaining to make their excessive claims on producers effective; and the producers must be price makers in the markets where they sell their products to recoup their losses. In other words, excess claims inflation and its cost- or wage-price spiral arise when producers are price makers in the markets where they sell but lack that advantage in some of the factor markets where they buy.[7]

All that work originated in my trying to find out what keeps prices from clearing markets and, while it gave me interesting insights into the workings of our economy, I am still working on the original question, this time by seeking the determinants of the floor below which price makers will not lower their prices for fear of bankruptcy.[8]

My work on international economics also started with my interest in exploitation, this time with governmental tariffs' exploiting domestic firms' monopoly–monopsony power in foreign markets to the country's advantage, when competition among the firms themselves kept them from exploiting it with their own pricing policies to their own advantage. This was a popular topic as early as the turn of the century with Edgeworth, Bickerdike and Marshall, but a purely theoretical one, because few countries imposed tariffs with a view to exploiting foreigners in those days. Most tariffs were import duties designed to protect domestic industries or improve the balance of payments, with increases in the country's share of the gains from trade only a welcome by-product.

The subject acquired practical importance during the 1930s depression when trade restrictions became an employment policy and retaliatory tariffs and trade wars entered the scene. I knew a little about that, because my father was Hungary's delegate to the many international trade conferences of the inter-war period, which aimed in the 1920s at restoring and expanding trade relations but after the depression merely tried, with scant success, to combat trade restriction and trade wars. In a 1942 paper I provided the theoretical underpinnings for the latter by showing that, just as each producer's quest for profit diminishes the profits of all, so each country's attempt to increase its own advantage from trade diminishes the advantage of all. That is why free trade cannot be trusted to persist or come about but must be imposed either by agreement or by a dominant power. Later I was able to add that Britain was in a unique position for enforcing free trade in the 19th century, because she had much to lose from other countries' trade restrictions and nothing to gain from imposing her own.[9]

I followed up that paper during the late 1950s and early 1960s with work on economic integration, balance-of-payments adjustment within and between countries, international liquidity and the conditions necessary for a unified currency. The guesses and predictions in my 1958 book on European integration[10] must have turned out better than I had hoped because, years later, when visiting a former student in the Community's offices in Brussels, I unexpectedly found myself dined and wined and the centre of attention.

In 1963, I became a member of the group of 32, also known as the Bellagio group, an assortment of academics from 11 countries concerned with international monetary problems, later joined by central bankers Paul Volcker and Ottmar Emminger. I enjoyed the group's periodic meetings, the lively discussions about practical problems and the contact with policy makers, but continued to feel like an intruder among them, suspecting that they, with their concentration on the problems of the day, would not share my theoretically oriented scale of values, which assigns equal weight to problems of the long and the short run.

For example, I worked on and later published a plan to link the creation of special drawing rights to grants-in-aid for third-world countries,[11] because I

had been disturbed by the gradual transformation of our generous development aid into loans and feared that the accumulation of the third-world
countries' foreign debt might lead to unmanageable transfer problems. The
Bellagio group would have been the ideal forum for a constructive discussion
of my plan, but I never dared to present it for fear that they would only see its
short-run difficulties and be blind to its long-term advantages.

That my fears were justified I learned at one of the meetings following the
1973 oil shock. It began with general elation and self-congratulation over the
successful recycling of OPEC's oil profits deposited in US banks and generously lent by them (at high interest) to third-world countries, thereby preventing the depression that the oil shock was generally expected to create.
Since the debt accumulation seemed enormous, I raised the question whether
the poor countries would ever be able to repay those loans, which did not
even contribute to their development. Having lived through the 1930s, whose
economic and political miseries seemed to an ex-European to have had much
to do with the transfer problem of reparations and debt repayment, I thought
that to be an obvious, important and opportune question; but many of the
others seemed to consider my raising it highly inappropriate. At any rate, the
chairman hastened to shut me up and change the subject, some people looked
at me as if I had said something obscene and I relearned the lesson that
practical people deal with problems of the moment and let the future take
care of itself.

My writing on international economic problems came to an end when
divorce changed my life. To ease the pains of divorce with geographic distance, I accepted a two-year appointment at the Development Centre of
OECD in Paris, which kept me busy full-time with development problems. I
enjoyed the work, because it was my first close encounter with industrialists
and real-world economies, my first chance to apply theory to practical problems, and my only opportunity for prolonged cooperation with stimulating
colleagues, which led to close friendships and a joint book.[12]

But my most enjoyable work in the field was a survey of Taiwan's and
South Korea's economic development.[13] The two countries looked like identical twins, equal in race, culture, religion and their recent history, and growing at almost the same, exceptionally fast, rate. Economic and social indicators showed Taiwan to be considerably ahead of Korea but only because the
Korean War delayed the latter's development and its devastation made her
start from a lower base.

To make my paper interesting, I had to discover differences between the
two and to track them down required detective work more than economic
analysis. My first clue was Seoul's more prosperous, modern and elegant
look than Taipei's, although Korea was much the poorer country. I had never
seen such glaring conflict between the statistical evidence and my tourist's

impressions and guessed that greater inequalities in Korean incomes might explain it. That was borne out by statistics; but what explained the difference between two such very similar countries' income distributions?

Identical land reforms and the confiscation of the rich Japanese settlers' property in both countries had enabled them to start their postwar development with the same egalitarian income distribution; and while development was known to increase income inequalities, why did that occur only in late-starting Korea, not in Taiwan? The reason seems to have been Taiwan's unique adherence to a high interest rate policy throughout the postwar period. Its effect on income distribution seemed paradoxical because, according to conventional wisdom, high interest rates make rich creditors richer and poor debtors poorer. That wisdom, however, had been stood on its head in the third world where the creditors were the poor, whom the lack of social security compelled to save for their old age, and the main debtors were the rich corporations and their owner-managers. That is why Taiwan's tight monetary policy slowed the growth of her firms and not only helped the poor but encouraged them to save more, making the country's personal saving rate the world's second highest, thereby enabling her to minimize her foreign debt and her economy to grow, not by the increasing size of large firms, but by the proliferation of small firms, founded by small savers out of their own and their relatives' and neighbours' savings. A related effect of the high interest rate policy was to eliminate the excess demand for investment funds, thereby greatly limiting government's ability to ration credit and control private investment.

Taiwan's monetary policy was best known, however, for the speed with which it stopped inflation in its tracks. After the first oil shock, South Korea adopted a similar anti-inflationary policy with good but much less spectacular success; and she soon abandoned it in order to regain her tight control over investment and the direction in which the economy was going.

In other words, of the two countries' equally autocratic governments, South Korea's kept tight reins on its economy with the aid of giant corporations whose investments it could plan and control, whereas Taiwan's equally authoritarian government willy-nilly allowed a surprisingly liberal, almost 19th-century type of small-scale free enterprise economy to develop. The key to that difference was undoubtedly Taiwan's much tighter monetary policy, and that raised two questions: why has Taiwan's government adopted and stuck to a monetary policy that limited its direct control over the economy and was very much out of fashion at the time; and why was that policy so very effective in maintaining both full employment and reasonable price stability?

The probable answer to the first question is that Chiang Kai-shek and his advisers were the only non-communist rulers to experience hyperinflation in the flesh (in mainland China) and that made preventing a repetition of that experience their highest priority. More puzzling was the uncanny effectiveness of Taiwan's monetary policy in assuring both price stability and full employment at the same time. When the 1973 oil shock raised wholesale prices by 40 per cent within a year, Taiwan's raising of interest rates not only stopped the inflation within the next year but rolled prices back by 5 per cent, while employment and real output continued to grow. That may look like an incredible accomplishment to us, who live in economies with downwardly sticky prices, but it is what, say, Wicksell's theory of the natural rate of interest, with its tacit assumption of flexible prices, predicted.

In my latest paper, referred to earlier,[14] I argued that downward price flexibility is likely to be assured whenever and wherever firms are small enough for managers to have personal relations with their employees and suppliers; and I believe that condition to have been pretty well fulfilled in Taiwan, not quite so well in South Korea. The problem of price flexibility appears to have haunted me throughout my professional career.

My other new interest, whose beginning also dates from Paris days, was motivational psychology, the study of the various sources of people's satisfactions, whose pursuit motivates their behaviour. Some of my colleagues were shocked by that change of venue, perceiving it, I suspect, as a sign of incipient senility; but to me it seemed a logical extension of my interests. After all, much of my work had a welfare orientation: what more natural than to look also at the effect on consumers' welfare of their own behaviour? Besides, my main contribution to economics was to introduce and analyse the asymmetric market rendered asymmetrical by the participants' incomplete and unequal market-relevant information: in psychology, I set out to explore the implication of the individual's incomplete knowledge of sources of satisfaction on his or her own welfare. Finally, as an immigrant, transplanted from an easy-going yet varied and interesting life in Hungary into America's industrious and puritan atmosphere, I was especially interested in the sources and implications of the difference between the two cultures.

In an early note,[15] I explored the geometry of the difference between maximizing profit or money income and maximizing satisfaction – activities the profession in those days considered more or less synonymous, though attributing the former to firms, the latter to people. I showed that when (or if) entrepreneurs and managers maximize their firms' profit, they reveal a particular preference pattern, which also characterizes misers, persons who love money for the security and power it gives, for the worldly success it symbolizes, or for the spiritual salvation it signifies to Calvinist believers in predestination, and even, to some extent, people who find complete satisfaction in their work. In short, not only entrepreneurs, but puritans, the money-minded and the workaholics are all income maximizers; and they constitute a large part of the population in most of the advanced industrial countries. One can probably attribute to that those countries' economic superiority and fast growth – as did Max Weber and R.H. Tawney in their theories of the rise of capitalism, though they put much the same argument into very different language.

But if a country's superior economic performance is due to its inhabitants' ambition to maximize their profits or money income, is there no danger that their enjoyment of life might suffer as a result? The very question must seem preposterous to those who unquestioningly accept the economist's assumption that everybody can be trusted to know best what gives him or her the most satisfaction and to act accordingly; for in that case, those who maximize money income can be assumed thereby also to maximize their satisfaction. That, indeed, was the underlying assumption of my 1943 note.

The situation is not that simple, however, because, while economists usually assume people to be rational and knowledgeable, that assumption must, at the very least, be taken with a grain of salt. To begin with, people's consumption patterns are highly suggestive and depend largely on tradition, habit, imitation and fashion. Secondly, the enjoyment of life and many of the satisfactions that contribute to it have to be learned like everything else. Indeed, the most enjoyable sources of satisfaction usually require the most skill and learning; and our educational system is much too imbued with the puritan work ethic to provide more than a modicum of that learning. Thirdly, money is general purchasing power, considered to give access to most of the good things in life; and when we make money, we often do not know, and do not have to know how and on what we are going to spend it. That is why money appears to most of us as the gateway to future pleasures and comforts even when we do not know of what these will consist.

I probably have always been more aware of these problems than my American-born colleagues; but returning to continental Europe after 25-years' stay in America was a vivid reminder and made me realize more than I did before that the difference between the two continents' lifestyles had more to do with differences in education and attitude to life than with affluence and élitism.

Needless to say, I was not the first economist to realize this and try to distinguish the different sources of human satisfactions. On the contrary, I may be one of the last. As long as economics was part of philosophy, economist-philosophers learnt about the various sources of man's satisfaction as a matter of course; but when it became a separate discipline, economists lost interest in the subject, assuming that each person knew best what he or she wanted. That seemed justified in earlier days; but Alfred Marshall already knew that there was something wrong with it. For he criticized Jevons for regarding human wants as the sole scientific basis of economics, arguing that activities that are their own reward are no less and possibly even more important. When Schumpeter spoke about the entrepreneur's creative urge and Keynes about his animal spirits without which there might not be much investment, they had one such rewarding activity in mind – Marx had another when he blamed the excessive division of labour under capitalism for alienating the worker from his work and depriving him of work satisfaction. These, however, are only two of many activities that are their own reward.

One crucial difference between wants and rewarding activities is that a want, as its very name implies, is a source of satisfaction that is already familiar to, and desired by, the person who wants it; whereas most rewarding activities require a skill for their exercise and enjoyment and are neither enjoyed nor even wanted by people who have not learned that skill. With respect to such activities, therefore, our customary assumption that most people know what gives or would give them satisfaction is not fulfilled.

Marshall may not have been aware of that difference; had he been, he would have made more of it than merely to criticize Jevons's neglect of rewarding activities. But having often questioned consumers' rationality and knowledgeability, I suspected the subject to have important consequences and to be well worth exploring. Finding little on it in economists' writings, I turned to motivational psychology for enlightenment and found its literature so rich and fascinating that I read everything I could lay hands on and ended up by writing a book on the subject.[16] It became a summary in layman's language of the motivational psychologists' theories and the findings and experiments on which they were based; but I also managed to supplement some of those findings with a few simple economic statistics and to round out the psychologists' theories by adding a few of my own economist's observations.

It was the most difficult and most enjoyable of all my writings: the former, because organizing many disparate bits of material into a coherent whole proved a formidable undertaking; the latter, because overcoming difficulties is always enjoyable and also because working on that book has greatly added to my self-knowledge and understanding of others.

In the past, most of what I enjoyed writing was also appreciated by its readers; but this book turned out to be an exception – possibly because I sent it to the wrong address. It was addressed to my fellow economists and they did not know what to do with it. For the book analysed the different sources of satisfaction and its message was that many of us do not know enough about what life and the market have to offer to make adequate use of it. That can create personal as well as social problems and the economy can be responsible for bringing about circumstances in which it creates them; but economists are not, as a rule, the people to eliminate those problems, at least not in their capacity as economists. The reason for this is a second crucial difference between wants and rewarding activities. To satisfy wants requires scarce resources, which renders their satisfaction an economic activity; whereas there is nothing scarce about rewarding activities, which means that to perform them just to enjoy the stimulus satisfaction they provide is not an economic activity, although it becomes one when performed to yield also income or a marketable product for sale.

Aware of that difference, Keynes, in a prophetic article,[17] defined the satisfaction of wants as *the* economic problem and called the finding and learning of activities with satisfying intrinsic rewards 'the permanent problem of the human race ... a fearful problem for the ordinary person, with no special talents, to occupy himself'. Bearing in mind the satiability of most human wants, he speculated that, barring wars, continued capital accumulation and technical progress could, within a century, bring us close to an economic utopia in which 'a quarter of the human effort to which we have been accustomed' would produce many times our present standard of living. Keynes feared that the resulting 'technological unemployment' might lead to 'a general nervous breakdown ... of the sort common enough in England and the United States among the wives of the well-to-do-classes'; and R.F. Harrod, looking at the same problem, envisaged a return to war, violence and blood sports – activities that the idle rich of the Middle Ages occupied themselves with.[18]

We are still very far, of course, from approaching that frightening Utopia but the problem already exists in our midst, plaguing not so much the idle rich as the involuntarily idle unemployed, unemployable youths and men, and the aged. For the idle rich, at least the *anciens riches* among them, follow an age-long tradition of giving their children an elitist education, which usually enables them to take up some scientific, artistic, cultural, philanthropic or other more-or-less benign activity that can be just as satisfying as work would be. It is mainly those with involuntary idleness thrust upon them who suffer psychological deprivation from lack of work or too little of it. The solution of that problem awaits a reform of our educational philosophy and lifestyle, which is bound to be a difficult and very slow process; and I had hoped and still hope that my book and other writings on psychology would contribute to a better understanding of the problem and of what needs to be done about it.

Let me conclude by pointing out an affinity between that problem and the one my first paper dealt with. There, I dealt with unemployment, which was considered to be a problem because it leads to loss of income; much of my work on psychology, focused on people's need for stimulus satisfaction and their difficulty in obtaining enough of it – a problem that is caused by no or not enough employment and the consequent loss of work satisfaction. Income and work satisfaction are equally important benefits of employment; but while society tries to compensate the unemployed for lack of the former, nothing or next to nothing is done to compensate them (and the underemployed) for lack of the latter. I did not set out to investigate that problem but stumbled upon it in the course of studying motivational psychology, which was prompted by sheer curiosity and my dislike of the unrealistic assumptions on which so much economic reasoning is based. The fact that I did come upon it makes me feel that satisfying my idle curiosity was not only fun for me but of some social value as well.

Notes

1. J.R. Hicks, 'Mr. Keynes and the "classics": a suggested interpretation', *Econometrica*, **V**, April 1937; and O. Lange, 'The rate of interest and the optimum propensity to consume', *Economica*, (1938), N.S., **V**, February.
2. 'A study of interest and capital', *Economica*, (1940), N.S., **VII**, August.
3. 'Growth in the affluent society', *Lloyds Bank Review*, no. 163, January 1987.
4. US Strategic Bombing Survey, *The Effects of Strategic Bombing on the German Economy* (1945).
5. *Welfare and Competition*, (Chicago, Ill: Richard D. Irwin, 1951), 2nd edn 1971.
6. 'Pricetakers' Plenty: a neglected benefit of capitalism', *Kyklos*, 1985, **XXXVIII**; 'The benefits of asymmetric markets', *Journal of Economic Perspectives*, 1990, **IV**, Winter.
7. 'Market power and inflation', *Economica*, (1978), **XLV**, August.
8. 'How our economy stands up to scrutiny', *American Economist*, (forthcoming).
9. 'A reconsideration of the theory of tariffs', *Review of Economic Studies*, (1942), **IX**; also my entry on 'Tariffs' in *The New Palgrave Dictionary of Economics*.
10. *Economic Theory and Western European Integration*, (London: Allen & Unwin, 1958).
11. 'A new approach to international liquidity', *American Economic Review*, (1966), **LVI**, March.
12. I.M.D. Little, T. Scitovsky and M. Scott, *Industry and Trade in Some Developing Countries*, (London: Oxford University Press, 1970).
13. 'Economic development in Taiwan and South Korea: 1965–81', *Food Research Institute Studies*, (1985), **XIX**, no. 3; also in L.J. Lau (ed.), *Models of Development*, (San Francisco: ICS Press, 1986).
14. See note 8 above.
15. 'A note on profit maximisation and its implications', *Review of Economic Studies*, (1943), **IX**.
16. *The Joyless Economy*, (New York: Oxford University Press, 1976).
17. J.M. Keynes, 'Economic possibilities for our grandchildren', in his *Essays in Persuasion*, (New York: W.W. Norton, 1963).
18. R.F. Harrod, 'The possibility of economic satiety', in Committee for Economic Development, *Problems of Economic Development*, (New York, 1958).

Index

adverse selection 75
Ainslie, George 84n, 85n
Akerlof, George 74, 75, 84, 85n
alienation 204, 236
altruism *see* righteous behaviour;
    compassion
ancillary services 6, 159
animal spirits 123, 133, 236
antiques ix, 100–103, 115–17
    see also market for collectables
antitrust legislation 8, 89
Arrow, Kenneth 74, 85, 197
art
    index (Sotheby and Times–Sotheby
      index) 104, 116
    see also market for collectables
asymmetric markets 64–5

bargaining
    bilateral 65
    collective 68
    strength of workers 69
Barone, Enrico 16–17, 25, 31
Bastable, Charles 35
Bellagio group 231–2
Bickerdike, C.F. 36, 55
bonus system 95, 140, 165

capital consumption 190–91
    adjustment 192
capitalism
    competitive vii, 19–20
    merchant 65
    monopolistic ix, 1, 19
    rise of 235
Chiang Kai-shek 233–4
collective goods x, 199–201, 205–6
    how made available 200–201
commodity exchanges 14–15
communist manifesto 20
compassion 201
    see also righteous behaviour
competition
    asymmetric 2–10, 229

    imperfect 20, 88
    monopolistic 4, 5, 7, 10–11, 86, 87
    non-price 5–15, 20, 75, 87, 200, 230
    perfect 2, 3, 18, 19, 21, 65, 67, 86, 88,
      91, 224
    predatory 131
    price 10–13
conspicuous consumption 99
consumers'
    rationality x
    sovereignty (freedom of choice) 17,
      31, 88, 215
    surplus 30
counterspeculation 26, 36, 49, 54
countervailing power 65, 73
credit rationing 146

Darwin, Charles 78, 85
deficit financing *see* Keynes, policies'
    versus 'sound finance'
depreciation *see* capital consumption
development policies 135–87, 232
    agricultural 151–4
    export promotion 155–6, 157, 160–61
    high interest rate 145–8, 167, 180,
      233
    import substitution 154–5
    low interest rate 148–9, 171
    tax incentives 150–51, 153, 155, 162,
      170, 171
    vulnerability to world depression
      156–7, 159
Dickinson, Henry D. 17, 18, 25
distribution
    egalitarian 137, 141, 147–8, 233
    equal 17, 21, 201
    equal opportunity 201
    equitable 161, 200–201
    of income 137, 161, 209, 233
    increasingly unequal 135, 209
    Gini index of inequality 138
    optimal 33–4
    of taxes 200–201
    of wealth and property 140, 161

Economists of the Twentieth Century

The Liberal Economic Order
Volume I Essays on International Economics
Volume II Money, Cycles and Related Themes
Gottfried Haberler
Edited by Anthony Y.C. Koo

Economic Growth and Business Cycles
Prices and the Process of Cyclical Development
Paolo Sylos Labini

International Adjustment, Money and Trade
Theory and Measurement for Economic Policy, Volume I
Herbert G. Grubel

International Capital and Service Flows
Theory and Measurement for Economic Policy, Volume II
Herbert G. Grubel

Unintended Effects of Government Policies
Theory and Measurement for Economic Policy, Volume III
Herbert G. Grubel

The Economics of Competitive Enterprise
Selected Essays of P.W.S. Andrews
Edited by Frederic S. Lee and Peter E. Earl

The Repressed Economy
Causes, Consequences, Reform
Deepak Lal

Economic Theory and Market Socialism
Selected Essays of Oskar Lange
Edited by Tadeusz Kowalik

Trade, Development and Political Economy
Selected Essays of Ronald Findlay
Ronald Findlay

General Equilibrium Theory
The Collected Essays of Takashi Negishi, Volume I
Takashi Negishi

The History of Economics
The Collected Essays of Takashi Negishi, Volume II
Takashi Negishi

Studies in Econometric Theory
The Collected Essays of Takeshi Amemiya
Takeshi Amemiya

Exchange Rates and the Monetary System
Selected Essays of Peter B. Kenen
Peter B. Kenen

Econometric Methods and Applications (2 volumes)
G.S. Maddala

National Accounting and Economic Theory
The Collected Papers of Dan Usher, Volume I
Dan Usher

Welfare Economics and Public Finance
The Collected Papers of Dan Usher, Volume II
Dan Usher

Economic Theory and Capitalist Society
The Selected Essays of Shigeto Tsuru, Volume I
Shigeto Tsuru

Methodology, Money and the Firm
The Collected Essays of D.P. O'Brien (2 volumes)
D.P. O'Brien

Economic Theory and Financial Policy
The Selected Essays of Jacques J. Polak (2 volumes)
Jacques J. Polak

Sturdy Econometrics
Edward E. Leamer

The Emergence of Economic Ideas
Essays in the History of Economics
Nathan Rosenberg

Productivity Change, Public Goods and Transaction Costs
Essays at the Boundaries of Microeconomics
Yoram Barzel

Reflections on Economic Development
The Selected Essays of Michael P. Todaro
Michael P. Todaro

The Economic Development of Modern Japan
The Selected Essays of Shigeto Tsuru, Volume II
Shigeto Tsuru

Money, Credit and Policy
Allan H. Meltzer

Macroeconomics and Monetary Theory
The Selected Essays of Meghnad Desai, Volume I
Meghnad Desai

Poverty, Famine and Economic Development
The Selected Essays of Meghnad Desai, Volume II
Meghnad Desai

Explaining the Economic Performance of Nations
Essays in Time and Space
Angus Maddison

Economic Doctrine and Method
Selected Papers of R.W. Clower
Robert W. Clower

Economic Theory and Reality
Selected Essays on their Disparity and Reconciliation
Tibor Scitovsky

Doing Economic Research
Essays on the Applied Methodology of Economics
Thomas Mayer

Institutions and Development Strategies
The Selected Essays of Irma Adelman, Volume I
Irma Adelman

Dynamics and Income Distribution
The Selected Essays of Irma Adelman, Volume II
Irma Adelman

The Economics of Growth and Development
The Selected Essays of A.P. Thirlwall
A.P. Thirlwall

Theoretical and Applied Econometrics
The Selected Papers of Phoebus J. Dhrymes
Phoebus J. Dhrymes

Innovation, Technology and the Economy
The Selected Essays of Edwin Mansfield (2 volumes)
Edwin Mansfield

Economic Theory and Policy in Context
The Selected Essays of R.D. Collison Black
R.D. Collison Black

Capitalism, Socialism and Post-Keynesianism
Selected Essays of G.C. Harcourt
G.C. Harcourt

Time Series Analysis and Macroeconometric Modelling
The Collected Papers of Kenneth F. Wallis
Kenneth F. Wallis

Foundations of Modern Econometrics
The Selected Essays of Ragnar Frisch (2 volumes)
Olav Bjerkholt